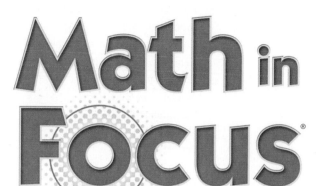

# Math in Focus

## Singapore Math
### by Marshall Cavendish

## Student Book

### 1A

**Consultant and Author**
Dr. Fong Ho Kheong

**Authors**
Chelvi Ramakrishnan and Bernice Lau Pui Wah

**U.S. Consultants**
Dr. Richard Bisk, Andy Clark,
and Patsy F. Kanter

**Marshall Cavendish**
Education

HOUGHTON
MIFFLIN
HARCOURT

© 2009 Marshall Cavendish International (Singapore) Private Limited

**Published by Marshall Cavendish Education**
*An imprint of Marshall Cavendish International (Singapore) Private Limited*
Times Centre, 1 New Industrial Road, Singapore 536196
Customer Service Hotline: (65) 6411 0820
E-mail: tmesales@sg.marshallcavendish.com
Website: www.marshallcavendish.com/education

Distributed by
**Houghton Mifflin Harcourt**
222 Berkeley Street
Boston, MA 02116
Tel: 617-351-5000
Website: www.hmheducation.com/mathinfocus

First published 2009
Reprinted 2010, 2011 (thrice), 2012 (twice)

Math in Focus® Grade 1 Student Book A
ISBN 978-0-669-01086-2

Printed in United States of America

7  8                    1897      16  15  14  13  12
4500360932                        B  C  D  E

# Contents

Look for **Practice and Problem Solving**

| Student Book A and Student Book B | Workbook A and Workbook B |
|---|---|
| • **Let's Practice** in every lesson | • **Independent Practice** for every lesson |
| • Put on Your Thinking Cap! in every chapter | • Put on Your Thinking Cap! in every chapter |

# CHAPTER
# 2 Number Bonds

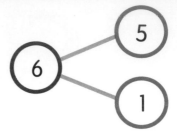

Look for **Assessment Opportunities**

| Student Book A and Student Book B | Workbook A and Workbook B |
|---|---|
| • **Quick Check** at the beginning of every chapter to assess chapter readiness<br>• **Guided Practice** after every example or two to assess readiness to continue | • **Chapter Review/Test** in every chapter to review or test chapter material<br>• **Cumulative Reviews** eight times during the year<br>• **Mid-Year** and **End-of-Year Reviews** to assess test readiness |

# CHAPTER 3 Addition Facts to 10

CHAPTER

# 4 Subtraction Facts to 10

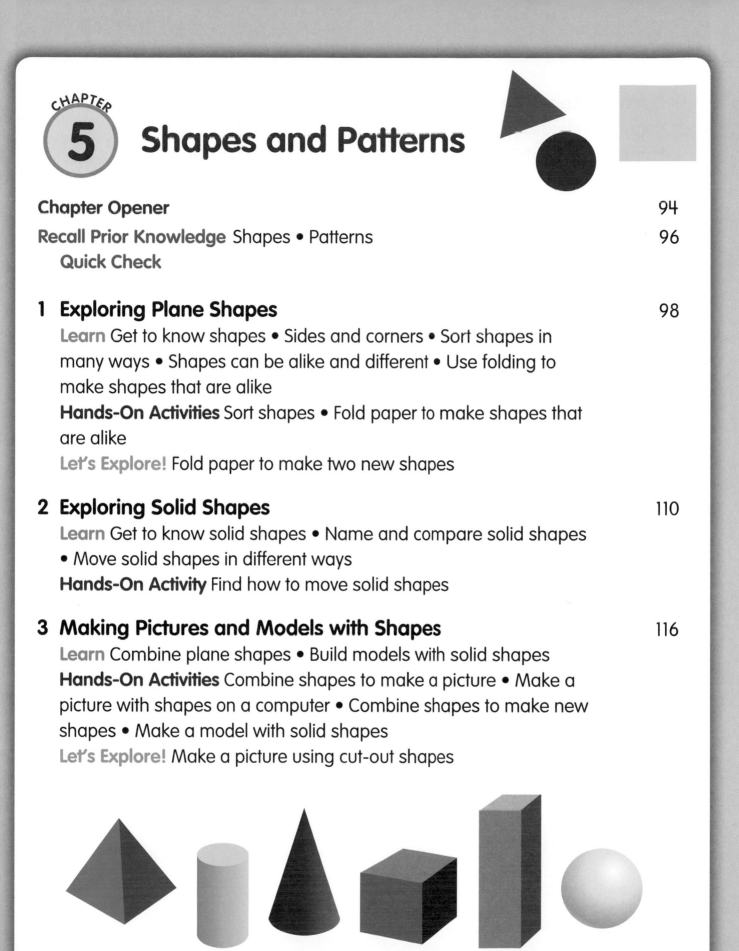

CHAPTER

# 6 Ordinal Numbers and Position

| Tens | Ones |
|------|------|
| | |

x

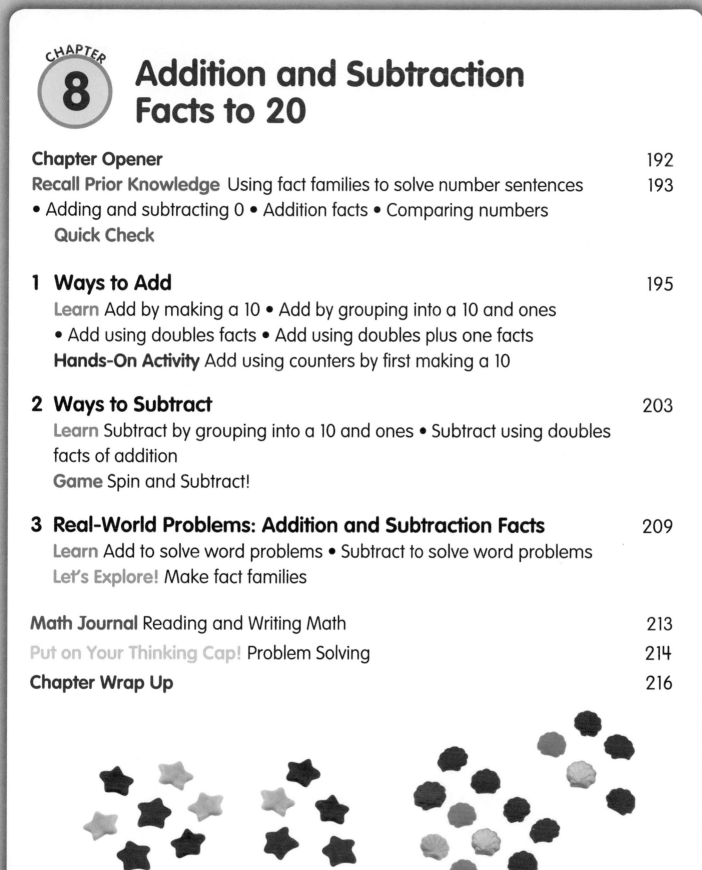

CHAPTER

**8**

# Addition and Subtraction Facts to 20

# CHAPTER
# 9  Length

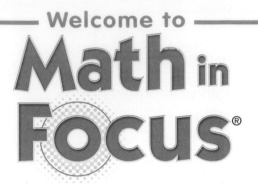

## Welcome to

# Math in Focus®

This exciting math program comes to you all the way from the country of Singapore. We are sure you will like all the different ways to learn math.

## What makes *Math in Focus®* different?

- **Two books** You don't write in the ▢ in this textbook. This book has a matching **Workbook.** When you see  ON YOUR OWN ✎ you will write in the **Workbook.**

- **Longer lessons** Some lessons may last more than a day, so you can really understand the math.

- **Math will make sense** Learn to use number bonds to understand better how numbers work.

## In this book, look for

| **Learn** | **Guided Practice** | **Let's Practice** | ■ ON YOUR OWN ✎ |
|---|---|---|---|
| This means you learn something new. | Your teacher helps you try some problems. | Practice. Make sure you really understand. | Now try some problems in your own **Workbook.** |

**Also look forward to** *Games, Hands-On Activities, Put on Your Thinking Cap!,* and more. Enjoy some real math challenges!

# What's in the Workbook?

*Math in Focus*® will give you time to learn important math ideas and do math problems. The **Workbook** will give you different types of practice.

- *Practice* problems will help you remember the new math idea you are learning. Watch for this **ON YOUR OWN** in your book. That will tell you which pages to use for practice.

- *Put on Your Thinking Cap!*

    *Challenging Practice* problems invite you to think in new ways to solve harder problems.

    *Problem Solving* gives you opportunities to solve questions in different ways.

- *Math Journal* activities ask you to think about thinking, and then write about that!

Students in Singapore have been using this kind of math program for many years. Now you can too — are you ready?

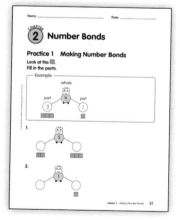

Blank

One, two, three, four,
Hear the mighty ocean roar!
Five, six, seven, eight,
Time to play, so don't be late!
What's next? Nine and ten.
Let's start all over again!

**Lesson 1** Counting to 10

**Lesson 2** Comparing Numbers

**Lesson 3** Making Number Patterns

**BIG IDEA**

Count and compare numbers to 10.

## Recall Prior Knowledge

### Counting

The toys are matched to show the same number.

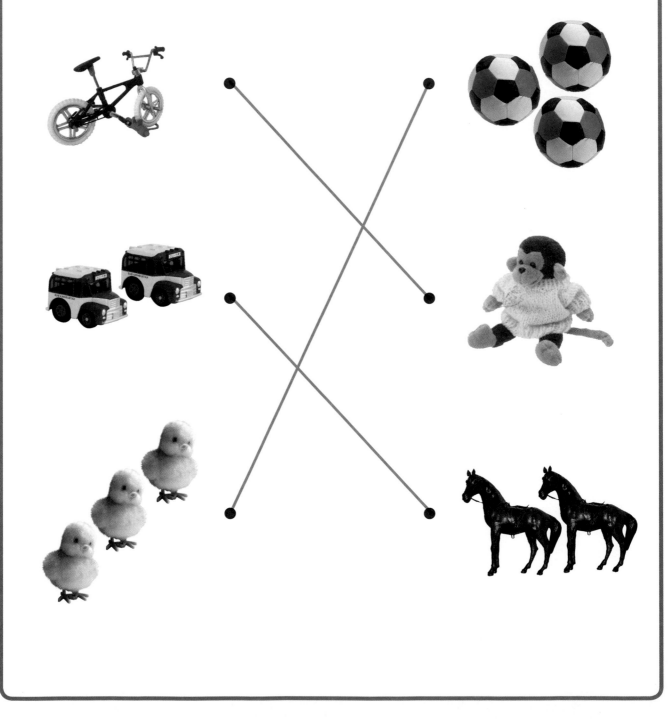

Match the 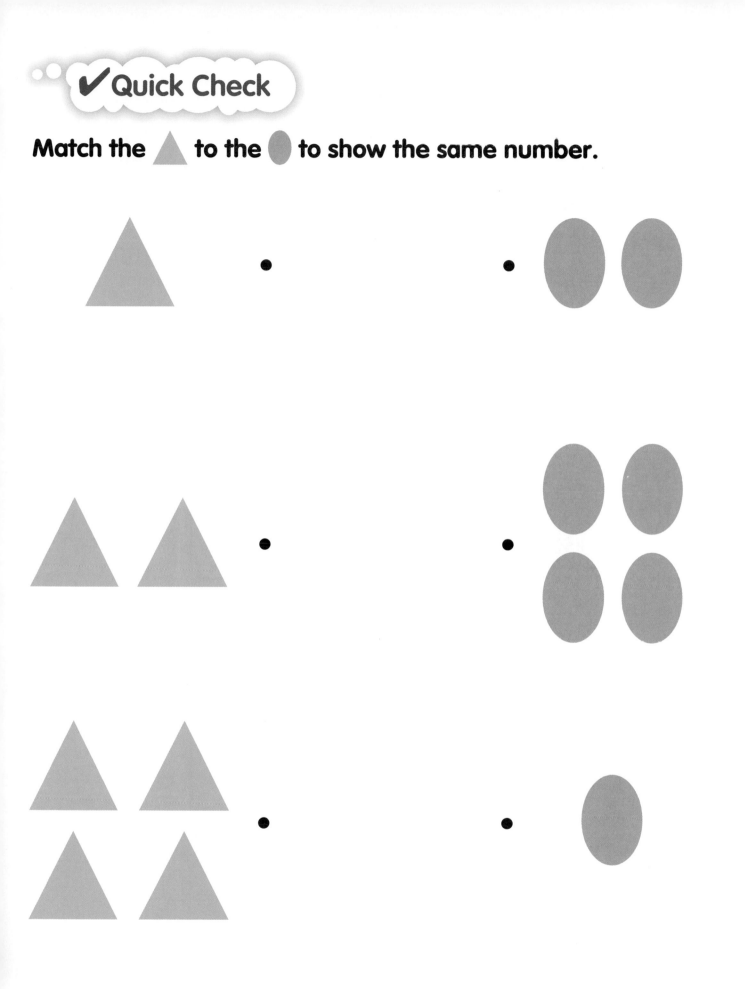 to the ⬭ to show the same number.

# Counting to 10

## Lesson Objectives

- Count from 0 to 10 objects.
- Read and write 0–10 in numbers and words.

**Vocabulary**

| | | |
|---|---|---|
| zero | one | two |
| three | four | five |
| six | seven | eight |
| nine | ten | |

**Learn** **Point with your finger and count.**

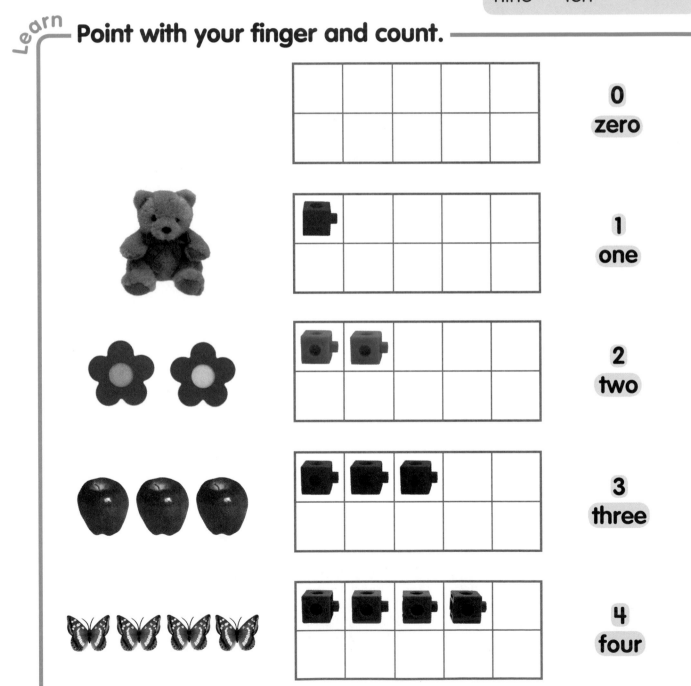

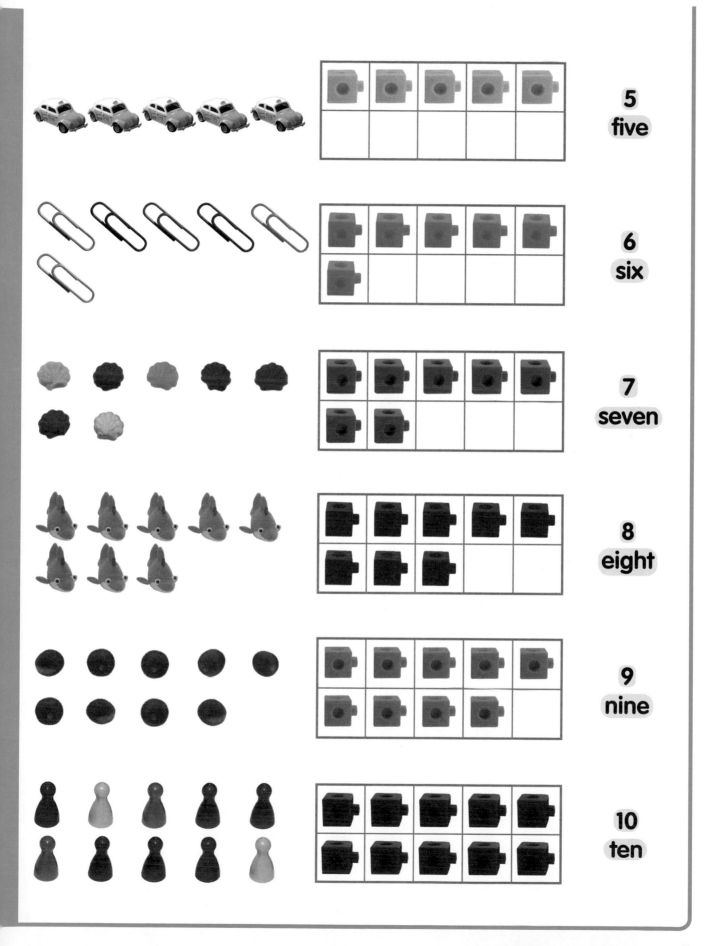

5 five

6 six

7 seven

8 eight

9 nine

10 ten

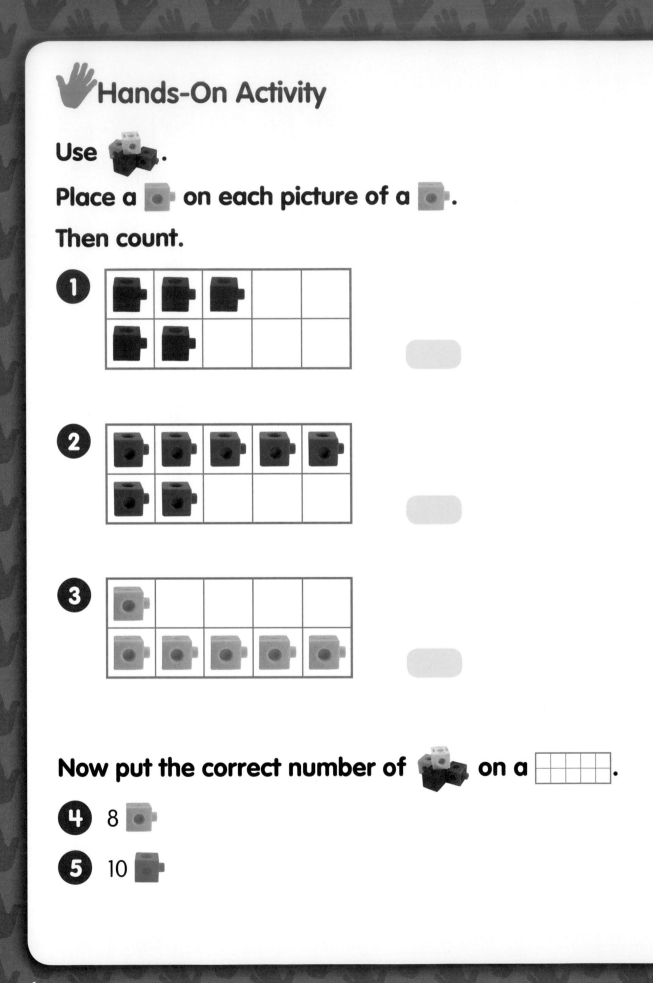

# ✋ Hands-On Activity

Use 🧊.

Place a 🔲 on each picture of a 🔲.

Then count.

1

2

3

Now put the correct number of 🧊 on a ⬜⬜.

4   8 🔲

5   10 🔲

# Guided Practice

## Count.
## Write the number.

Example

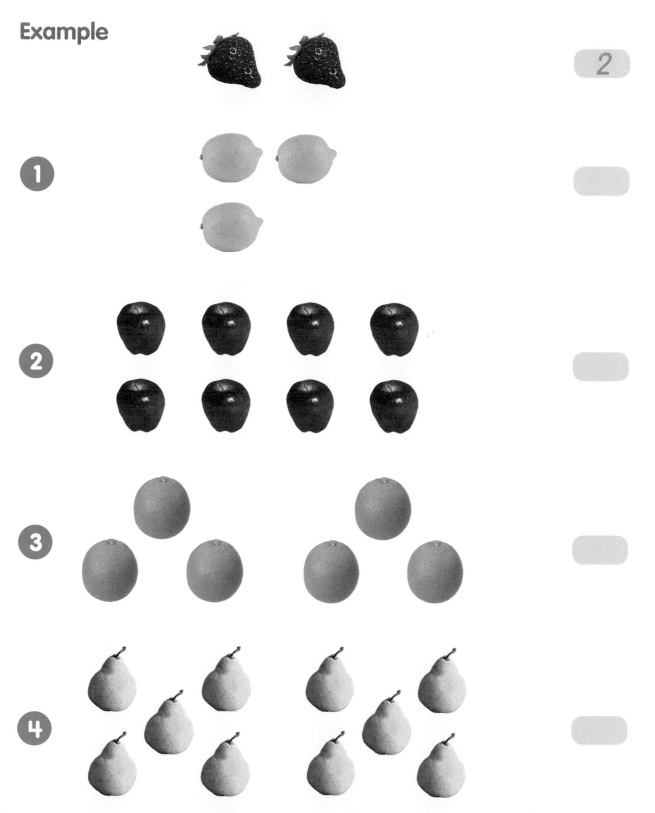

2

1

2

3

4

# Point to the bugs and count.
# Write in numbers and in words.

**Example**

3    three

5

6

7

# How many are there?
## Count. Write the number.

# Let's Explore!

Work in groups of 3 or 4.

**STEP 1** Pick a number from 2 to 10.

**STEP 2** Use 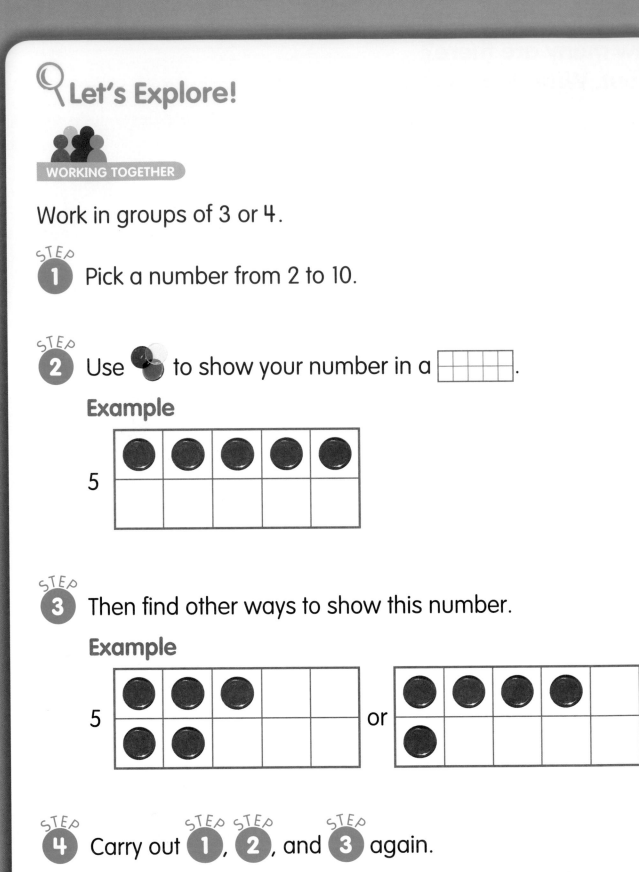 to show your number in a ⬚.

**Example**

5

**STEP 3** Then find other ways to show this number.

**Example**

5 or

**STEP 4** Carry out **1**, **2**, and **3** again.

Use a different number.

# Land on 10!

Players: 3

**How to play:** Use only 1, 2, or 3 fingers to count.

**STEP 1** Player 1 starts counting from 1.

**STEP 2** Player 2 counts on.

**STEP 3** Player 3 counts on.

End

The player who lands on 10 wins!

**What is the number? Count.
Write the number.**

**1**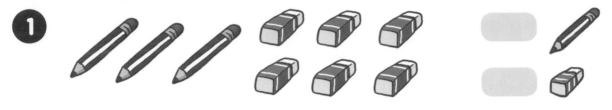

**2**

**3**

**ON YOUR OWN**

**Go to Workbook A:
Practice 1, pages 1–6**

# LESSON 2 Comparing Numbers

**Lesson Objectives**

- Compare two sets of objects by using one-to-one correspondence.
- Identify the set that has more, fewer, or the same number of objects.
- Identify the number that is greater than or less than another number.

**Vocabulary**

same

more

fewer

greater than

less than

## Learn Match and compare.

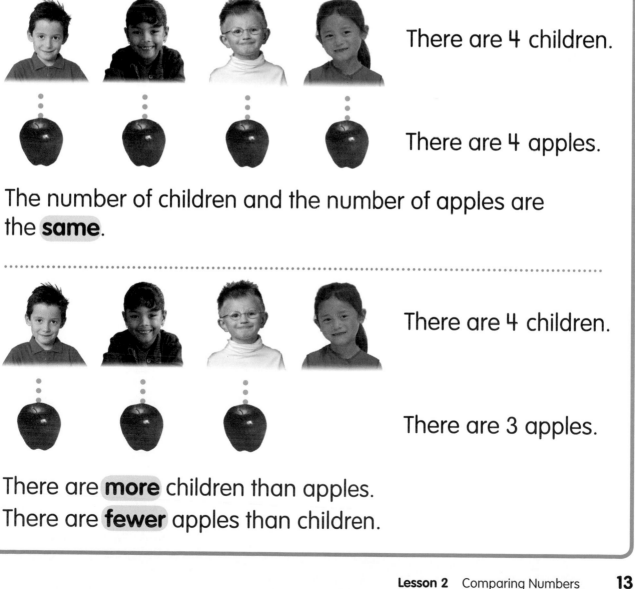

There are 4 children.

There are 4 apples.

The number of children and the number of apples are the **same**.

There are 4 children.

There are 3 apples.

There are **more** children than apples.
There are **fewer** apples than children.

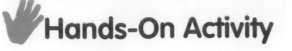 **Hands-On Activity**

**Use a copy of these socks and shoes.**

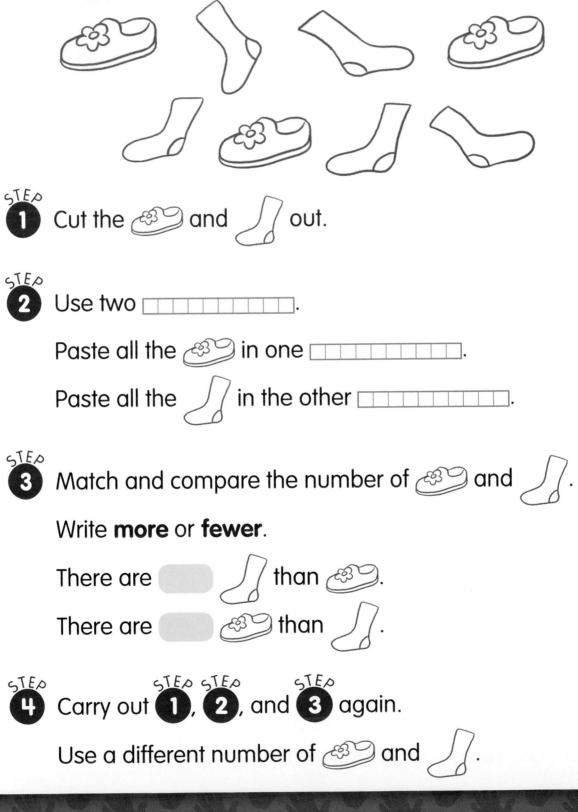

**STEP 1** Cut the and out.

**STEP 2** Use two ⬚⬚⬚⬚⬚⬚⬚⬚⬚.

Paste all the in one ⬚⬚⬚⬚⬚⬚⬚⬚⬚.

Paste all the in the other ⬚⬚⬚⬚⬚⬚⬚⬚⬚.

**STEP 3** Match and compare the number of and .

Write **more** or **fewer**.

There are ⬚⬚⬚ than .

There are ⬚⬚⬚ than .

**STEP 4** Carry out **STEP 1**, **STEP 2**, and **STEP 3** again.

Use a different number of and .

# Guided Practice

## Match and compare.
## Write more or fewer.

**1**

There are ⬚ 🌼 than 🦋.

There are ⬚ 🦋 than 🌼.

**2**

More or fewer?

There are ⬚ 🐱 than 🐟.

There are ⬚ 🦆 than 🐟.

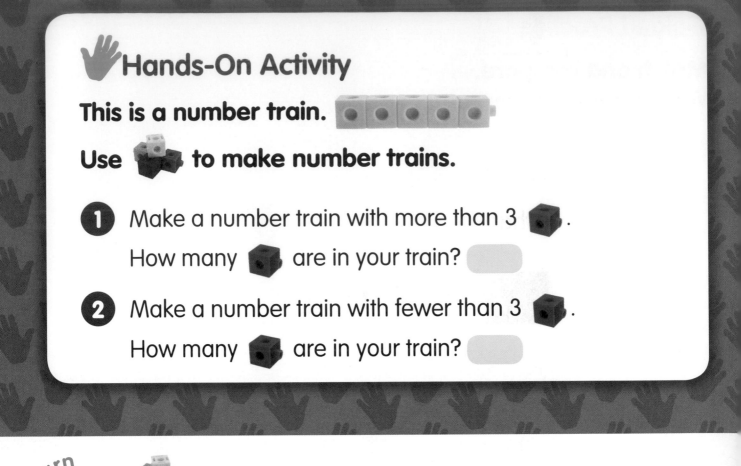

## Hands-On Activity

This is a number train.

Use ✋ to make number trains.

**1** Make a number train with more than 3 🔲.

How many 🔲 are in your train?

**2** Make a number train with fewer than 3 🔲.

How many 🔲 are in your train?

*Learn* Use 🔲 to count and compare.

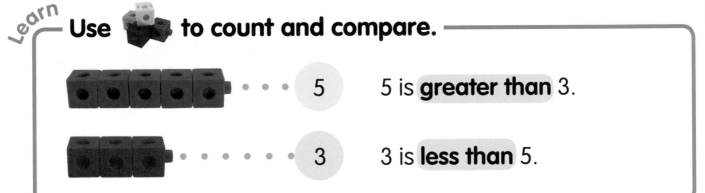

5       5 is **greater than** 3.

3       3 is **less than** 5.

## Guided Practice

**Find the missing numbers.**

**3**

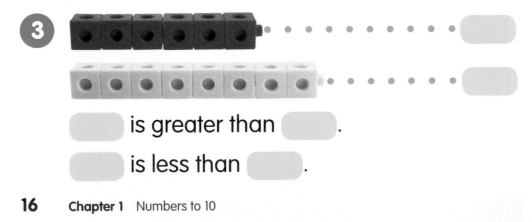

[    ] is greater than [    ].

[    ] is less than [    ].

**4**

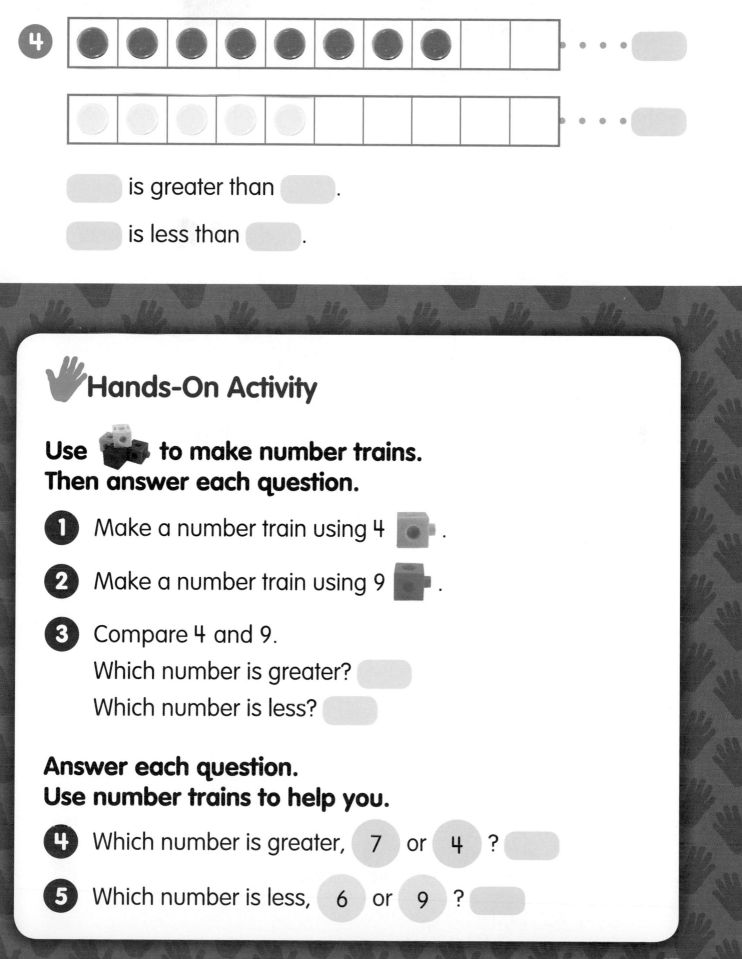

_____ is greater than _____ .

_____ is less than _____ .

## Hands-On Activity

Use [cubes] to make number trains.
Then answer each question.

**1** Make a number train using 4 [cube].

**2** Make a number train using 9 [cube].

**3** Compare 4 and 9.
Which number is greater? _____
Which number is less? _____

**Answer each question.**
**Use number trains to help you.**

**4** Which number is greater, 7 or 4 ? _____

**5** Which number is less, 6 or 9 ? _____

# Let's Practice

**Solve.**

 Point to the two groups that show the same number.

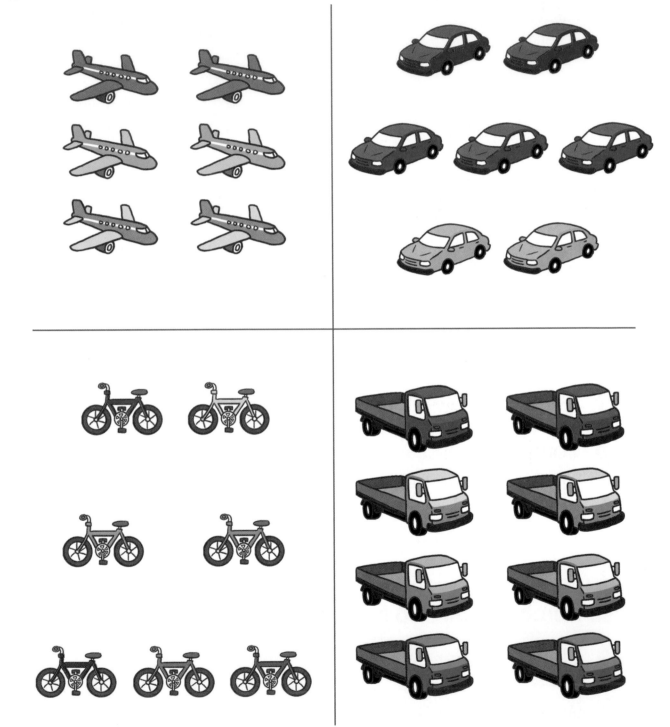

**2** Which tank has more fish, A or B?

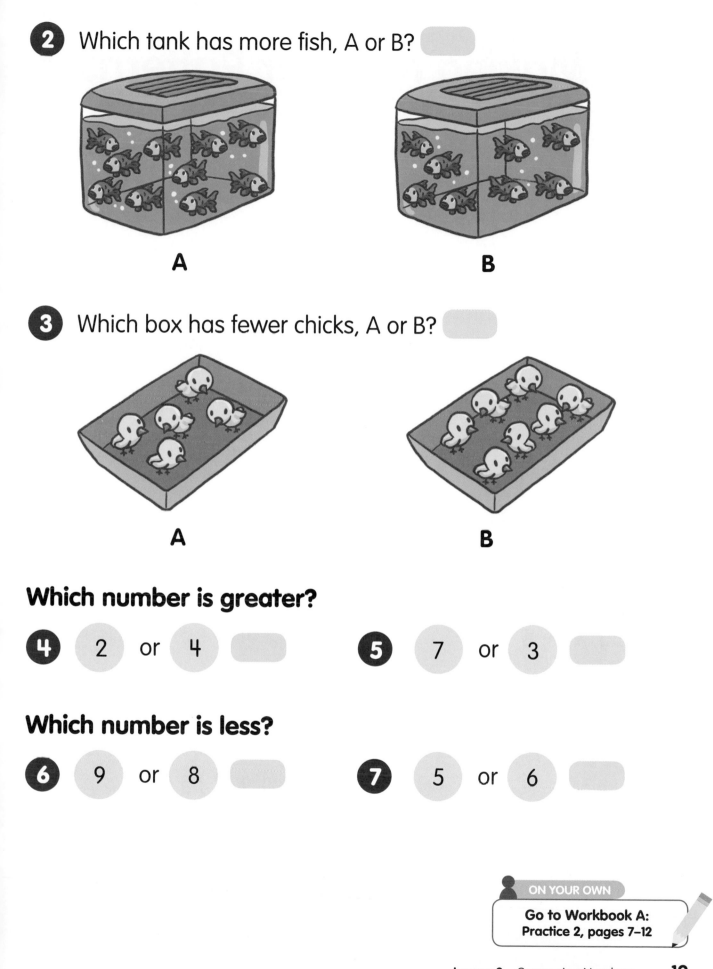

A

B

**3** Which box has fewer chicks, A or B?

A

B

# Which number is greater?

**4** 2 or 4

**5** 7 or 3

# Which number is less?

**6** 9 or 8

**7** 5 or 6

ON YOUR OWN

Go to Workbook A:
Practice 2, pages 7–12

# 3 Making Number Patterns

## Lesson Objective
• Make number patterns.

### Learn Make a pattern.

Joe makes the **pattern** below using .

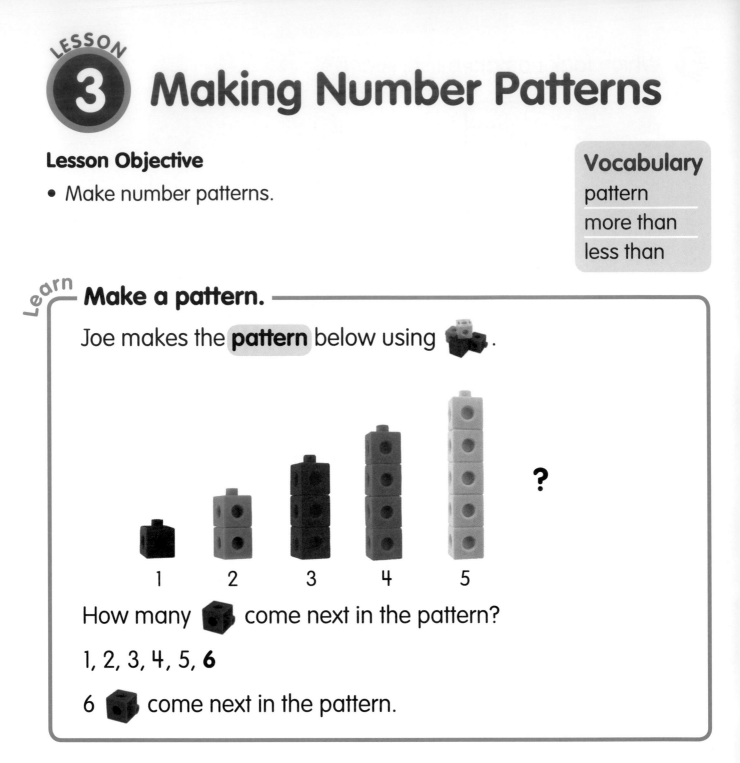

1   2   3   4   5

How many ☐ come next in the pattern?

1, 2, 3, 4, 5, **6**

6 ☐ come next in the pattern.

## Guided Practice

## Solve.

1 Megan makes a pattern with beads.

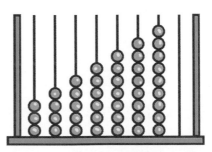

How many beads come next in the pattern?

**2** John makes a pattern.

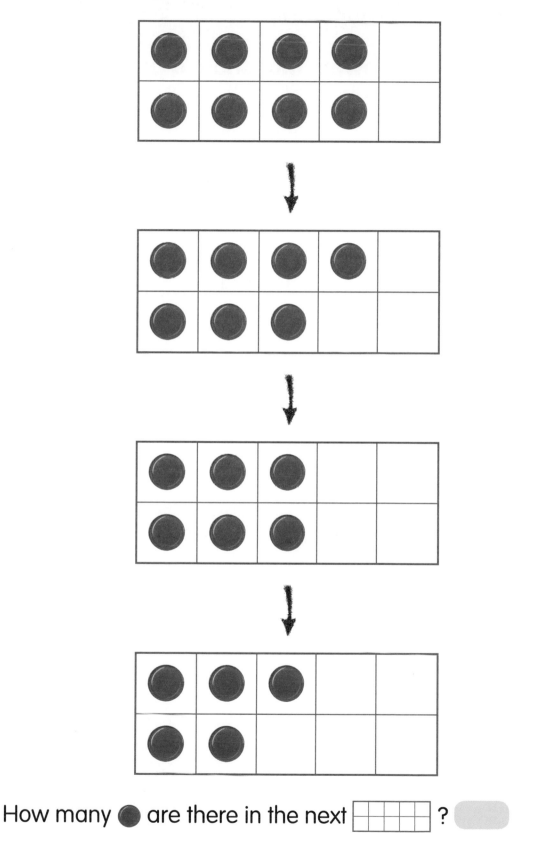

How many ⬤ are there in the next ▭▭▭▭▭ ?

Use 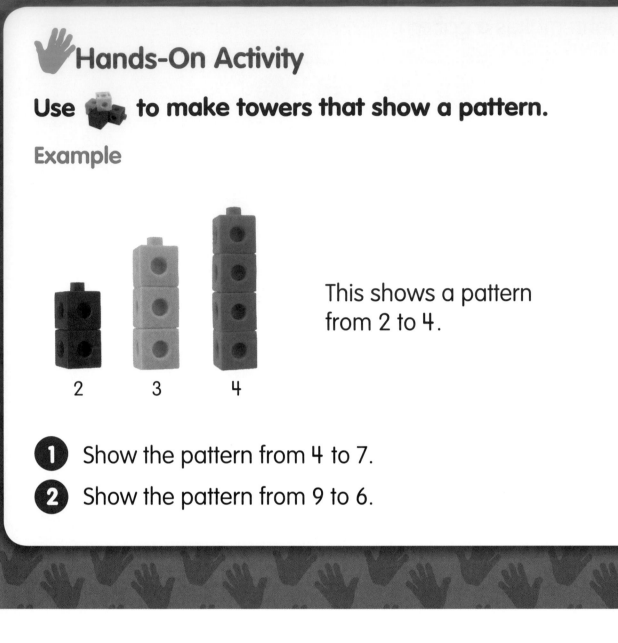 to make towers that show a pattern.

**Example**

This shows a pattern
from 2 to 4.

2    3    4

**1** Show the pattern from 4 to 7.

**2** Show the pattern from 9 to 6.

## Guided Practice

### Solve.

**3** Count on.
Find the next number in the pattern.

1, 2, 3, 4, [    ]

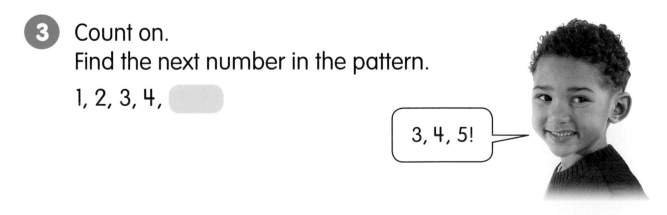

3, 4, 5!

**4** Find the missing numbers in the number patterns.

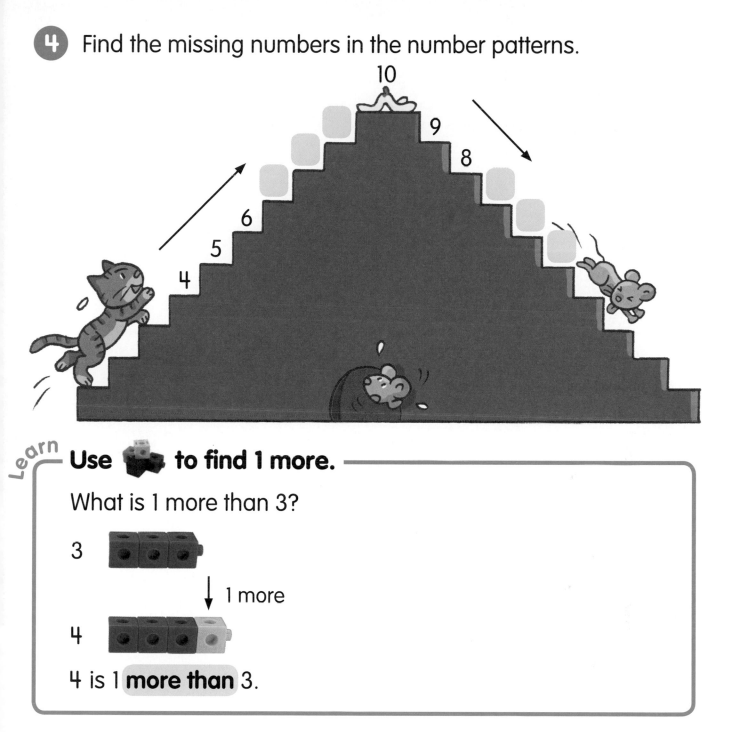

10

9

8

6

5

4

**Use  to find 1 more.**

What is 1 more than 3?

3

↓ 1 more

4

4 is 1 **more than** 3.

## Guided Practice

**Solve.**

**5** What is 1 more than 8?

        is 1 more than 8.

# Learn

## Use 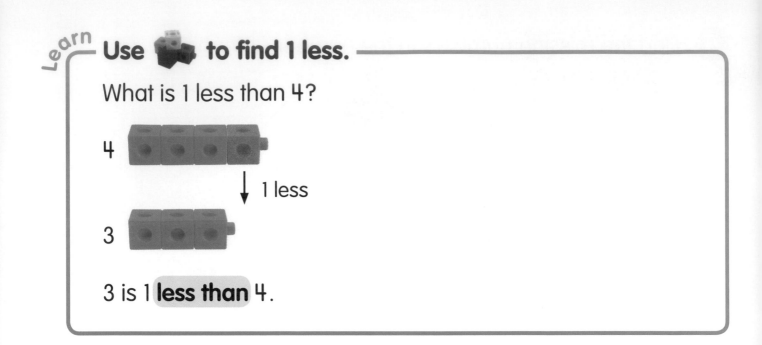 to find 1 less.

What is 1 less than 4?

4

↓ 1 less

3

3 is 1 **less than** 4.

## Guided Practice

### Solve.

**6** What is 1 less than 6?

_____ is 1 less than 6.

### Count and answer.

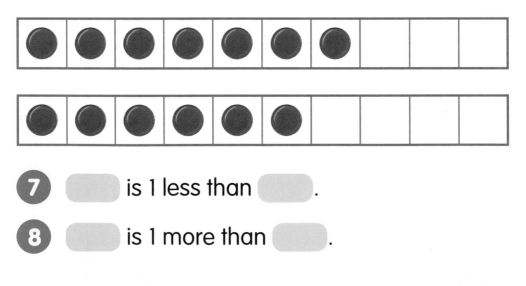

**7** _____ is 1 less than _____.

**8** _____ is 1 more than _____.

# Let's Practice

**Solve.**

**1**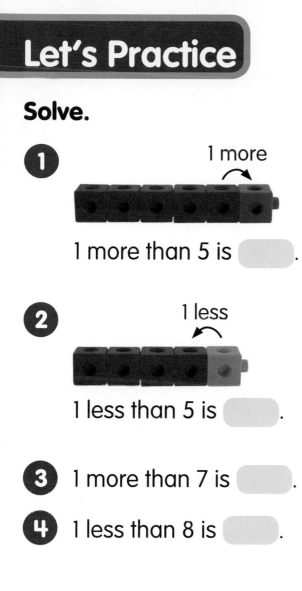

1 more

1 more than 5 is [    ].

**2**

1 less

1 less than 5 is [    ].

**3** 1 more than 7 is [    ].

**4** 1 less than 8 is [    ].

## Find the missing numbers in each pattern.

**5** 1, 2, 3, [    ], [    ]

**6** 2, 3, 4, [    ], [    ], 7, 8

**7** [    ], 7, 8, 9, [    ]

**8** 10, 9, [    ], [    ], [    ], 5, 4

**9** 5, 4, 3, [    ], [    ], [    ]

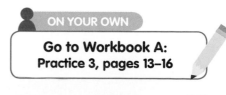

ON YOUR OWN

**Go to Workbook A:**
**Practice 3, pages 13–16**

# Math Journal

**Which sentences are true?**

1 A bicycle has 2 wheels.

2 A cat has 4 legs.

3 5 is more than 7.

4 8 is 1 less than 9.

# Put On Your Thinking Cap!

**PROBLEM SOLVING**

Here are some counters.

Group the numbers this way.

| Numbers Less Than 5 | Numbers from 5 to 7 | Numbers Greater Than 7 |
|---|---|---|
|  |  |  |

What can you say about the counters in each group?

**ON YOUR OWN**

**Go to Workbook A:
Put on Your Thinking Cap!
pages 17–18**

# Chapter Wrap Up

Count and compare numbers to 10.

You have learned...

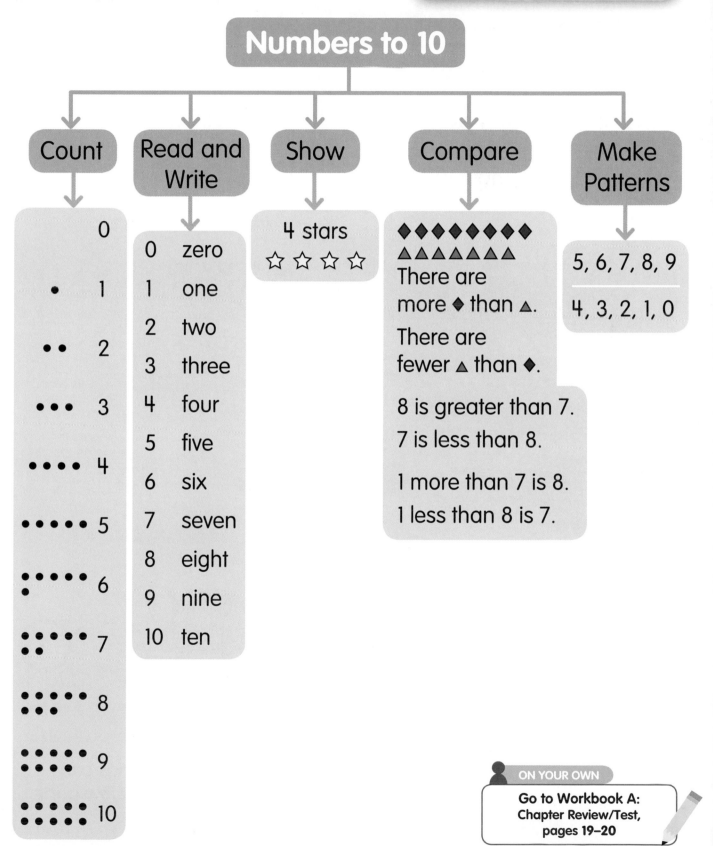

**Numbers to 10**

**Count**

0

• 1

•• 2

••• 3

•••• 4

••••• 5

•••••• 6

••••••• 7

•••••••• 8

••••••••• 9

•••••••••• 10

**Read and Write**

0 zero

1 one

2 two

3 three

4 four

5 five

6 six

7 seven

8 eight

9 nine

10 ten

**Show**

4 stars

☆ ☆ ☆ ☆

**Compare**

◆◆◆◆◆◆◆◆◆

△△△△△△△△

There are more ◆ than △.

There are fewer △ than ◆.

8 is greater than 7.

7 is less than 8.

1 more than 7 is 8.

1 less than 8 is 7.

**Make Patterns**

5, 6, 7, 8, 9

4, 3, 2, 1, 0

ON YOUR OWN

Go to Workbook A:
Chapter Review/Test,
pages 19–20

# CHAPTER 2 Number Bonds

Kittens, kittens, cute little kittens,
How I love them so!
Seven on the inside,
Three on the outside,
Each dressed up in a bow!

How many kittens are there?

7

3

?

**Lesson 1** Making Number Bonds

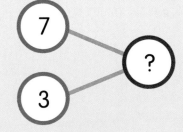

**BIG IDEA**

Number bonds can be used to show parts and whole.

# Recall Prior Knowledge

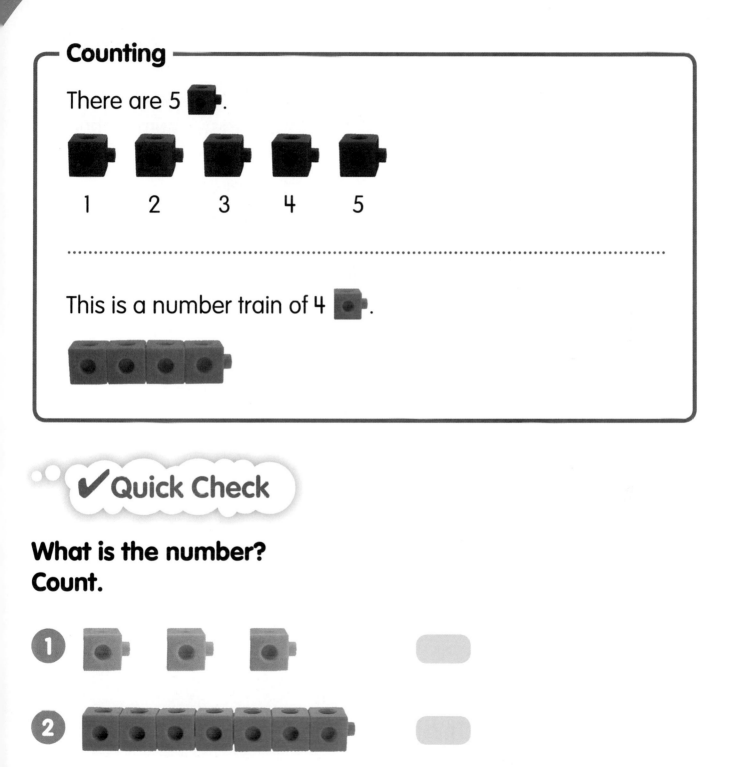

## Counting

There are 5 ▪.

1   2   3   4   5

This is a number train of 4 ▪.

## ✔ Quick Check

**What is the number?**
**Count.**

1

2

# 1 Making Number Bonds

### Lesson Objectives

- Use connecting cubes or a math balance to find number bonds.

- Find different number bonds for numbers to 10.

**Vocabulary**
part
whole
number bond

**Learn** **You can make number bonds with 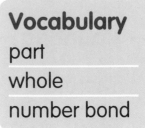.**

You can use a number train to make number bonds.

Sam put [number train] into two parts.

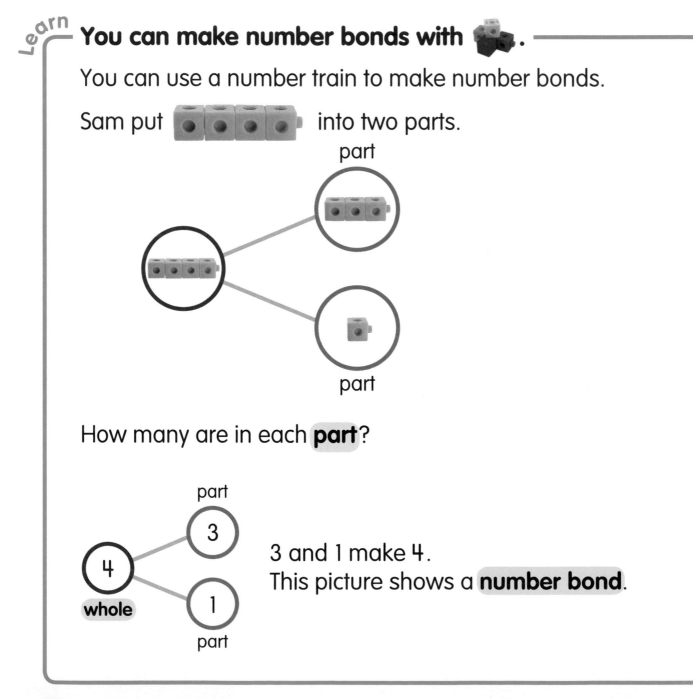

part

part

How many are in each **part**?

part

3

4
whole

1

part

3 and 1 make 4.
This picture shows a **number bond**.

# Hands-On Activity

Use 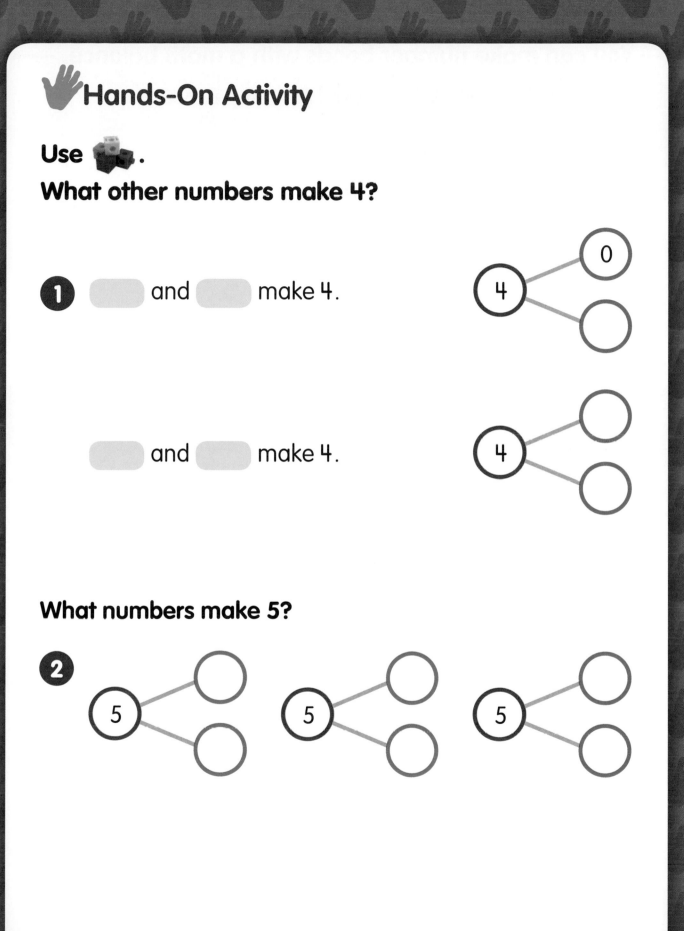 .

**What other numbers make 4?**

**1** ⬜ and ⬜ make 4.

4 — 0

4

**What numbers make 5?**

**2** 5

5

5

**You can make number bonds with a math balance.**

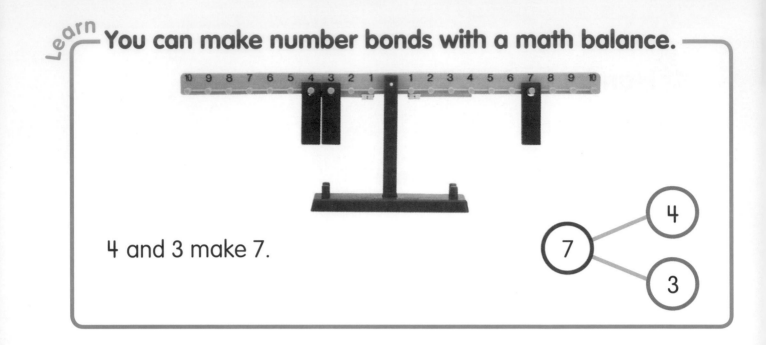

4 and 3 make 7.

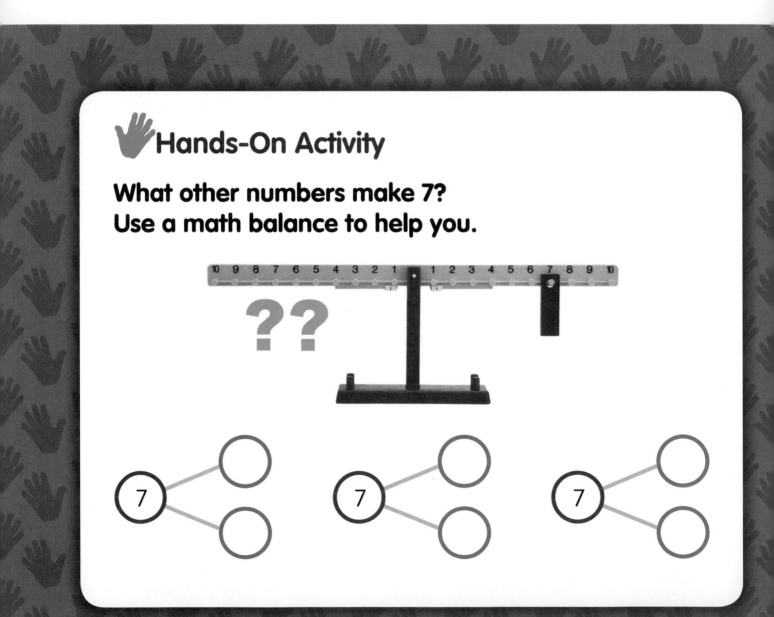

# Hands-On Activity

**What other numbers make 7?**
**Use a math balance to help you.**

??

# Let's Practice

Make number bonds for these numbers.
Use 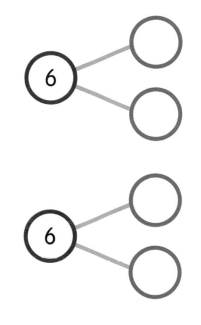 or a math balance to help you.

**1**

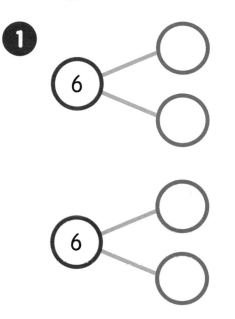

**2**

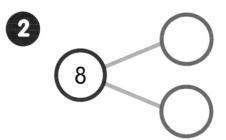

**3**

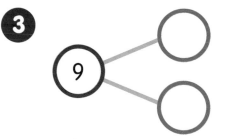

**ON YOUR OWN**

**Go to Workbook A:**
Practice 1 to 3, pages 21–30

READING AND WRITING MATH

# Math Journal

**Look at the picture.
Make two number bonds.**

red stool and ⬜ blue stools
make ⬜ stools.

# Let's Explore!

**Use 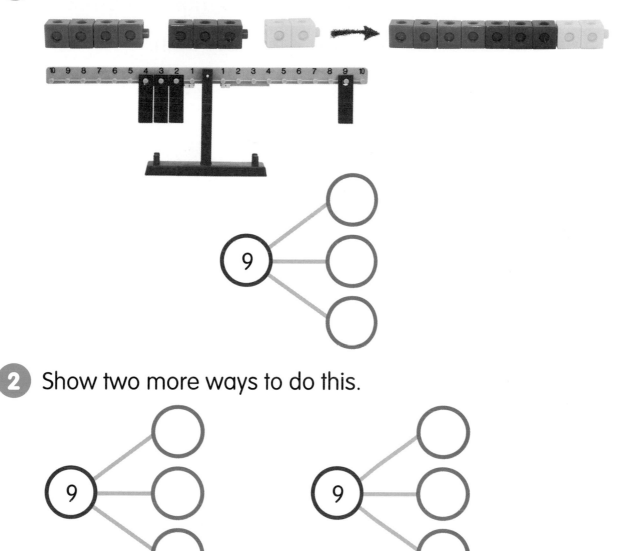 or a math balance to help you.**

**1** Find three numbers that make 9.

**2** Show two more ways to do this.

**3** Find three numbers that make 10.
Show two more ways to do this.

# Let's Explore!

**Use .**

**STEP 1** Put some 🟦 and ⬛ together to make a number train.

Now add some 🟨 to your number train.

Make sure your number train has 10 or less 🧊.

**STEP 2** Count the total number of 🟦 and ⬛. ⬭

Count the number of 🟨. ⬭

Add the total number of 🟦 and ⬛ to the number of 🟨.

What number do you get? ⬭

**STEP 3** Count the total number of ⬛ and 🟨. ⬭

Count the number of 🟦. ⬭

Add the number of 🟦 to the total number of ⬛ and 🟨.

What number do you get? ⬭

Did you get the same number for **STEP 2** and **STEP 3** ?

Choose different numbers of 🟦, ⬛, and 🟨.

Carry out **STEP 1**, **STEP 2**, and **STEP 3** again.

What do you notice?

**PROBLEM SOLVING**

## Find the number of beads.
## Use number bonds to help you.

**1** There are 6 beads under the two cups.

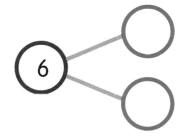

**2** There are 8 beads under the two cups.

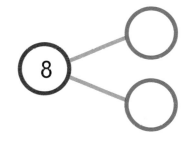

**3** There are 10 beads under the three cups.

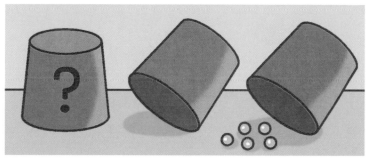

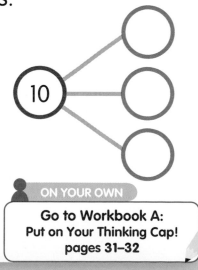

ON YOUR OWN

Go to Workbook A:
Put on Your Thinking Cap!
pages 31–32

# Chapter Wrap Up

**You have learned...**

## Numbers Bonds

to make a number bond.

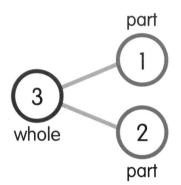

part

1

3 whole

2

part

1 and 2 make 3.
1, 2, and 3 make a number bond.

that there are more than one set of parts for a whole.

part

1

4 whole

3

part

part

2

4 whole

2

part

part

4

4 whole

0

part

to use a math balance to help you make number bonds.

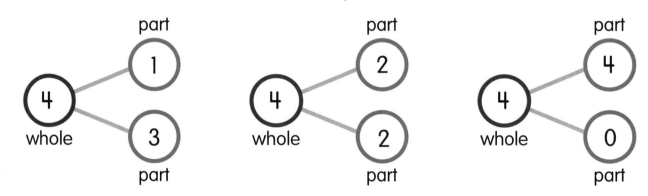

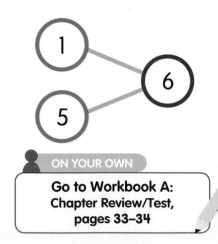

1

5

6

**ON YOUR OWN**

**Go to Workbook A: Chapter Review/Test, pages 33–34**

# CHAPTER
# 3  Addition Facts to 10

I'm riding on the school bus,
On my way to school,
On hops Lou and that makes two.

On goes the school bus,
Down the street, not too fast,
On leaps Sheree and that makes three!

On goes the school bus,
Up the hill, oh so slow!
On jumps Paul and then there are four!

On goes the school bus,
Round the corner, hold on tight!
On climbs Clive and then there are five!

On goes the school bus,
Stopping at the lights,
On plod Sam and Ben and that makes... seven!

**BIG IDEA**

Addition can be used to find how many in all.

# Recall Prior Knowledge

## Counting

There are 6 toys.

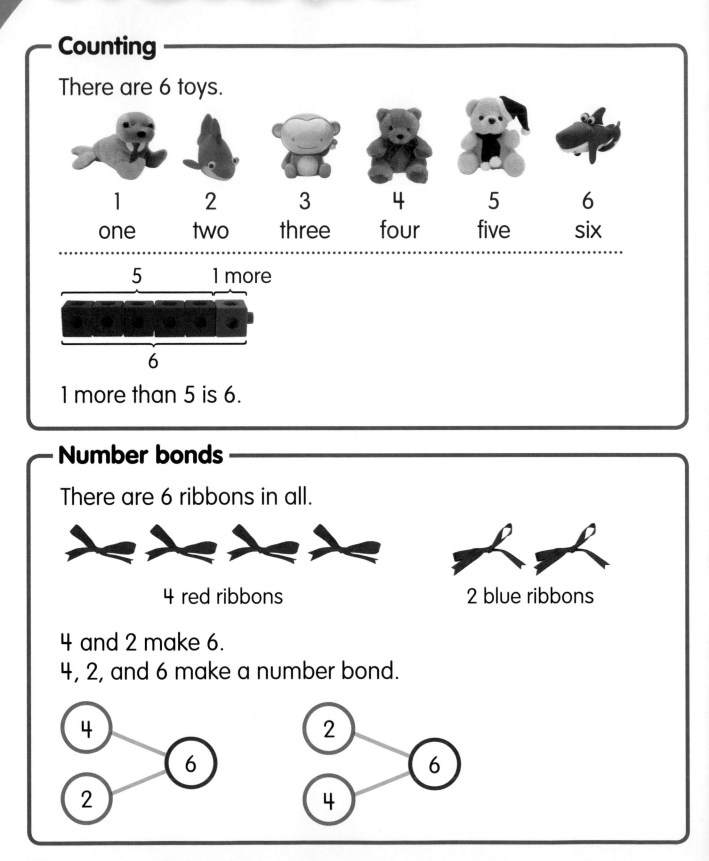

| 1 | 2 | 3 | 4 | 5 | 6 |
|---|---|---|---|---|---|
| one | two | three | four | five | six |

5    1 more

6

1 more than 5 is 6.

## Number bonds

There are 6 ribbons in all.

4 red ribbons          2 blue ribbons

4 and 2 make 6.
4, 2, and 6 make a number bond.

4
6
2

2
6
4

# ✔ Quick Check

## Count.

**1**  1, 2, 3, _____, _____, _____

**2**

There are _____ flowers.

1 more than 6 is _____.

**3**  There are 7 butterflies in all.

_____ white butterflies          _____ black butterflies

## Complete the number bonds.

**4**  5 and 2 make 7.
What other numbers make 7?

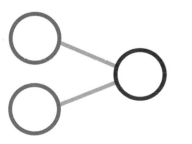   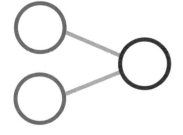   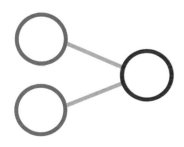

**Chapter 3** Addition Facts to 10     **41**

# Ways to Add

**LESSON 1**

## Lesson Objectives

- Count on to add.
- Use number bonds to add in any order.
- Write and solve addition sentences.

**Learn** **You can add by counting on.**

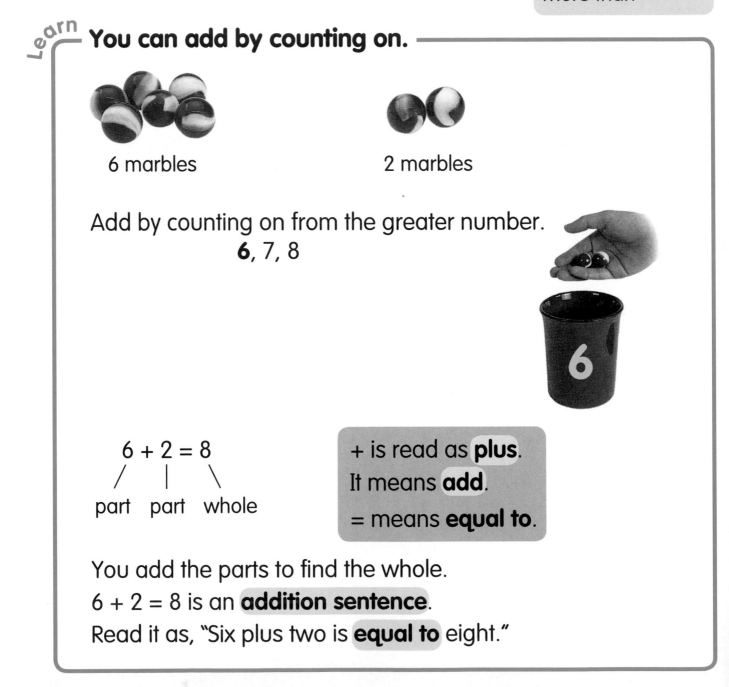

6 marbles

2 marbles

Add by counting on from the greater number.
**6**, 7, 8

$$6 + 2 = 8$$

part  part  whole

+ is read as **plus**.
It means **add**.
= means **equal to**.

You add the parts to find the whole.
$6 + 2 = 8$ is an **addition sentence**.
Read it as, "Six plus two is **equal to** eight."

## Guided Practice

**Find the missing numbers.**
**Count on from the greater number.**

**1** 2 + 5 = ?

5, ____ , ____

**2** 7 + 3 = ?

7, ____ , ____ , ____

---

 **Hands-On Activity**

Use  .
**Make the number trains.**
**Count on from the greater number.**
**Complete the addition sentence.**

**1** 8

2

____ , ____ , ____

____ + ____ = ____

**2** 4

5

5, ____ , ____ , ____ , ____

4 + 5 = ____

**Count on from the greater number.
Complete the addition sentence.**

**3**

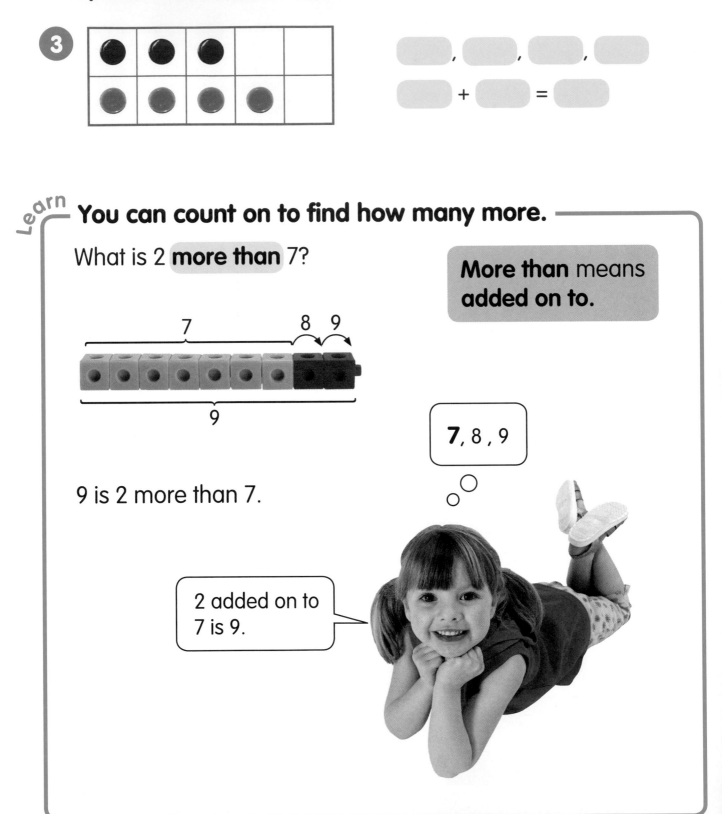

☐ , ☐ , ☐ , ☐

☐ + ☐ = ☐

**Learn** **You can count on to find how many more.**

What is 2 **more than** 7?

**More than** means
added on to.

7    8   9

**7**, 8 , 9

9 is 2 more than 7.

2 added on to
7 is 9.

## Guided Practice

### Find the missing numbers.

**4** What is 3 more than 5?

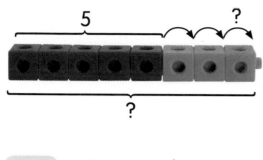

5, ____, ____, ____

_____ is 3 more than 5.

**5** What is 2 more than 6?

6, ____, ____

_____ is 2 more than 6.

# Card Fun!

Players: 3

You need:
- 2 packs of cards

## How to play:

 **STEP 1** Make two packs of cards.

Pack X

| 1 | 2 | 3 | 0 |
|---|---|---|---|

| 1 | 2 | 3 |
|---|---|---|

Pack Y

| 1 | 2 | 3 | 4 | 5 |
|---|---|---|---|---|

| 6 | 7 |
|---|---|

 **STEP 2** Player 1 picks a card from Pack X.

**STEP 3** Player 2 picks a card from Pack Y.

**STEP 4** Player 3 adds the numbers on the cards, then says the answer.

**STEP 5** Players 1 and 2 check the answer.

$5 + 3 = 8$

Correct!

**STEP 6** Player 3 gets one point if the answer is correct. Take turns to pick cards and add.

After six rounds, the player with the most points wins!

# Let's Practice

**Add.**
**Count on from the greater number.**

1. $4 + 2 = $ ⬚

2. $6 + 1 = $ ⬚

3. $2 + 3 = $ ⬚

4. $7 + 3 = $ ⬚

5. $3 + 5 = $ ⬚

6. $2 + 8 = $ ⬚

7. What is 4 more than 5? ⬚

8. What is 3 more than 6? ⬚

9. What is 2 more than 7? ⬚

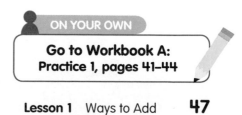

ON YOUR OWN

Go to Workbook A:
Practice 1, pages 41–44

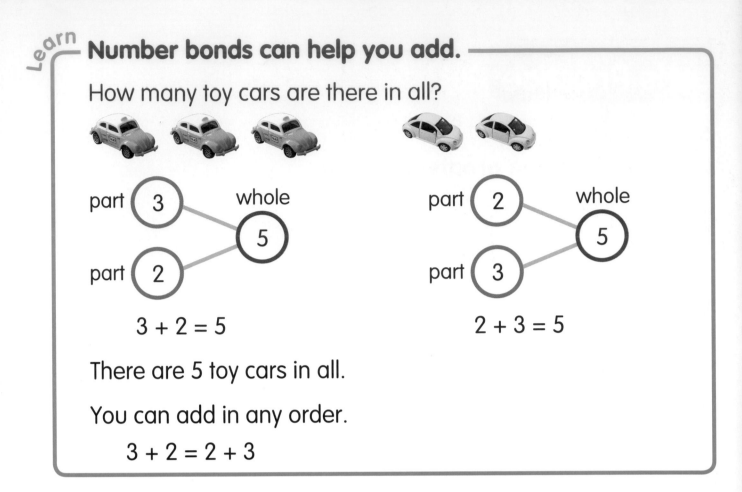

## Learn Number bonds can help you add.

How many toy cars are there in all?

part ( 3 )   whole
          ( 5 )
part ( 2 )

$$3 + 2 = 5$$

part ( 2 )   whole
          ( 5 )
part ( 3 )

$$2 + 3 = 5$$

There are 5 toy cars in all.

You can add in any order.

$$3 + 2 = 2 + 3$$

## Guided Practice

## Add. Use number bonds to help you.

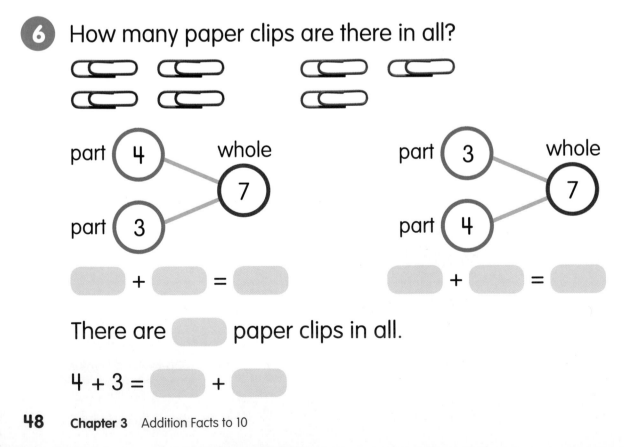

**6**   How many paper clips are there in all?

part ( 4 )   whole
          ( 7 )
part ( 3 )

part ( 3 )   whole
          ( 7 )
part ( 4 )

[   ] + [   ] = [   ]          [   ] + [   ] = [   ]

There are [   ] paper clips in all.

$$4 + 3 = [\quad] + [\quad]$$

# Number bonds can help you add.

How many lemons are there in all?

5 + 3 = 8

3 + 5 = 8

There are 8 lemons in all.

You can add in any order.

5 + 3 = 3 + 5

3 added on to 5 is equal to 8.
⬜ added on to ⬜ is also equal to 8.

# Add.
# Use number bonds to help you.

**7** How many monkeys are there in all?

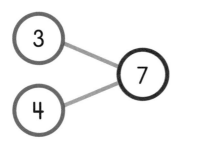  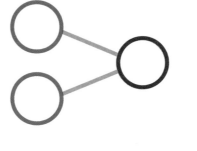

⬜ + ⬜ = ⬜          ⬜ + ⬜ = ⬜

There are ⬜ monkeys in all.

You can add in any order.

4 added on to 3 is equal to 7.
⬜ added on to ⬜ is
also equal to 7.

## 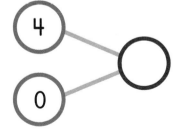Hands-On Activity

**Use ⬤◯ and two ▢▢▢▢▢.**

Show 2 + 8.

| | | | | |
|---|---|---|---|---|
| | | | | |

Show 8 + 2.

| | | | | |
|---|---|---|---|---|
| | | | | |

What can you say about 2 + 8 and 8 + 2?

# Let's Practice

**Complete the number bonds.**

**1**

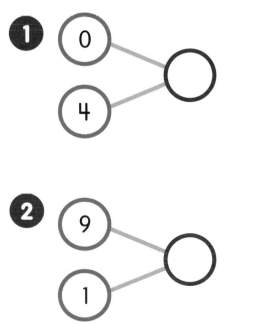

0
4
◯

4
0
◯

**2**

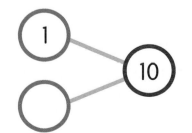

9
1
◯

1
◯
10

# Complete the number bonds.
# Find the missing numbers.

**3** How many crayons are there in all?

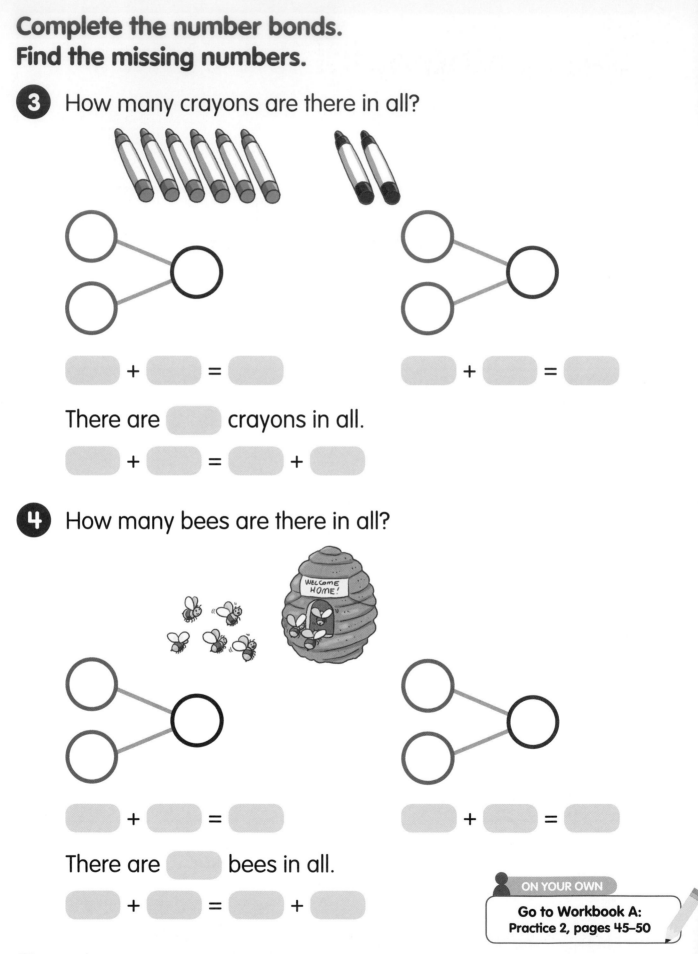

+ = 

There are ___ crayons in all.

+ = + 

**4** How many bees are there in all?

+ = 

There are ___ bees in all.

+ = + 

**ON YOUR OWN**

Go to Workbook A:
Practice 2, pages 45–50

# LESSON 2 Making Addition Stories

**Lesson Objectives**

- Tell addition stories about pictures.
- Write addition sentences.

**Vocabulary**
addition story

**Learn** — **You can tell addition stories about a picture.**

5 🦆 are in a pond.

4 🦆 join them.

5 + 4 = 9

There are 9 🦆 in all.

5
4
9

## Guided Practice

**Look at the pictures.**
**Tell an addition story.**

**1**

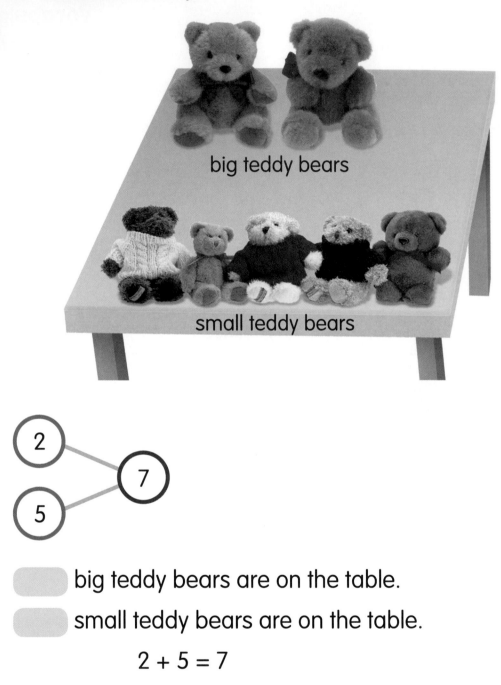

big teddy bears

small teddy bears

There are ⬜ big teddy bears are on the table.

⬜ small teddy bears are on the table.

$$2 + 5 = 7$$

There are ⬜ teddy bears in all.

**2**

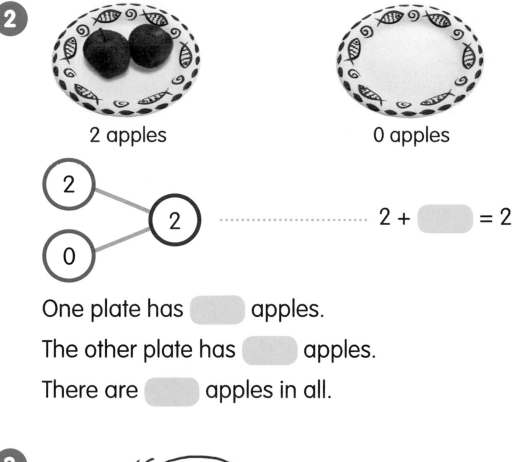

2 apples                  0 apples

2 + [   ] = 2

One plate has [   ] apples.

The other plate has [   ] apples.

There are [   ] apples in all.

**3**

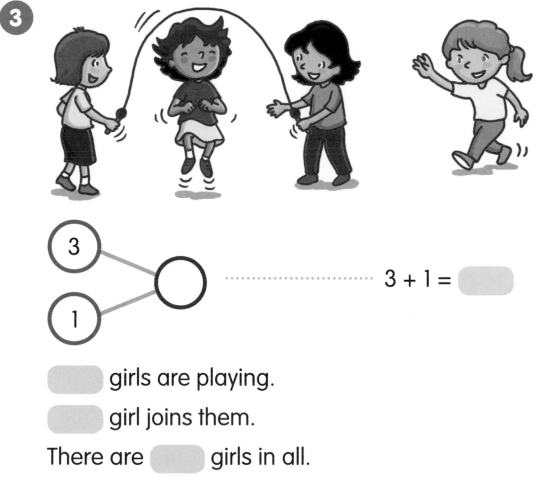

3 + 1 = [   ]

[   ] girls are playing.

[   ] girl joins them.

There are [   ] girls in all.

## Look at the picture.
## Tell an addition story about each thing.

**1** the birds

**2** the bicycles

**3** the turtles

ON YOUR OWN

Go to Workbook A:
Practice 3, pages 51–54

# LESSON 3 Real-World Problems: Addition

## Lesson Objectives

- Write addition sentences.
- Solve real-world problems.

**Learn** Read and understand a word problem.

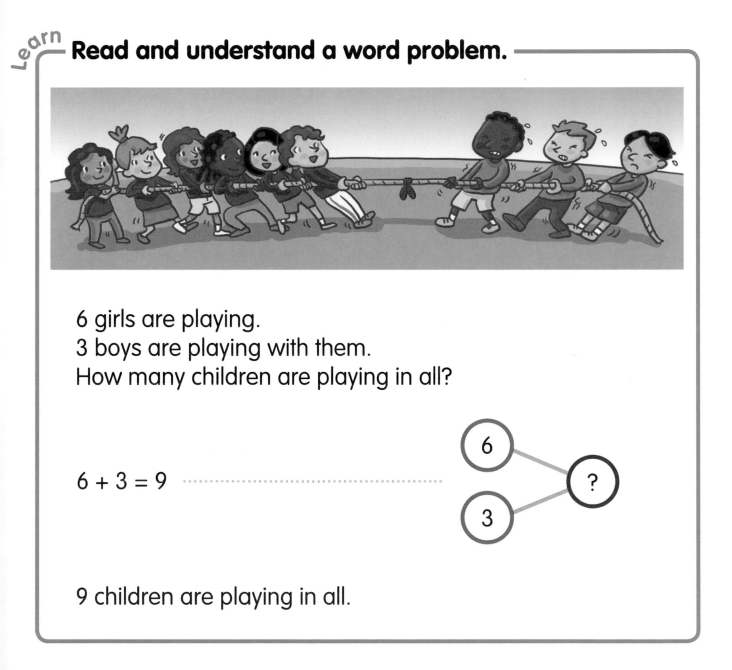

6 girls are playing.
3 boys are playing with them.
How many children are playing in all?

6 + 3 = 9 ·········································

6
3
?

9 children are playing in all.

## Guided Practice

### Solve.

**1** John has 2 baseball cards.
He has 4 football cards.
How many cards does John have in all?

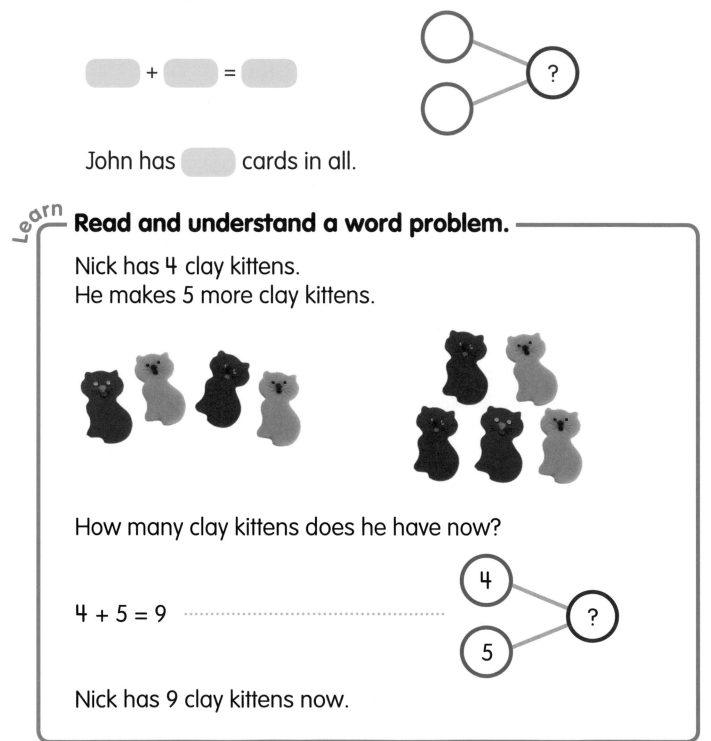

[____] + [____] = [____]

John has [____] cards in all.

### Learn **Read and understand a word problem.**

Nick has 4 clay kittens.
He makes 5 more clay kittens.

How many clay kittens does he have now?

4 + 5 = 9

Nick has 9 clay kittens now.

## Guided Practice

**Solve.**

**2**

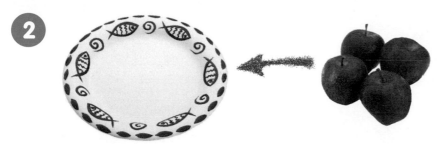

Mary has no apples on her plate.
Tara puts 4 apples on Mary's plate.
How many apples does Mary have now?

[ ] [ ] [ ] = [ ]

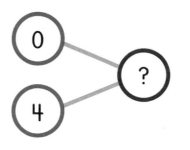

Mary has [ ] apples now.

---

# Let's Practice

**Solve.**

**1** Megan has 4 red markers.
She has 3 blue markers.
How many markers does she have in all?

**2** 2 children are dancing.
7 children join them.
How many children are dancing now?

**3**

Jar A          Jar B

Jar A has 5 marbles.
Jar B has 0 marbles.
How many marbles are there in all?

ON YOUR OWN

Go to Workbook A:
Practice 4, pages 55–56

**PROBLEM SOLVING**

Find the missing numbers.

Fill in the ⬜ with 1, 2, 3, 4, 6, or 7.

Use each number once.

Then find the missing number in ⬜, ⬜, and ⬜.

The numbers may be 10 or less than 10.

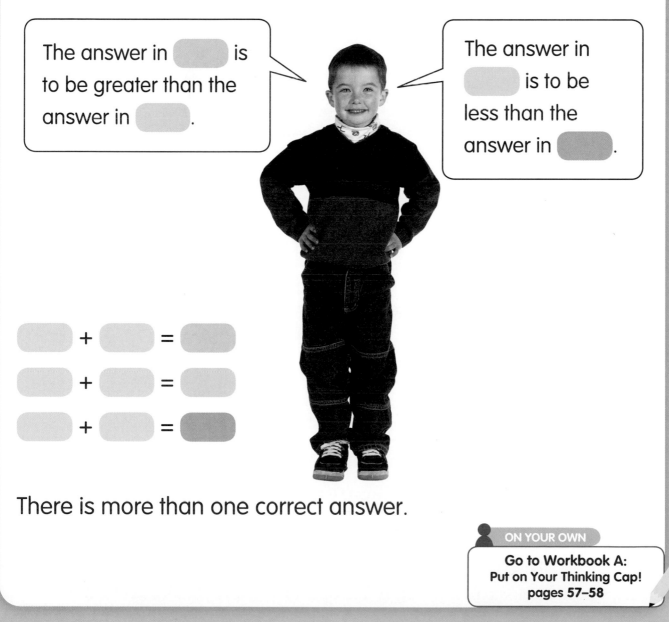

The answer in ⬜ is to be greater than the answer in ⬜.

The answer in ⬜ is to be less than the answer in ⬜.

⬜ + ⬜ = ⬜

⬜ + ⬜ = ⬜

⬜ + ⬜ = ⬜

There is more than one correct answer.

ON YOUR OWN

Go to Workbook A:
Put on Your Thinking Cap!
pages 57–58

# Chapter Wrap Up

**You have learned...**

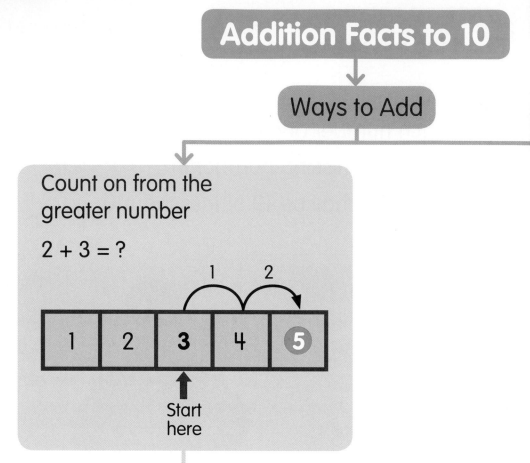

Addition Facts to 10

Ways to Add

Count on from the greater number

2 + 3 = ?

1  2

| 1 | 2 | **3** | 4 | 5 |

Start here

Tell addition stories about a picture and write an addition sentence for each story.

There is 1 yellow bean.
There are 2 green beans.

1 + 2 = 3

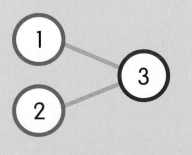

1

2

3

There are 3 beans in all.

Number Bonds

$3 + 5 = 8$

$5 + 3 = 8$

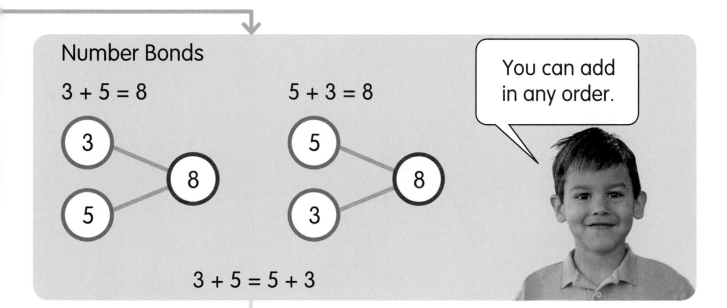

You can add in any order.

$3 + 5 = 5 + 3$

Solve real-world problems

Kelly has 6 stickers.
Her friend gives her 2 stickers.
How many stickers does Kelly have now?

$6 + 2 = 8$

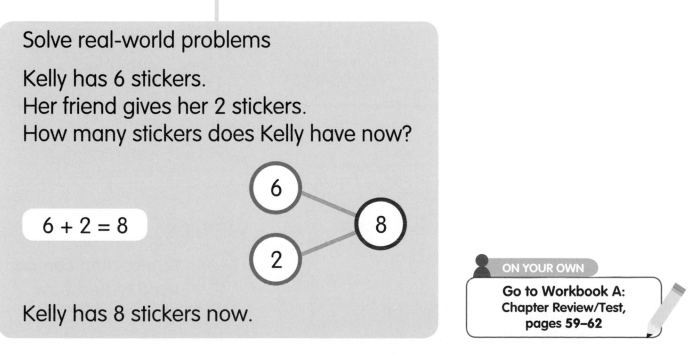

Kelly has 8 stickers now.

ON YOUR OWN

Go to Workbook A:
Chapter Review/Test,
pages 59–62

# Subtraction Facts to 10

BIG IDEA

Subtraction can be used to find how many are left.

# Recall Prior Knowledge

## Counting

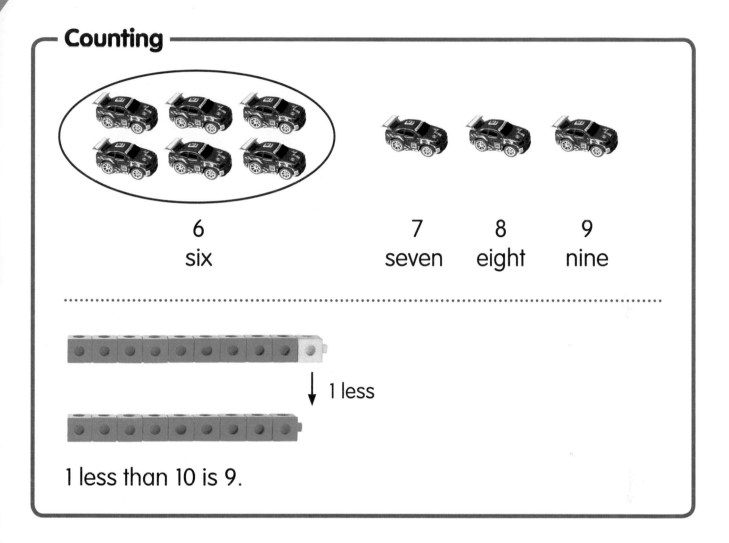

6
six

7
seven

8
eight

9
nine

↓ 1 less

1 less than 10 is 9.

## Number bonds

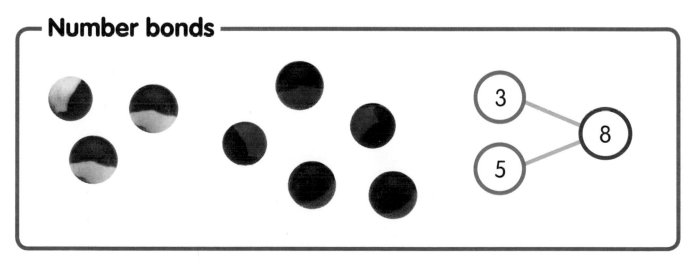

3

5

8

## Quick Check

**Find the missing numbers in each pattern.**

**1**  2, 3, 4, ⬚, ⬚, ⬚

**2**  9, 8, 7, ⬚, ⬚, ⬚

## Look at the picture.
## Complete the number bond.

**3**

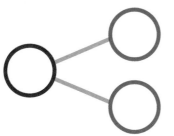

## Solve.

**4**

⬚ is 1 less than 7.

# LESSON 1 Ways to Subtract

## Lesson Objectives

- Take away to subtract.
- Count on to subtract.
- Count back to subtract.
- Use number bonds to subtract.
- Write and solve subtraction sentences.

**Vocabulary**

take away

subtract

minus (−)

subtraction sentence

less than

---

*Learn* **You can subtract by taking away.**

9 spiders are having breakfast.
6 spiders walk away.
How many spiders are left?

> Crossing out 6 spiders **takes away** 6 spiders.

You subtract one part from the whole to find the other part.

9 − 6 = 3
whole  part  part

> − is read as **minus**.
> It means **subtract**.

3 spiders are left.

9 − 6 = 3 is a **subtraction sentence**.

Read it as, "Nine minus six is equal to three."

## Guided Practice

**Find how many are left.**

**1**

10 − 4 = ⬭

**2**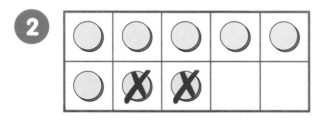

8 − 2 = ⬭

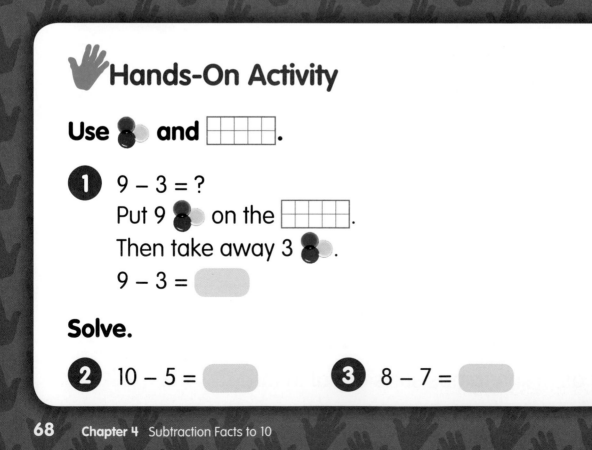

## 🖐 Hands-On Activity

**Use 🔵 and ▭▭▭▭▭.**

**1** 9 − 3 = ?

Put 9 🔵 on the ▭▭▭▭▭.

Then take away 3 🔵.

9 − 3 = ⬭

**Solve.**

**2** 10 − 5 = ⬭   **3** 8 − 7 = ⬭

# You can take away to find how many less.

What is 2 less than 6?

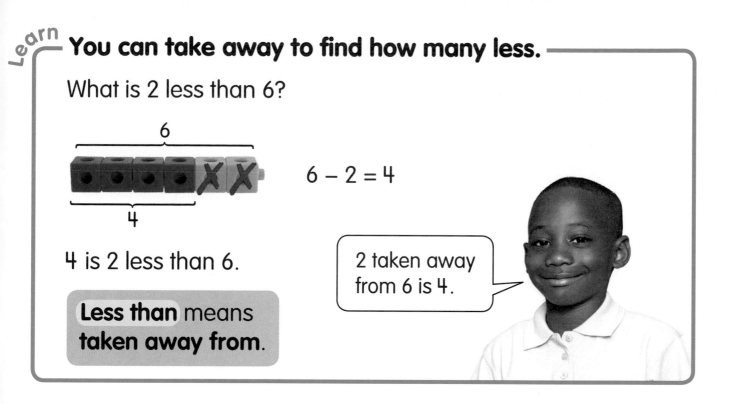

$6 - 2 = 4$

4 is 2 less than 6.

2 taken away from 6 is 4.

**Less than** means **taken away from**.

## Guided Practice

**Solve.**

**3** What is 5 less than 8?

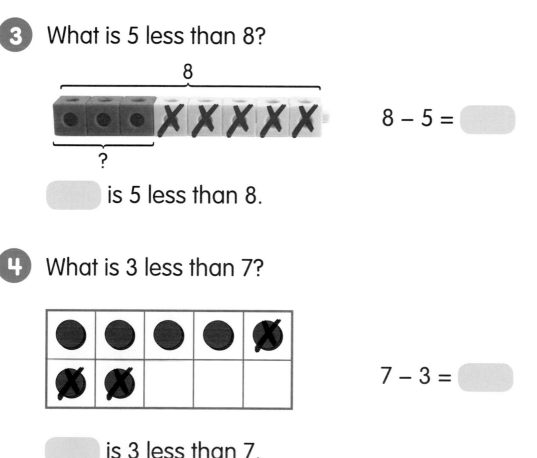

$8 - 5 = $ ☐

☐ is 5 less than 8.

**4** What is 3 less than 7?

$7 - 3 = $ ☐

☐ is 3 less than 7.

Learn **You can count on to subtract.**

9 birds are on a wire.
6 birds fly away.
How many birds are still on the wire?

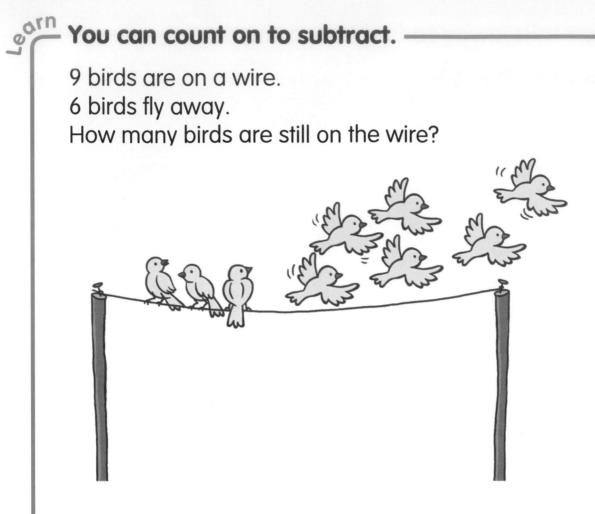

Find 9 – 6.
Count on from the number that is less, 6.
Stop at 9.

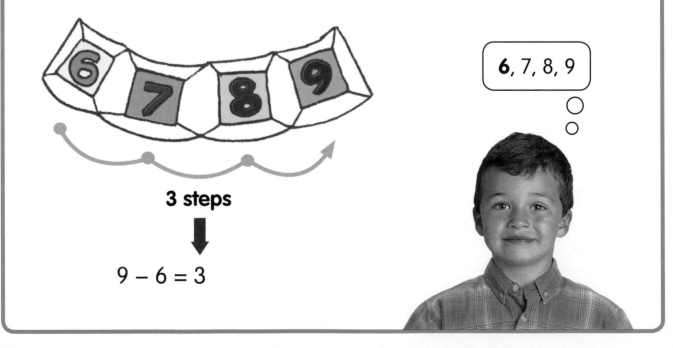

**6**, 7, 8, 9

**3 steps**

9 – 6 = 3

# What's Hidden?

Players: 3-4
You need:

**How to play:**

STEP **1** Player 1 chooses a number of 🎲 and shows them to the other players.

STEP **2** Player 1 hides some of them.

STEP **3** The other players must tell the number of 🎲 Player 1 hid. Count on to find out.

There were 8.

Now there are 5.

**5**, 6, 7, 8
You hid 3 🎲!

STEP **4** Check their answer. Take turns to play!

Correct!

## Guided Practice

**Count on from the number that is less to subtract.**

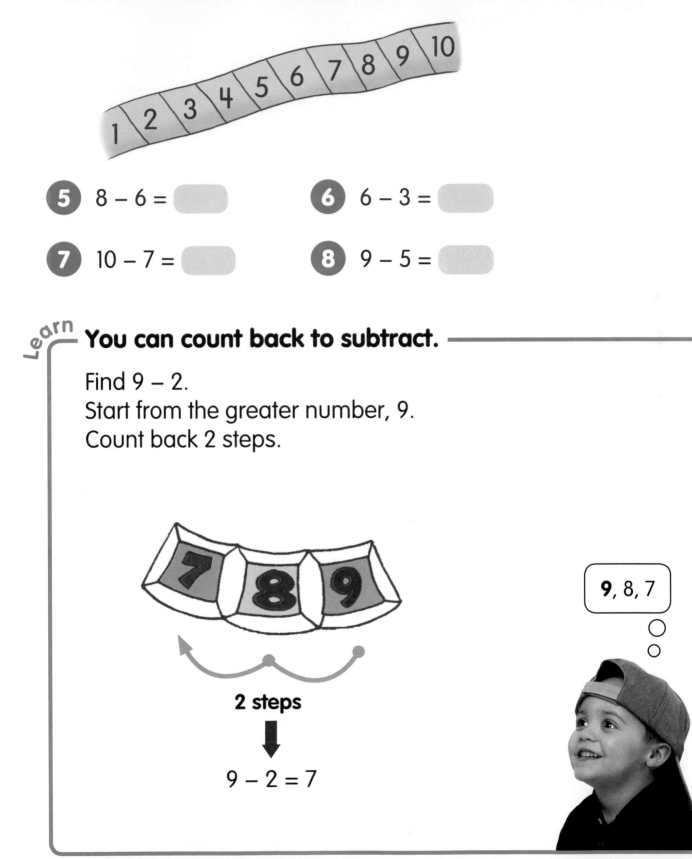

**5** $8 - 6 = $ 〇

**6** $6 - 3 = $ 〇

**7** $10 - 7 = $ 〇

**8** $9 - 5 = $ 〇

*Learn*

### You can count back to subtract.

Find $9 - 2$.
Start from the greater number, 9.
Count back 2 steps.

**2 steps**

$9 - 2 = 7$

**9**, 8, 7

## Guided Practice

**Count back from the greater number to subtract.**

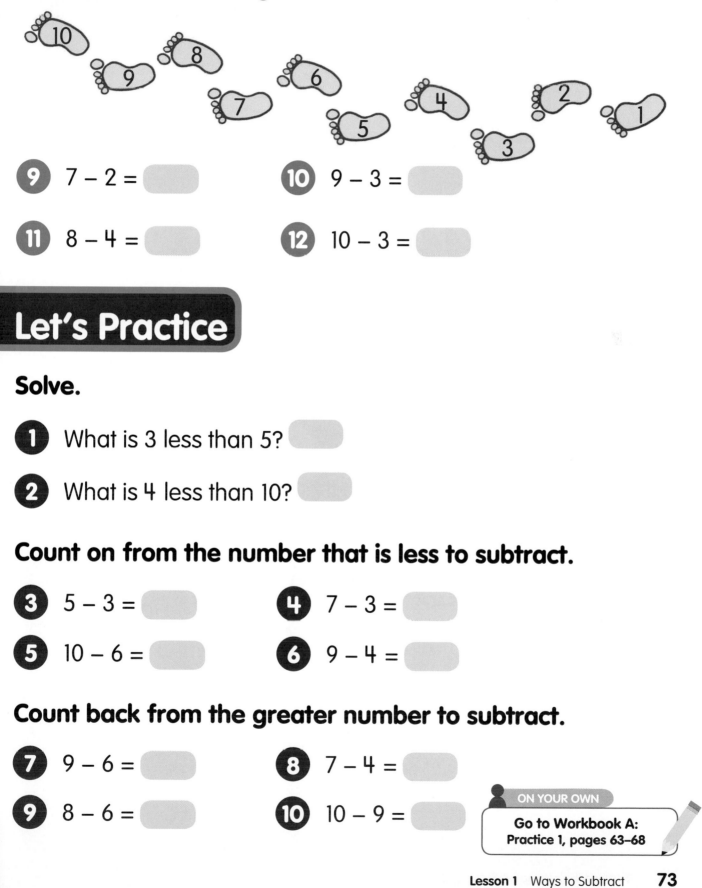

**9** 7 − 2 = ⬭      **10** 9 − 3 = ⬭

**11** 8 − 4 = ⬭      **12** 10 − 3 = ⬭

# Let's Practice

## Solve.

**1** What is 3 less than 5? ⬭

**2** What is 4 less than 10? ⬭

## Count on from the number that is less to subtract.

**3** 5 − 3 = ⬭      **4** 7 − 3 = ⬭

**5** 10 − 6 = ⬭      **6** 9 − 4 = ⬭

## Count back from the greater number to subtract.

**7** 9 − 6 = ⬭      **8** 7 − 4 = ⬭

**9** 8 − 6 = ⬭      **10** 10 − 9 = ⬭

**ON YOUR OWN**

Go to Workbook A:
Practice 1, pages 63–68

**You can use number bonds to help you subtract.**

How many beanbags are on the floor?

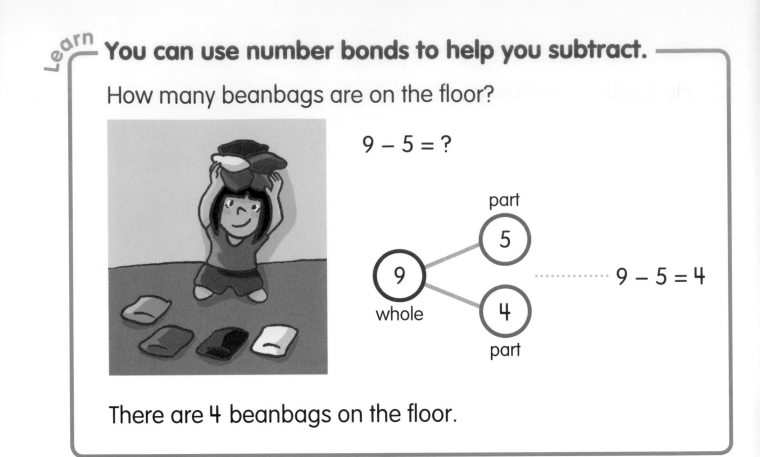

$9 - 5 = ?$

part

5

9

whole

4

part

$9 - 5 = 4$

There are 4 beanbags on the floor.

## Guided Practice

**Use number bonds to subtract.**

**13** How many yellow beans are there?

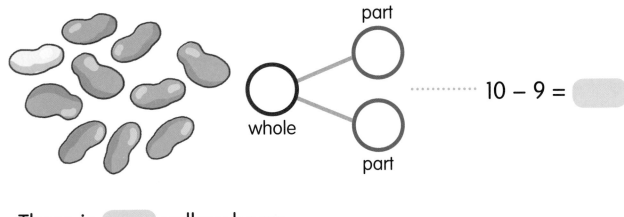

part

whole

part

$10 - 9 = $

There is ⬜ yellow bean.

## You can use number bonds to help you subtract.

How many strawberries are left on the plate?

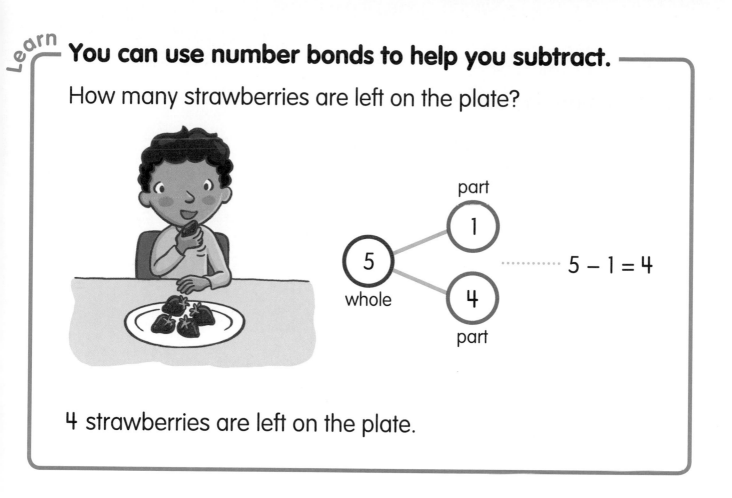

part

5 whole

1

4

part

............ 5 − 1 = 4

4 strawberries are left on the plate.

## Guided Practice

### Use number bonds to subtract.

**14** How many seahorses do not swim away?

part

whole

part

10 − ⬚ = ⬚

⬚ seahorses do not swim away.

# Let's Practice

**Fill in the number bonds.**
**Complete the subtraction sentences.**

**1** How many frogs are on a lily pad?

$8 - \boxed{\phantom{0}} = \boxed{\phantom{0}}$

$\boxed{\phantom{0}}$ frogs are on a lily pad.

**2** How many birds are left in the nest?

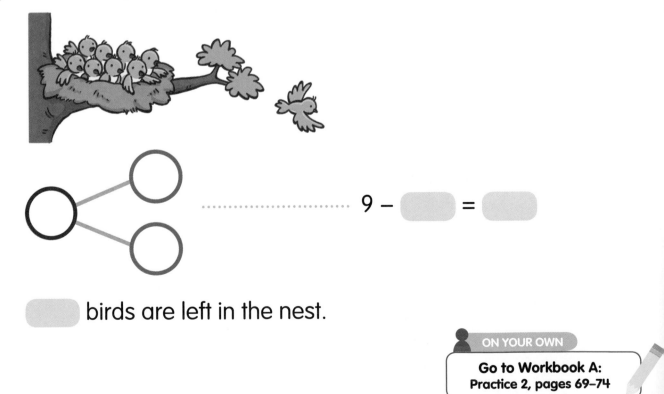

$9 - \boxed{\phantom{0}} = \boxed{\phantom{0}}$

$\boxed{\phantom{0}}$ birds are left in the nest.

ON YOUR OWN

Go to Workbook A:
Practice 2, pages 69–74

# 2 Making Subtraction Stories

## Lesson Objectives

- Tell subtraction stories about pictures.
- Write subtraction sentences.

**Vocabulary**
subtraction story

### Learn

**You can tell subtraction stories about a picture.**

There are 7 animals.
4 are squirrels.

7
4
3

$7 - 4 = 3$

3 are hamsters.

## Guided Practice

**Look at the picture.**
**Tell a subtraction story.**
**Complete the subtraction sentence.**

1

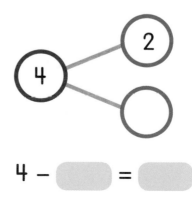

4
2

$4 - \boxed{\phantom{0}} = \boxed{\phantom{0}}$

Sarah has 10 apples.
Josh takes 2 apples
from Sarah.

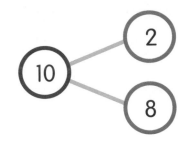

$$10 - 2 = 8$$

Sarah has 8 apples left.

## Guided Practice

**Look at the pictures.**
**Tell a subtraction story.**
**Complete the subtraction sentence.**

**2**

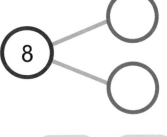

$$8 - \boxed{\phantom{0}} = \boxed{\phantom{0}}$$

#  Hands-On Activity

**Use**  **.**

**1** Put some counters on the table.
Then take away 0 counters.
How many counters are left on the table?

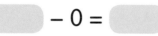 – 0 = ▢

**2** Try this again.
Put a different number of counters on the table.
Then take away 0 counters.
How many counters are left on the table?

▢ – 0 = ▢

What do you notice?

**3** Tell a story about taking away 0.

**Example**

I have 3 buttons on my jeans.
0 buttons fall off.
3 – 0 = 3

# Let's Practice

## Make a subtraction sentence for each picture.

**1**

 –  =

**2**

 –  =

# Look at the picture.
# Tell subtraction stories about it.
# Make a subtraction sentence for each story.

**3**

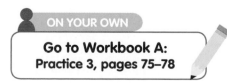

ON YOUR OWN

**Go to Workbook A:**
Practice 3, pages 75–78

Lesson 2   Making Subtraction Stories   **81**

# Real-World Problems: Subtraction

**Lesson Objectives**

- Write subtraction sentences.
- Solve real-world word problems.

*Learn* **Read and understand a word problem.**

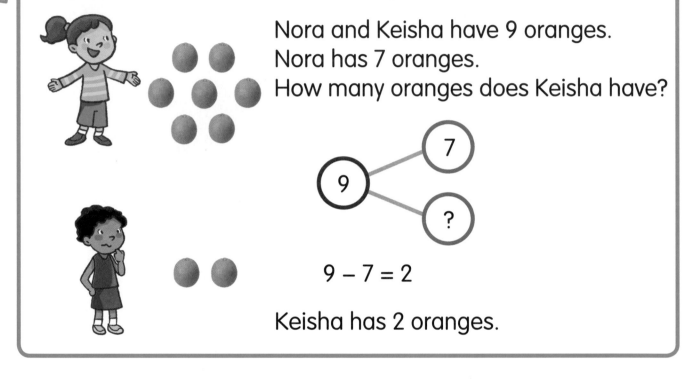

Nora and Keisha have 9 oranges.
Nora has 7 oranges.
How many oranges does Keisha have?

$9 - 7 = 2$

Keisha has 2 oranges.

## Guided Practice

**Solve.**

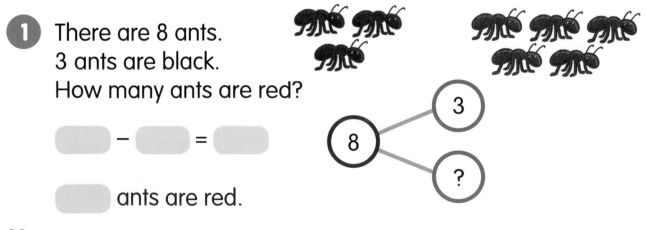

1  There are 8 ants.
3 ants are black.
How many ants are red?

☐ – ☐ = ☐

☐ ants are red.

**Subtract to solve word problems by taking away.**

There are 10 biscuits on a plate.
Luis takes some.
6 biscuits are left.
How many biscuits does he take?

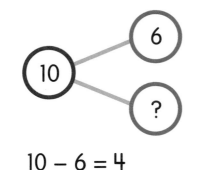

$$10 - 6 = 4$$

Luis takes 4 biscuits.

## Guided Practice

**Solve.**

**2** Jackie has 9 balloons.
2 balloons burst.
How many balloons does
Jackie have left?

 = 

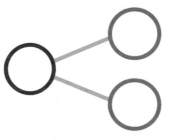

Jackie has ____ balloons left.

**Solve.**

A tree has 7 lemons.
2 of the lemons are yellow.
How many lemons are green?

There are 10 muffins.
Hector takes some.
3 muffins are left.
How many muffins does Hector take?

**ON YOUR OWN**

Go to Workbook A:
Practice 4, pages 79–80

# Making Fact Families

## Lesson Objectives

• Recognize related addition and subtraction sentences.

• Write fact families.

• Use fact families to solve real-world problems.

**Vocabulary**
fact family

**Learn** — **Addition and subtraction are related.**

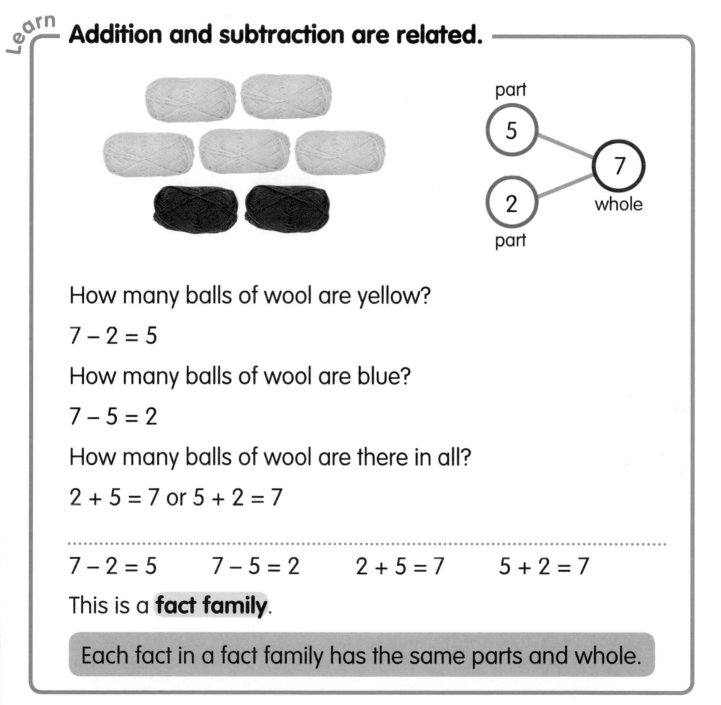

part
5
7
whole
2
part

How many balls of wool are yellow?

$7 - 2 = 5$

How many balls of wool are blue?

$7 - 5 = 2$

How many balls of wool are there in all?

$2 + 5 = 7$ or $5 + 2 = 7$

$7 - 2 = 5$      $7 - 5 = 2$      $2 + 5 = 7$      $5 + 2 = 7$

This is a **fact family**.

Each fact in a fact family has the same parts and whole.

# Guided Practice

## Look at the picture.
## Find the missing numbers in the fact family.

**1**

$4 + 2 = 6$ $\qquad$ $6 - 4 = 2$

◻ + ◻ = ◻ $\qquad$ ◻ − ◻ = ◻

## Make a fact family for each picture.

**2**

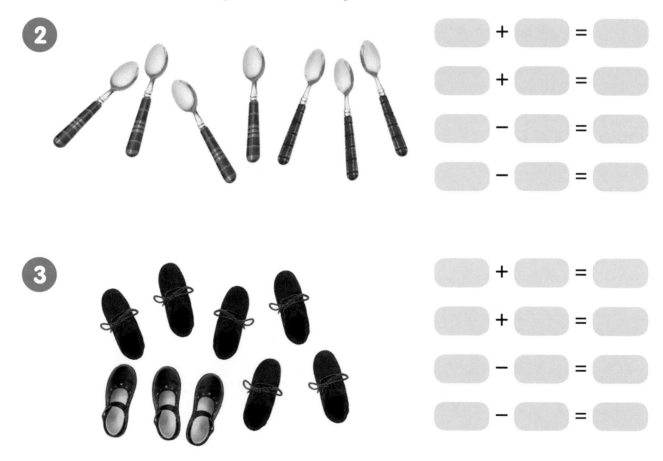

◻ + ◻ = ◻

◻ + ◻ = ◻

◻ − ◻ = ◻

◻ − ◻ = ◻

**3**

◻ + ◻ = ◻

◻ + ◻ = ◻

◻ − ◻ = ◻

◻ − ◻ = ◻

**Learn** **You can use related addition facts to solve subtraction sentences.**

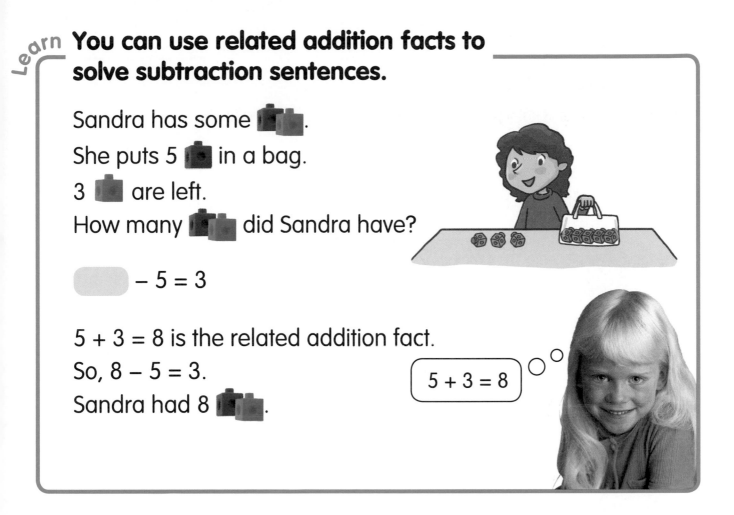

Sandra has some ▪▪.
She puts 5 ▪ in a bag.
3 ▪ are left.
How many ▪▪ did Sandra have?

☐ − 5 = 3

5 + 3 = 8 is the related addition fact.
So, 8 − 5 = 3.
Sandra had 8 ▪▪.

5 + 3 = 8

## Guided Practice

**Solve.**

**4** Sal has some granola bars.
He gives 4 to his brother.
Sal has 5 left.
How many granola bars did Sal have?

☐ − 4 = 5

4 + 5 = ☐ is the related addition fact.

So, ☐ − 4 = 5

Sal had ☐ granola bars.

# Learn You can use related subtraction facts to solve addition sentences.

Terrel has 3 pencils.
Joe gives him some pencils.
Terrel now has 7 pencils.
How many pencils does Joe give Terrel?

$3 +$ ⬚ $= 7$

$7 - 3 = 4$

$7 - 3 = 4$ is the related subtraction fact.
So, $3 + 4 = 7$.
Joe gives Terrel 4 pencils.

## Guided Practice

**Solve.**

**5** Jasmine has 6 ladybugs in a jar.
She finds some ladybugs in the garden.
Jasmine now has 10 ladybugs.
How many ladybugs does she find?

$6 +$ ⬚ $= 10$

$10 - 6 =$ ⬚ is the related subtraction fact.

So, $6 +$ ⬚ $= 10$.

Jasmine finds ⬚ ladybugs.

# Let's Practice

**Use the pictures to write a fact family.**

**1**

**Use the numbers to write a fact family.**

**2** 10    2    8

**Find the missing number.**
**Use related facts to help you.**

**3**  2 + [   ] = 7

**4**  6 + [   ] = 9

**5**  7 − [   ] = 3

**6**  10 − [   ] = 4

**7**  [   ] + 3 = 5

**8**  [   ] + 5 = 8

**9**  [   ] − 4 = 4

**10**  [   ] − 6 = 3

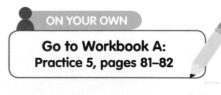

ON YOUR OWN

Go to Workbook A:
Practice 5, pages 81–82

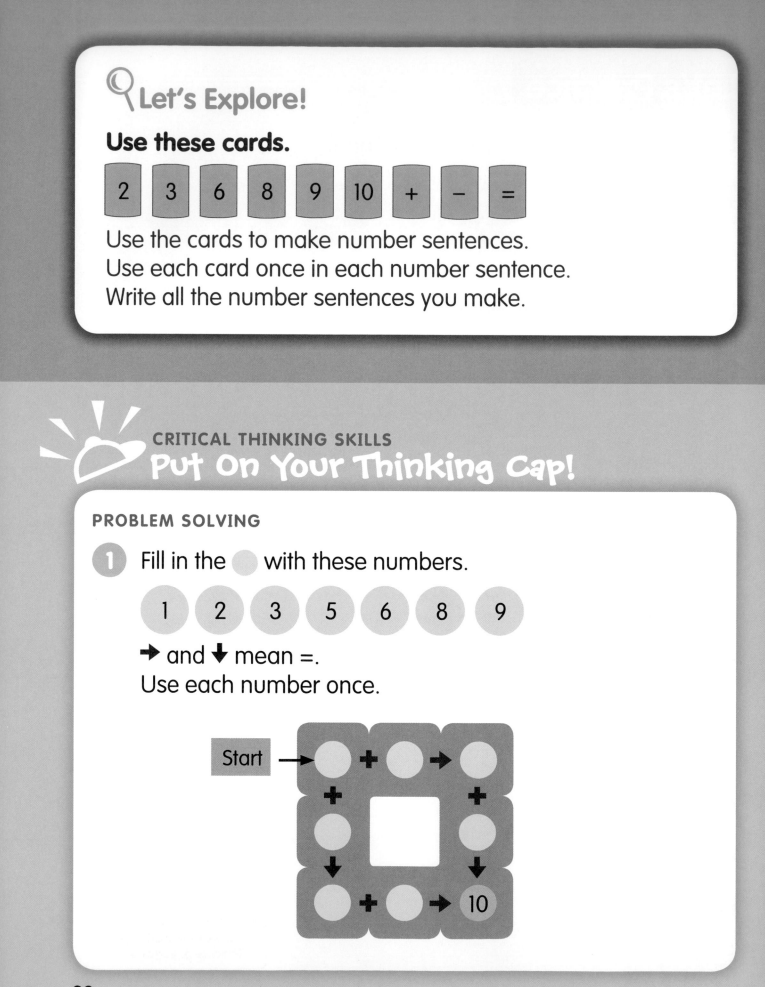

## Let's Explore!

### Use these cards.

| 2 | 3 | 6 | 8 | 9 | 10 | + | − | = |

Use the cards to make number sentences.
Use each card once in each number sentence.
Write all the number sentences you make.

**CRITICAL THINKING SKILLS**
## Put On Your Thinking Cap!

**PROBLEM SOLVING**

1 Fill in the ⬤ with these numbers.

1   2   3   5   6   8   9

➜ and ⬇ mean =.
Use each number once.

Start ➜ ⬤ + ⬤ ➜ ⬤
+            +
⬤           ⬤
⬇            ⬇
⬤ + ⬤ ➜ 10

**PROBLEM SOLVING**

**2** Fill in the ⬤ with these numbers.

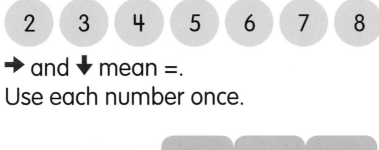

➡ and ⬇ mean =.
Use each number once.

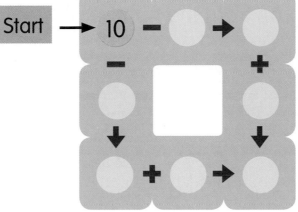

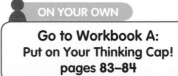

ON YOUR OWN

**Go to Workbook A:
Put on Your Thinking Cap!
pages 83–84**

# Chapter Wrap Up

**You have learned...**

to subtract by taking away.

$3 - 1 = 2$

........................................................

to subtract by counting on from the number that is less.

$5 - 3 = 2$

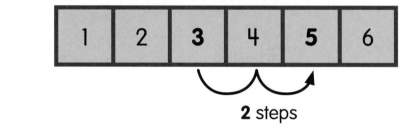

**2** steps

........................................................

to subtract by counting back from the greater number.

$10 - 3 = 7$

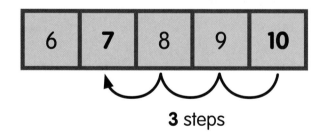

**3** steps

........................................................

to subtract using number bonds.

$9 - 8 = 1$

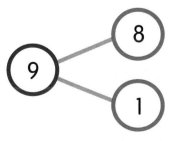

to tell subtraction stories about pictures and write a subtraction sentence for each story.

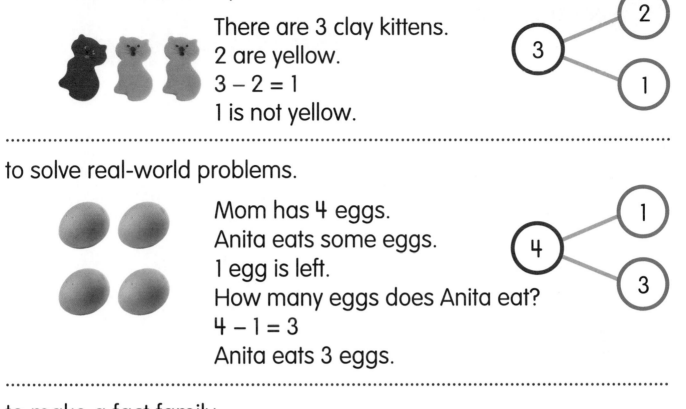

There are 3 clay kittens.
2 are yellow.
$3 - 2 = 1$
1 is not yellow.

to solve real-world problems.

Mom has 4 eggs.
Anita eats some eggs.
1 egg is left.
How many eggs does Anita eat?
$4 - 1 = 3$
Anita eats 3 eggs.

to make a fact family.

$2 + 6 = 8$        $6 + 2 = 8$        $8 - 2 = 6$        $8 - 6 = 2$

Each fact in fact family has the same parts and whole.

to use fact families to solve real-world problems.

James has 1 sock.
He finds more socks under his bed.
He has 3 socks now.
How many socks does he find?

$1 +$ [ ] $= 3$

$3 - 1 = 2$ is the related subtraction fact.

So, $1 + 2 = 3$.

James finds 2 socks under his bed.

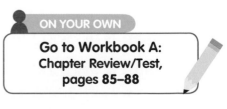

**ON YOUR OWN**

**Go to Workbook A: Chapter Review/Test, pages 85–88**

# 5 Shapes and Patterns

Once upon a time, there was a place called the Land of Shapes.
Many shapes lived there.
They worked, played, and ate together.

One day, a strange visitor came.
The visitor wanted to live in the Land of Shapes.
The shapes looked at the visitor.
One shape said,
"You are not like us.
How can you live here?"

**Lesson 1** Exploring Plane Shapes

**Lesson 2** Exploring Solid Shapes

**Lesson 3** Making Pictures and Models with Shapes

**Lesson 4** Seeing Shapes Around Us

**Lesson 5** Making Patterns with Plane Shapes

**Lesson 6** Making Patterns with Solid Shapes

The visitor smiled.
He said, "I am not only one shape, I can be any shape!"
He then turned himself into the different shapes.

The shapes thought this was great!
They decided to let the visitor stay.
So the visitor stayed and they all lived happily ever after.

BIG IDEA

Explore, identify, and compare plane and solid shapes in patterns and in the real world.

# Recall Prior Knowledge

## These are shapes.

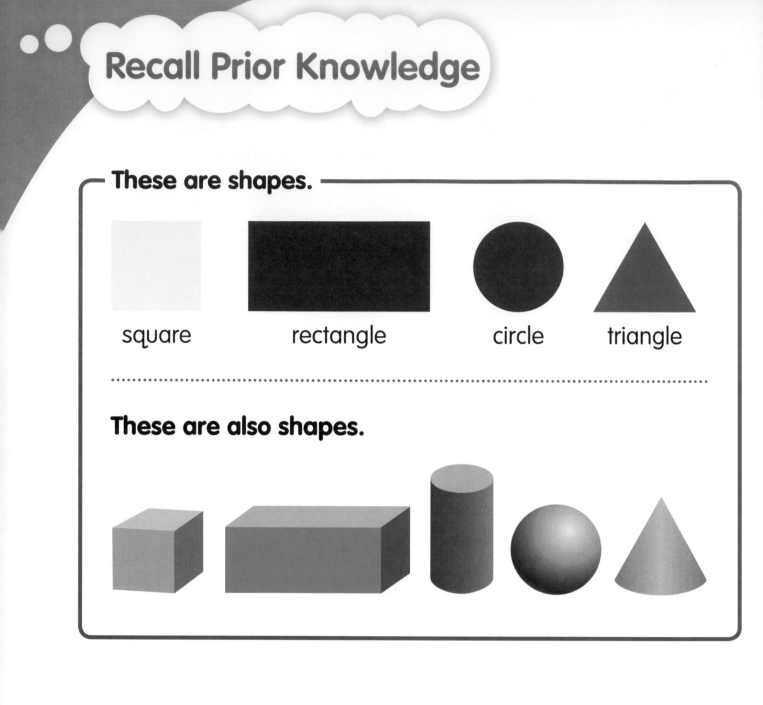

square          rectangle          circle          triangle

## These are also shapes.

## This is a pattern.

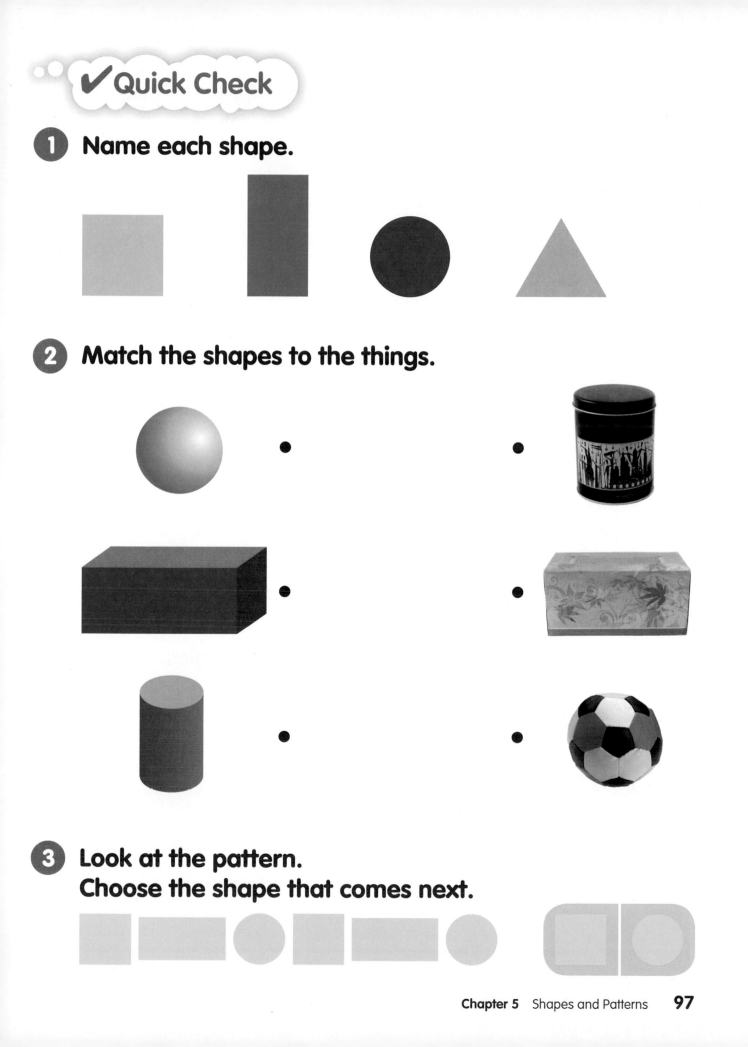

✔ Quick Check

1 Name each shape.

2 Match the shapes to the things.

3 Look at the pattern.
Choose the shape that comes next.

# Exploring Plane Shapes

## Lesson Objectives

- Identify, classify, and describe plane shapes.
- Make same and different shapes.

### Vocabulary

| | |
|---|---|
| circle | triangle |
| square | rectangle |
| side | corner |
| sort | color |
| alike | shape |
| size | different |

Learn

## Get to know shapes.

Trace these shapes with your finger.
Talk about them.

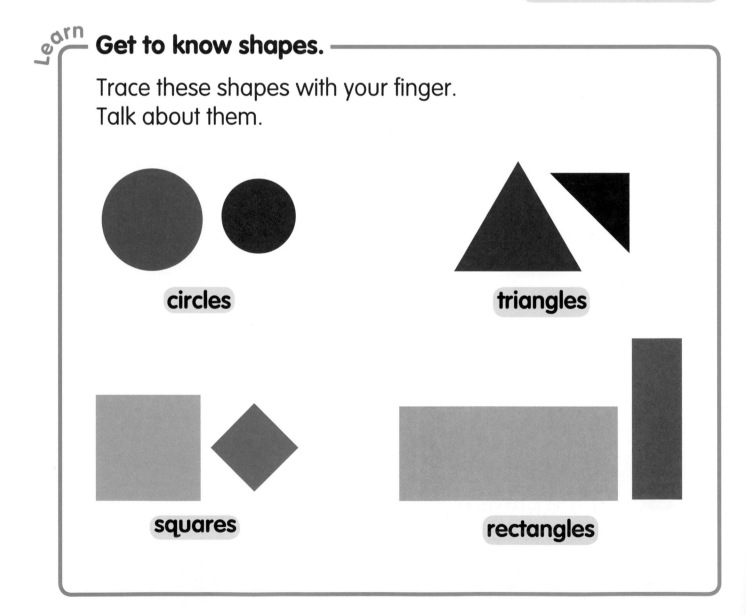

circles

triangles

squares

rectangles

# Guided Practice

## Find the shapes that are <u>not</u> squares.

**1**

## ℒℯarn About sides and corners.

Some shapes have **sides** and **corners**.

corner

side

Corners are where the sides meet.

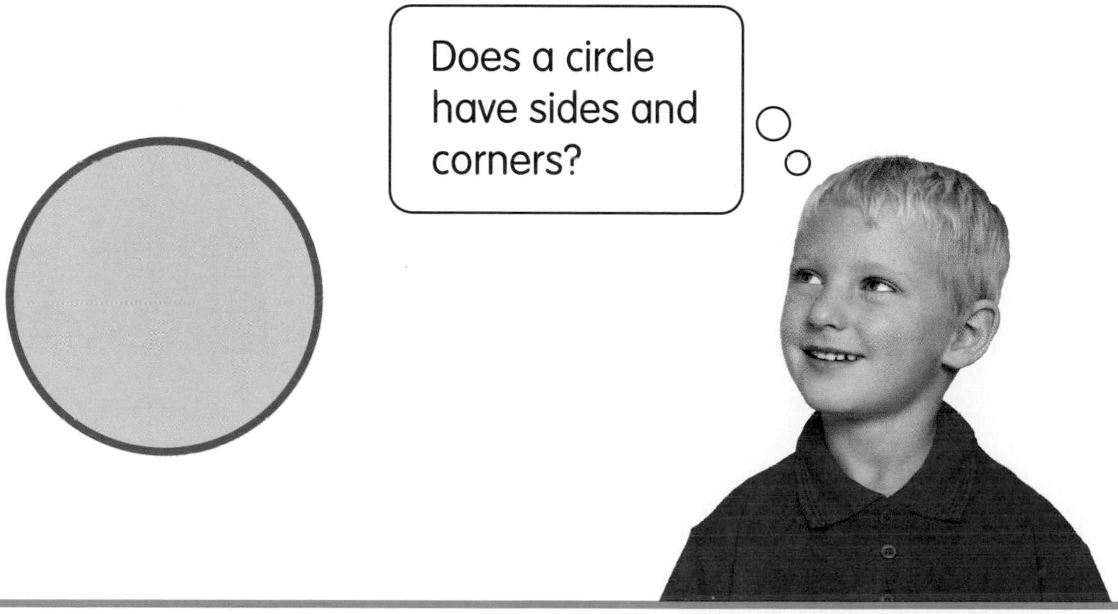

Does a circle have sides and corners?

## Guided Practice

**Count the number of sides.**
**Then count the number of corners.**

**2** square

| sides

| corners

**3** triangle

| sides

| corners

**4** rectangle

| sides

| corners

**5** circle

| sides

| corners

*Learn* **You can sort shapes in many ways.**

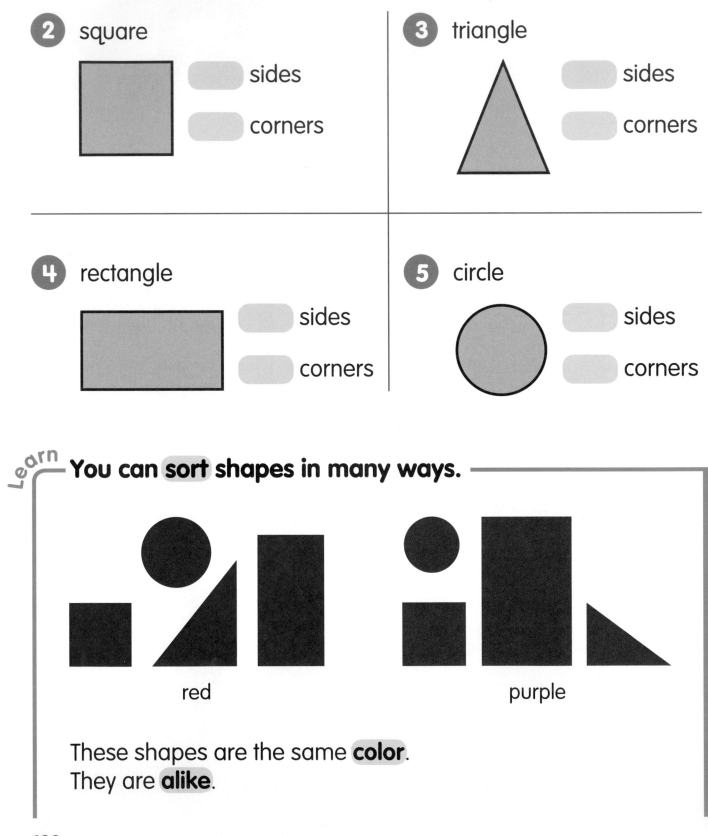

red

purple

These shapes are the same **color**.
They are **alike**.

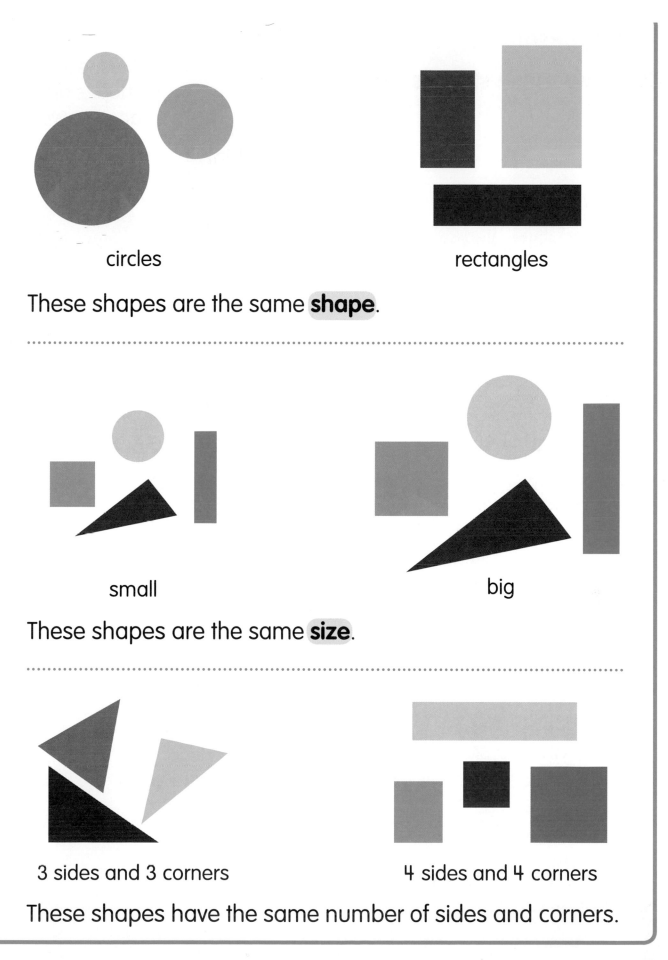

circles

rectangles

These shapes are the same **shape**.

small

big

These shapes are the same **size**.

3 sides and 3 corners

4 sides and 4 corners

These shapes have the same number of sides and corners.

## Guided Practice

**Tell how these shapes are alike.**

6

Are these shapes alike in another way?

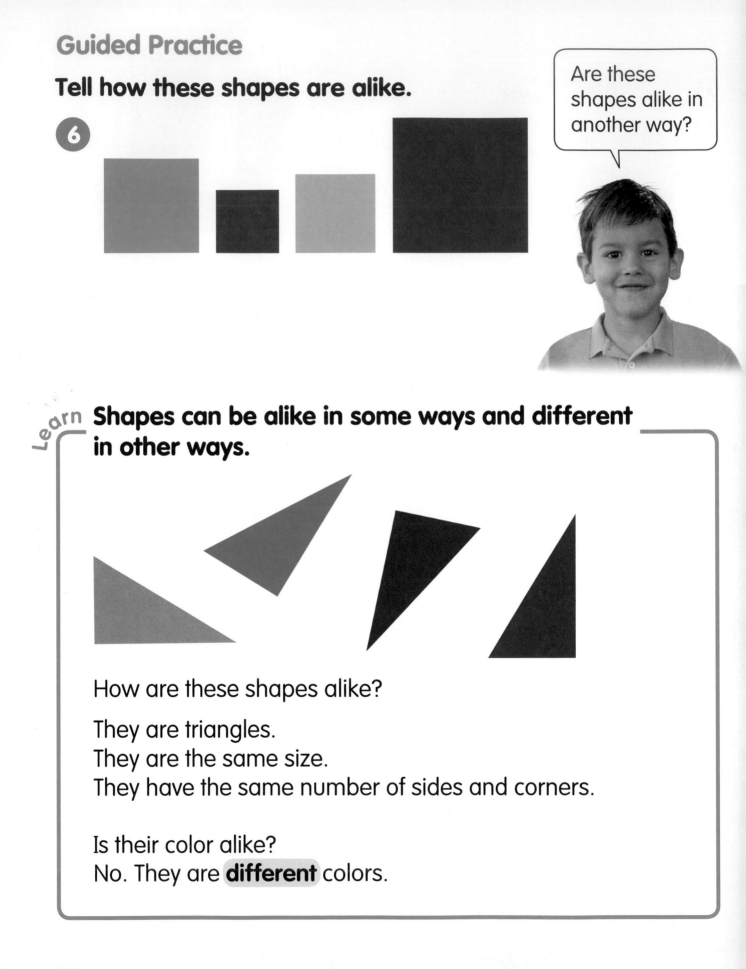

**Learn** **Shapes can be alike in some ways and different in other ways.**

How are these shapes alike?

They are triangles.
They are the same size.
They have the same number of sides and corners.

Is their color alike?
No. They are **different** colors.

# Guided Practice

**Tell how these shapes are different.**

> Are these shapes different in another way?

**7**

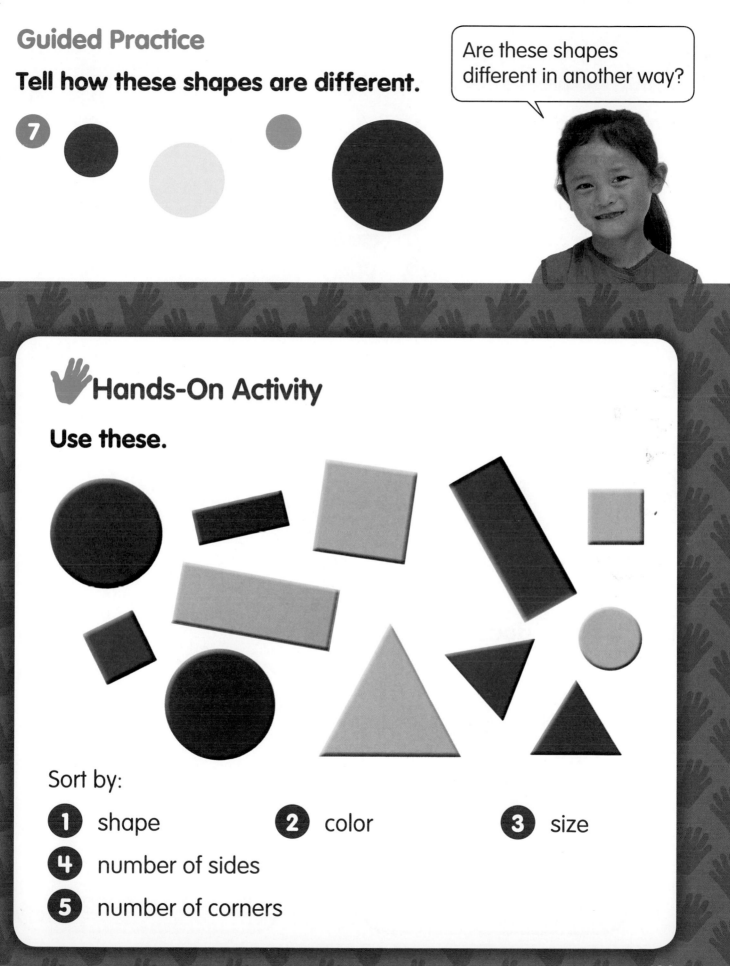

## Hands-On Activity

**Use these.**

Sort by:

**1** shape   **2** color   **3** size

**4** number of sides

**5** number of corners

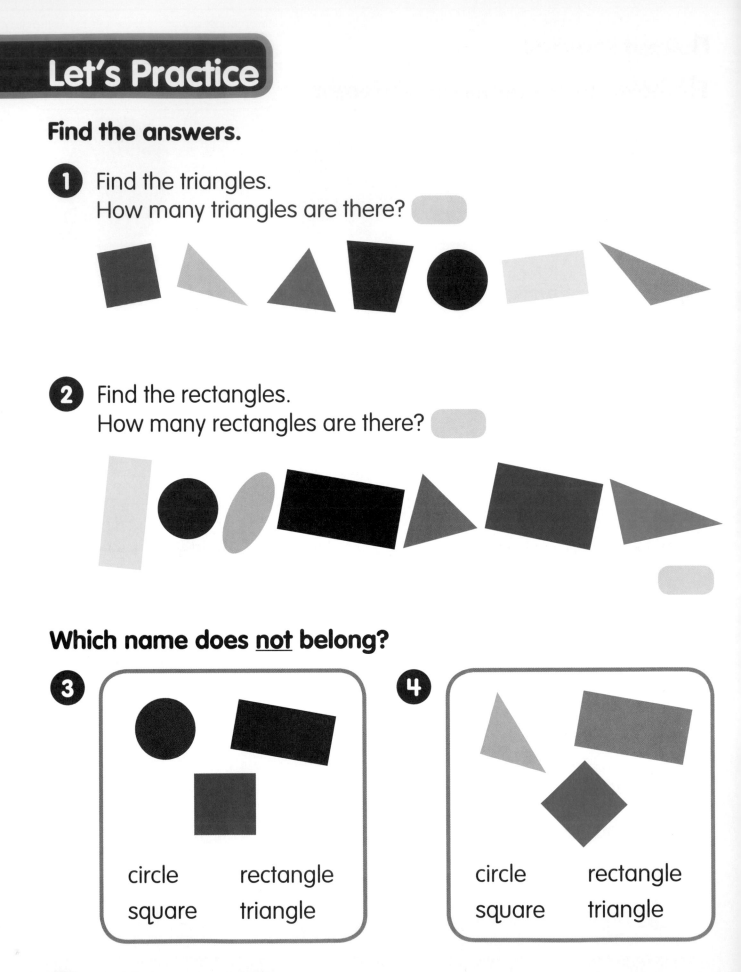

## Let's Practice

**Find the answers.**

**1** Find the triangles.
How many triangles are there?

**2** Find the rectangles.
How many rectangles are there?

## Which name does <u>not</u> belong?

**3**
circle     rectangle

square     triangle

**4**
circle     rectangle

square     triangle

# Find the answers.

 **5** Name the shape that has 3 sides and 3 corners.

 **6** Tell how these shapes are alike.
Tell how they are different.

**7** Find the shapes that are of the same size <u>and</u> the same shape.

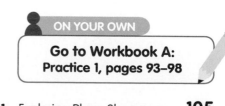

ON YOUR OWN

**Go to Workbook A:**
**Practice 1, pages 93–98**

# Use folding to make shapes that are alike.

Judy has a piece of paper.
It is the shape of a rectangle.

She folds it like this.

Then, she unfolds it and
draws a line along the fold.

Now she has two shapes
Shape A and Shape B.

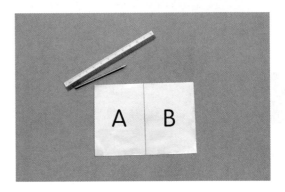

What can you say about the two shapes?

They have the same shape and color.
They have the same size.
They have the same number of sides.
They have the same number of corners.
They are alike.

Shapes A and B
fit exactly over
each other.

Is there anything
different about
the shapes?

# Guided Practice

**Look at the pictures.**
**Solve.**

**8**

Judy folds her piece of paper.   She unfolds it.

What can you say about the two shapes?
How are they alike?

 **Hands-On Activity**

**1** Fold a square piece of paper to make two shapes that are alike.

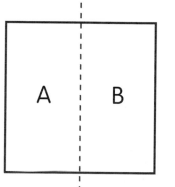

Can you make two triangles that are alike using a square piece of paper?

**2** Now fold another piece of paper a different way. Make two shapes that are alike.

# Let's Explore!

**Use a copy of these shapes.**
**Fold the shapes along the line to make two new shapes.**
**Draw a line along the fold.**

**1**

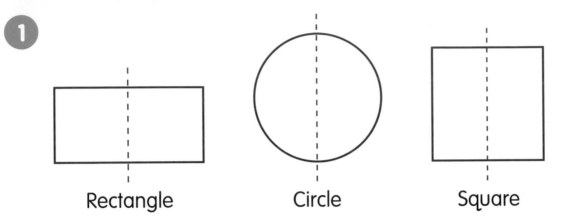

Rectangle          Circle          Square

What can you say about the two new shapes?
How are they alike?

**2**

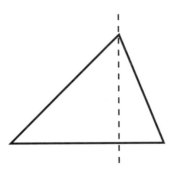

What can you say about the two shapes?
Can you fold the triangle in a different way to make two
shapes that are alike?

**3** **Answer the questions for** ⓐ **and** ⓑ **.**

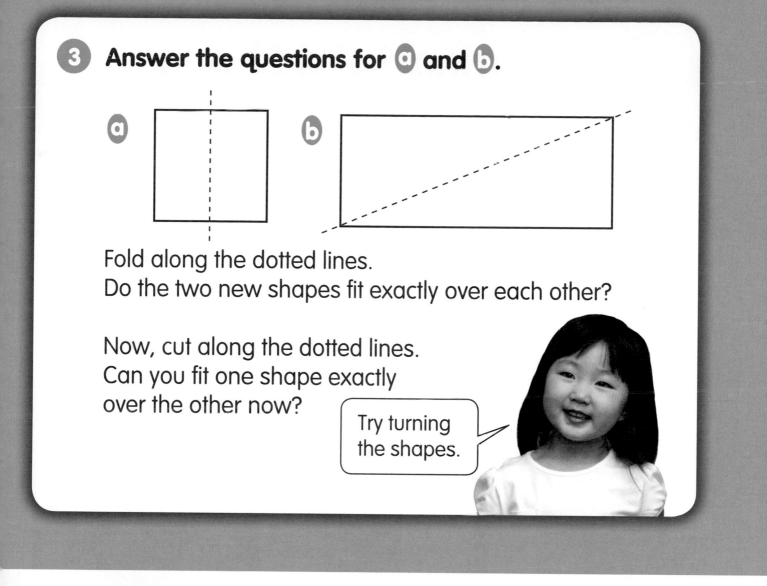

Fold along the dotted lines.
Do the two new shapes fit exactly over each other?

Now, cut along the dotted lines.
Can you fit one shape exactly
over the other now?

Try turning
the shapes.

# Let's Practice

**Solve.**

**1** What can you say about the two shapes?
How are they alike?
How are they different?

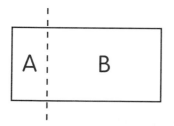

ON YOUR OWN
Go to Workbook A:
Practice 2, pages 99–100

# LESSON 2 Exploring Solid Shapes

**Lesson Objective**

• Identify, classify, and sort solid shapes.

**Vocabulary**

| rectangular prism | cube |
| --- | --- |
| cone | sphere |
| pyramid | cylinder |
| slide | stack |
| roll | |

**Learn** Get to know solid shapes.

Trace these solid shapes with your finger.
Talk about them.

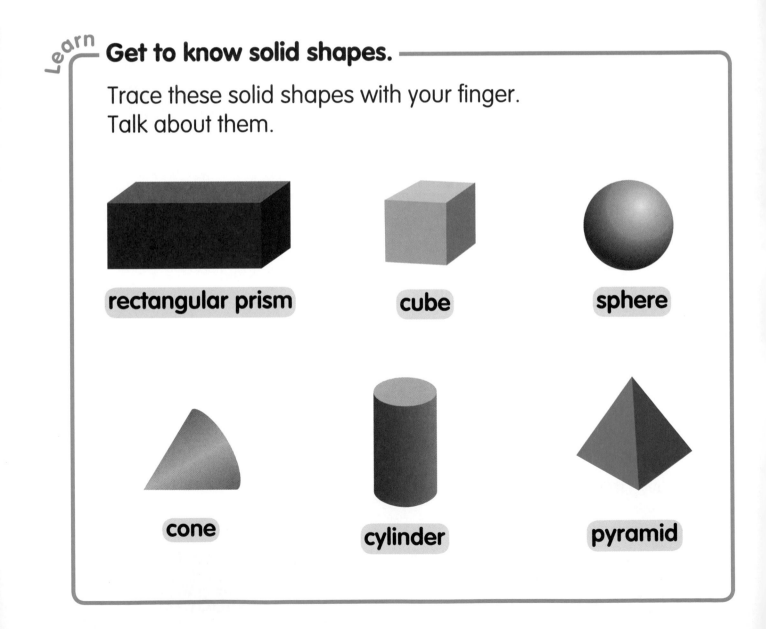

rectangular prism  cube  sphere

cone  cylinder  pyramid

# Name and compare solid shapes.

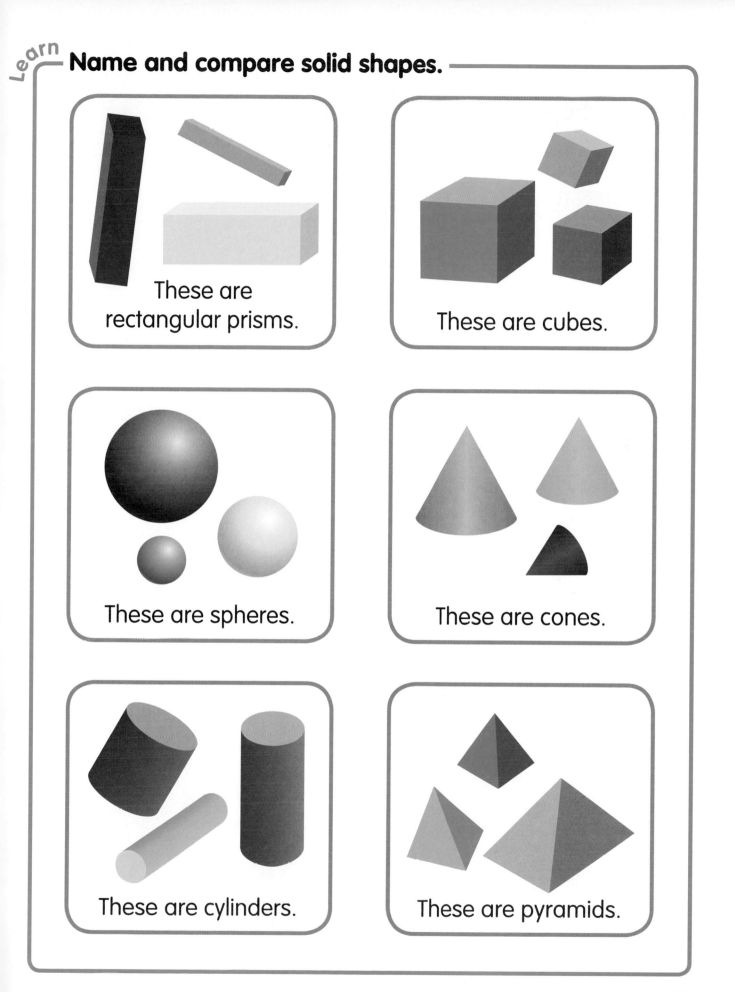

These are
rectangular prisms.

These are cubes.

These are spheres.

These are cones.

These are cylinders.

These are pyramids.

## Guided Practice

**Find the shapes that are <u>not</u> cubes.**

**1**

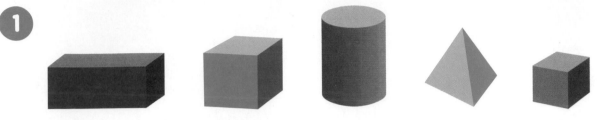

<sup>Learn</sup> **You can move solid shapes in different ways.**

You can **stack** and **slide** these shapes.

You can **roll** these shapes.

 **Hands-On Activity**

**1** Show your classmate the correct shape.
Can you make the shape stack, slide, or roll?
Make an ✗ in your table if you can.

| Solid Shape | | Stack | Roll | Slide |
|---|---|---|---|---|
| rectangular prism | | | | |
| sphere | | | | |
| cube | | | | |
| cylinder | | | | |
| cone | | | | |

## Now talk about the shapes.

**2** Which shapes can you stack?

**3** Which shapes can you roll?

**4** Which shapes can you <u>not</u> slide?

**5** Which two shapes can be moved in the same ways?

**6** Is there a shape that you can stack, roll, and slide?

# Let's Practice

**1** Find the cubes.

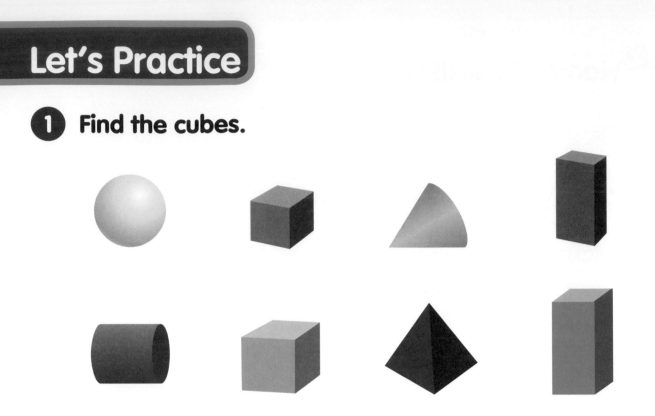

## Name each solid shape.

**2** **3**

**4** **5**

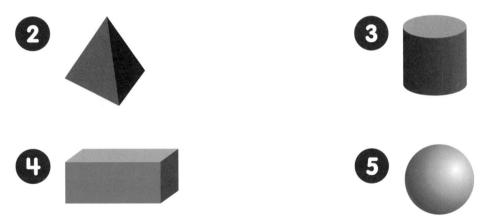

## Look around you.
## Find two things that look like these solid shapes.

**6** cylinder **7** cone

# Sort the solid shapes.

 **8** Find the shapes that can stack.

 **9** Find the shapes that can roll.

**10** Find the shapes that can slide.

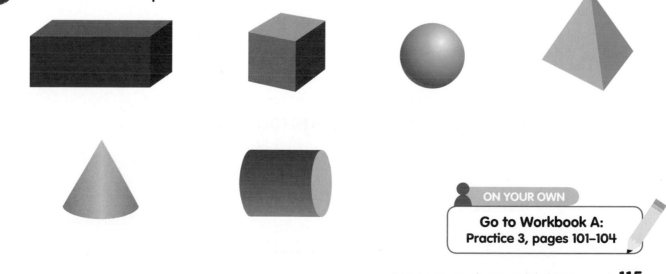

**ON YOUR OWN**

**Go to Workbook A:**
**Practice 3, pages 101–104**

# Making Pictures and Models with Shapes

**Lesson Objective**

• Combine and separate plane and solid shapes.

**Learn**

## You can combine plane shapes.

Here are 2 rectangles, 2 triangles, and a square.

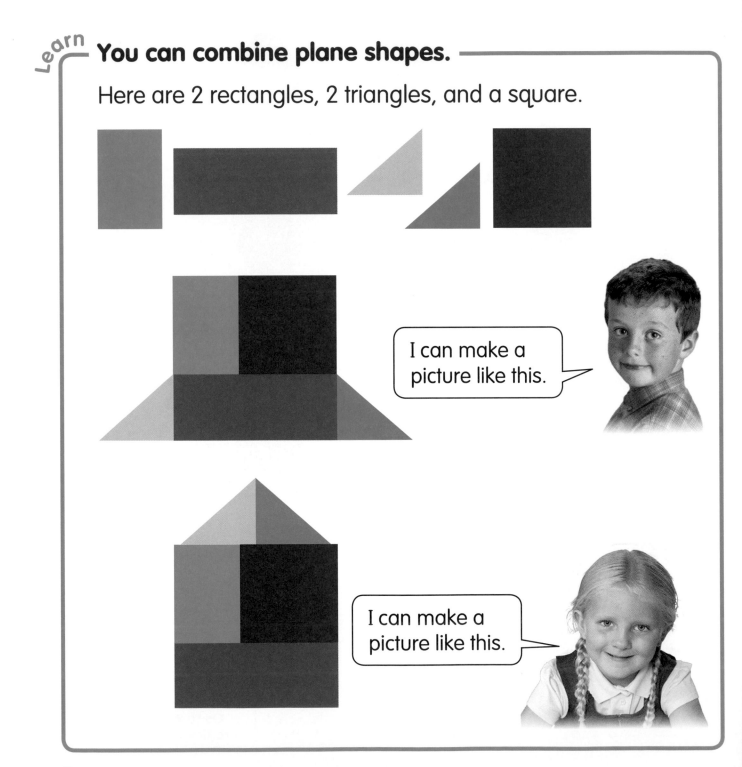

I can make a picture like this.

I can make a picture like this.

# Guided Practice

## Solve.

**1** Name the shapes that make this picture.

| Shapes | How many? |
|---|---|
| triangles | |
| rectangles | |
| squares | |
| circles | |

# Hands-On Activity

**1** Make a picture with these shapes.
How many of each shape are there?

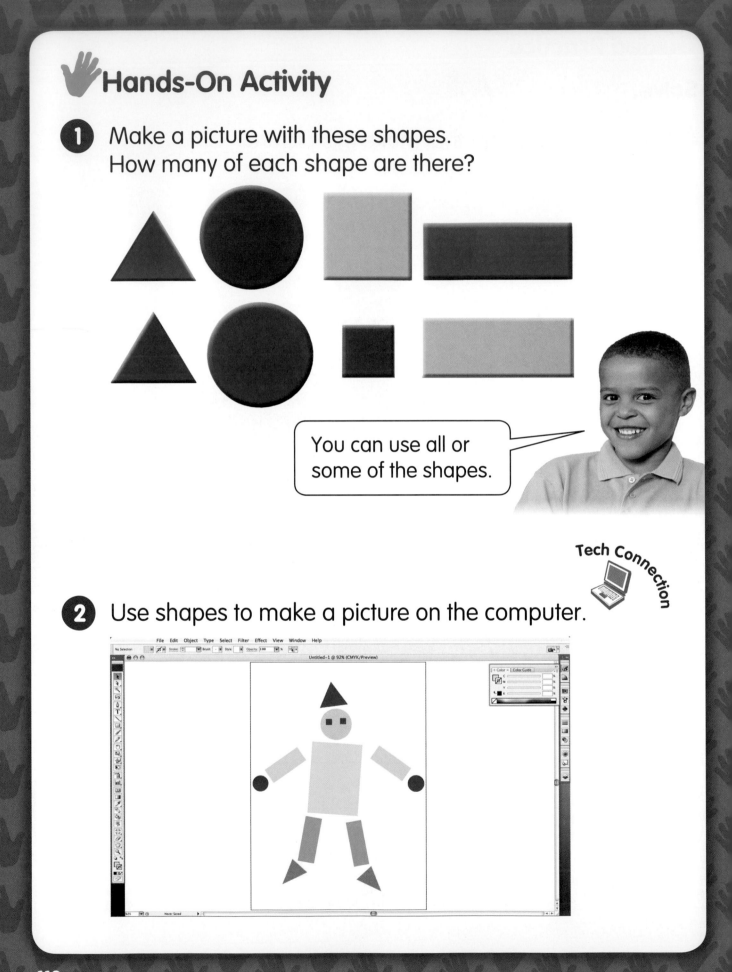

You can use all or some of the shapes.

**Tech Connection**

**2** Use shapes to make a picture on the computer.

# Hands-On Activity

**3** Cut out a copy of these shapes.

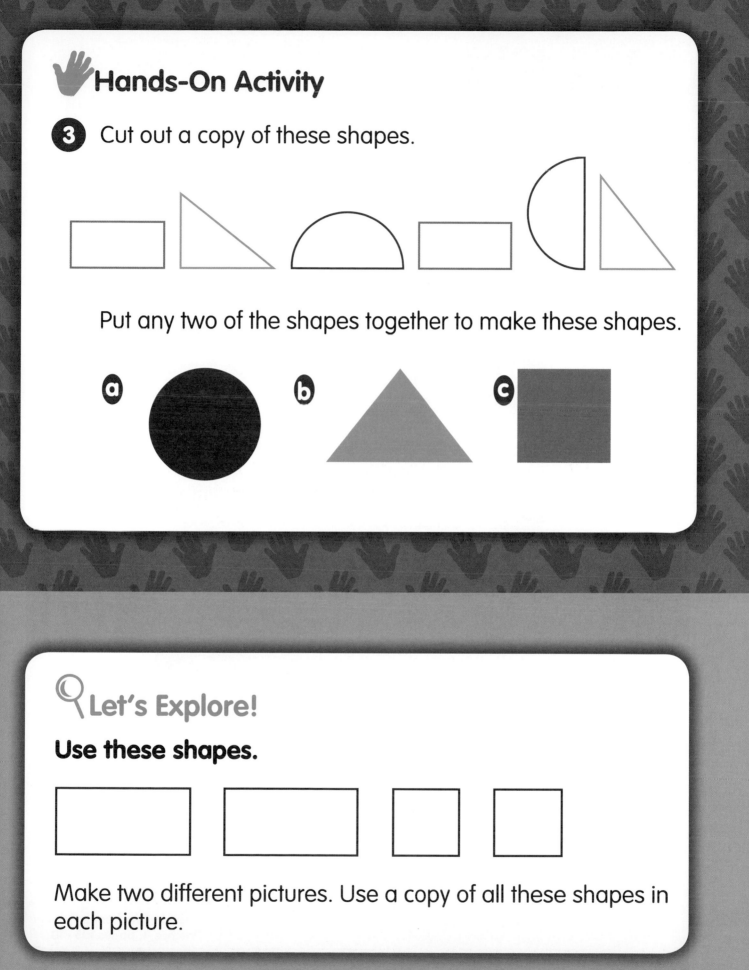

Put any two of the shapes together to make these shapes.

**a**

**b**

**c**

# Let's Explore!

**Use these shapes.**

Make two different pictures. Use a copy of all these shapes in each picture.

## Count.
## Look at the picture.

**1** This picture is made of many shapes.

How many of these shapes can you find?

| Shapes | How many? |
|--------|-----------|
| triangles | |
| rectangles | |
| squares | |
| circles | |

**ON YOUR OWN**

Go to Workbook A:
Practice 4, pages 105–110

# You can build models with solid shapes.

Here is 1 sphere, 2 pyramids, 4 cylinders, 2 cubes, 1 cone, and 1 rectangular prism.

I can make a model like this.

I can make a model like this.

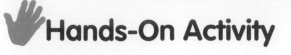 **Hands-On Activity**

Use .

Make your own model.

Find the number of each solid shape in your model.

| Solid | | How many? |
|-------|---|-----------|
| cube | | |
| sphere | | |
| rectangular prism | | |
| pyramid | | |
| cylinder | | |
| cone | | |

## Guided Practice

**Look at the model.**
**Find the number of each solid shape in the model.**

**2**

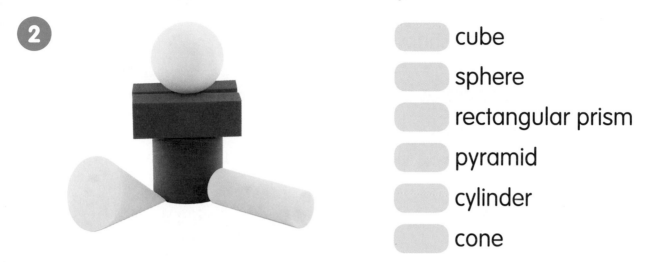

◯ cube

◯ sphere

◯ rectangular prism

◯ pyramid

◯ cylinder

◯ cone

# Let's Practice

**Look at the model.**
**Find the number of each solid shape in the model.**

**1**

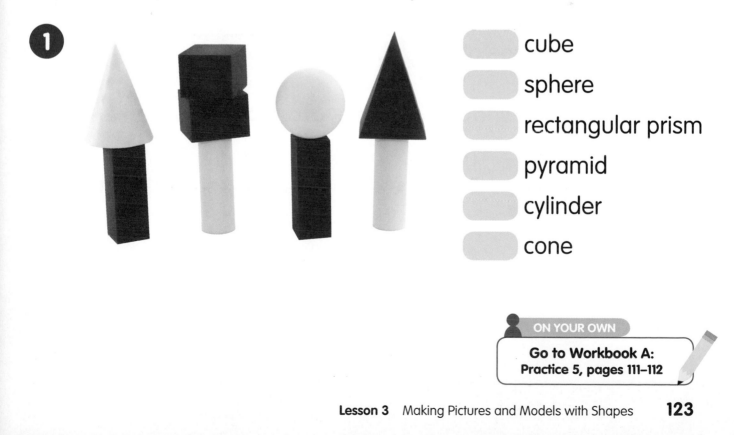

◯ cube

◯ sphere

◯ rectangular prism

◯ pyramid

◯ cylinder

◯ cone

ON YOUR OWN

**Go to Workbook A:**
**Practice 5, pages 111–112**

# LESSON

# 4 Seeing Shapes Around Us

## Lesson Objective

• Identify plane and solid shapes in real life.

**Learn** **You can see shapes in things around you.**

This is a CD.
It has the shape of a circle.

This is an envelope.
It has the shape of a rectangle.

## Guided Practice

**1** This is a slice of cheese.
It has the shape of a  .

**Learn** **You can see shapes in things around you.**

This is a container.
It has the shape of a rectangular prism.

This is a tennis ball.
It has the shape of a sphere.

# Guided Practice

**2** This is a popcorn tin.
It has the shape of a ▢ .

 Hands-On Activity

**Look around your classroom and school.**
**Find two things that have these shapes.**

**1** circle ▢                  **2** rectangle ▢

**3** square ▢                  **4** triangle ▢

**5** sphere ▢                  **6** rectangular prism ▢

**7** cube ▢

**Can you find one thing that has these shapes?**

**8** cone ▢                    **9** pyramid ▢

#  Hands-On Activity

Use 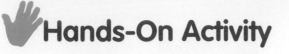.

Draw around each shape.
What shape do you make?

**1**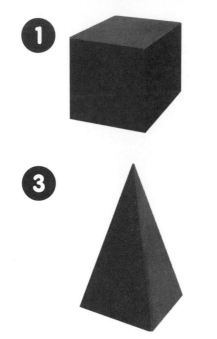

**2**

**3** 

**4**

Try turning the pyramid around.
Can you make a different shape?

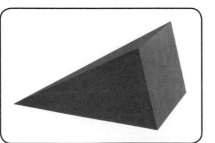

# Let's Practice

## Look at the pictures.
## Name the shapes you see.

**1**

**2**

**3**

**4**

## Answer the questions.

**5** This is a sponge.
What shape does it have?
What other shapes do you see?

**6** This is a sharpener.
What shape does it have?
What other shapes do you see?

**Look at the picture.**
**What solid shapes can you see?**
**What plane shapes can you see?**

**7**

ruler

eraser

glue

**8**

Cereal

cereal

granola bar

orange

ON YOUR OWN

Go to Workbook A:
Practice 6, pages 113–116

# Making Patterns with Plane Shapes

## Lesson Objective

- Use plane shapes to identify, extend, and create patterns.

**Vocabulary**
repeating pattern

Learn **These are repeating patterns.**

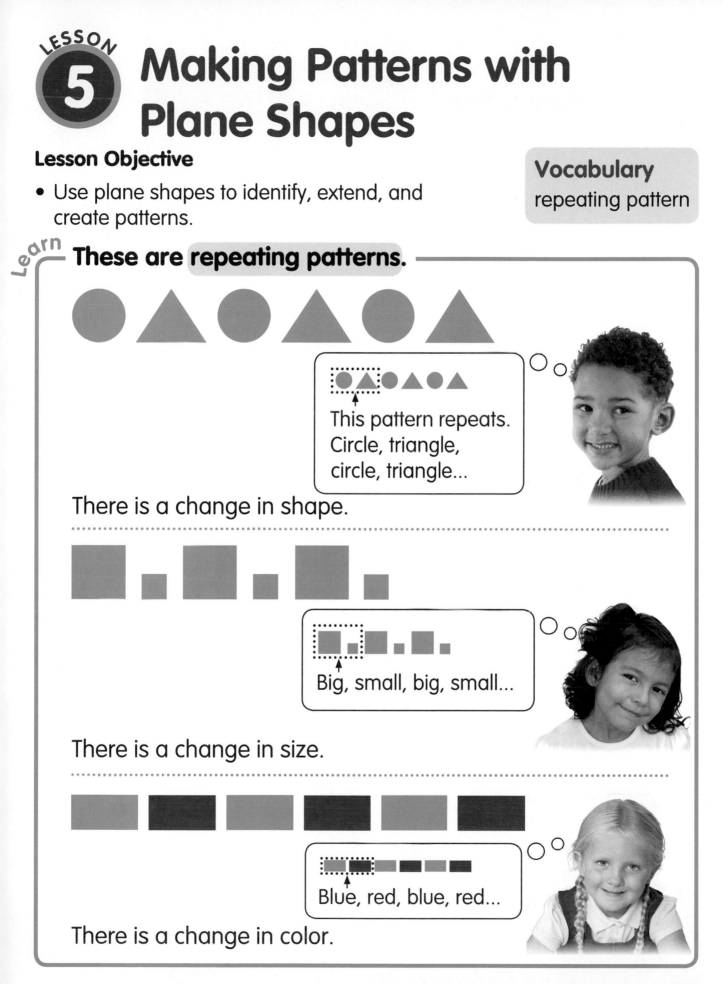

This pattern repeats.
Circle, triangle,
circle, triangle...

There is a change in shape.

Big, small, big, small...

There is a change in size.

Blue, red, blue, red...

There is a change in color.

## Guided Practice

**Complete the patterns.**

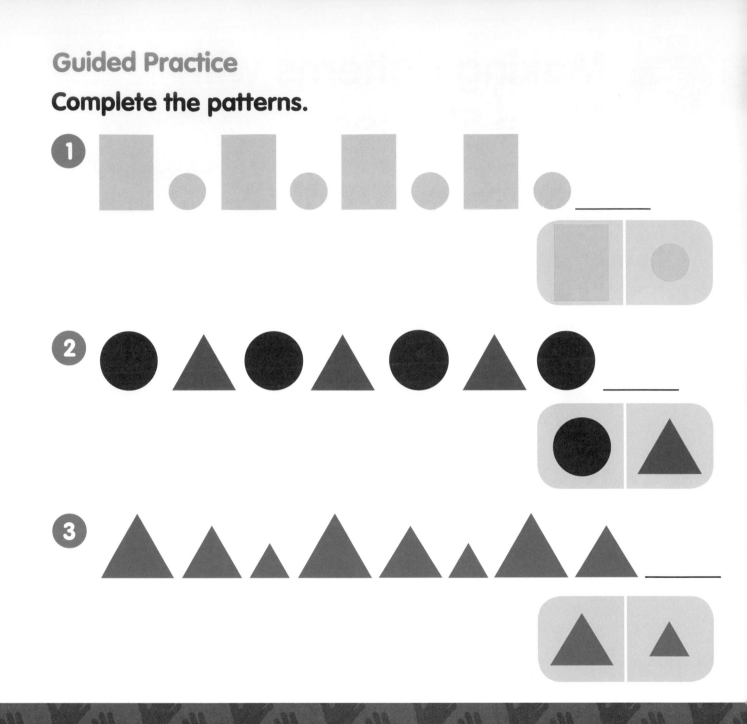

**1**

**2**

**3**

---

👋 **Hands-On Activity**

Tech Connection

Make a repeating pattern with two shapes
on the computer.
Print the pattern you have made.
Ask your classmates what comes next.

# Let's Practice

## Complete the patterns.

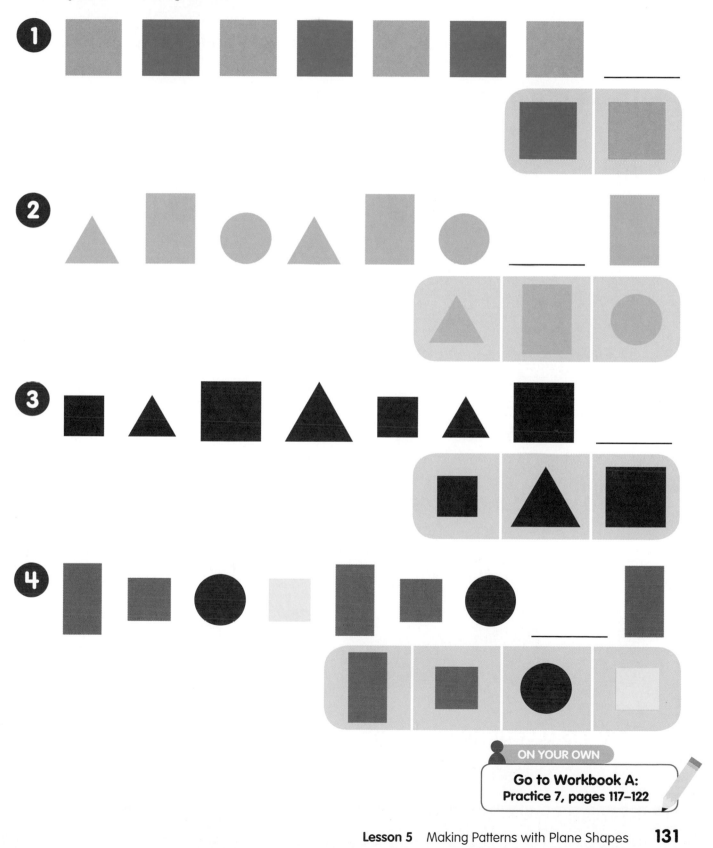

**ON YOUR OWN**

**Go to Workbook A:**
Practice 7, pages 117–122

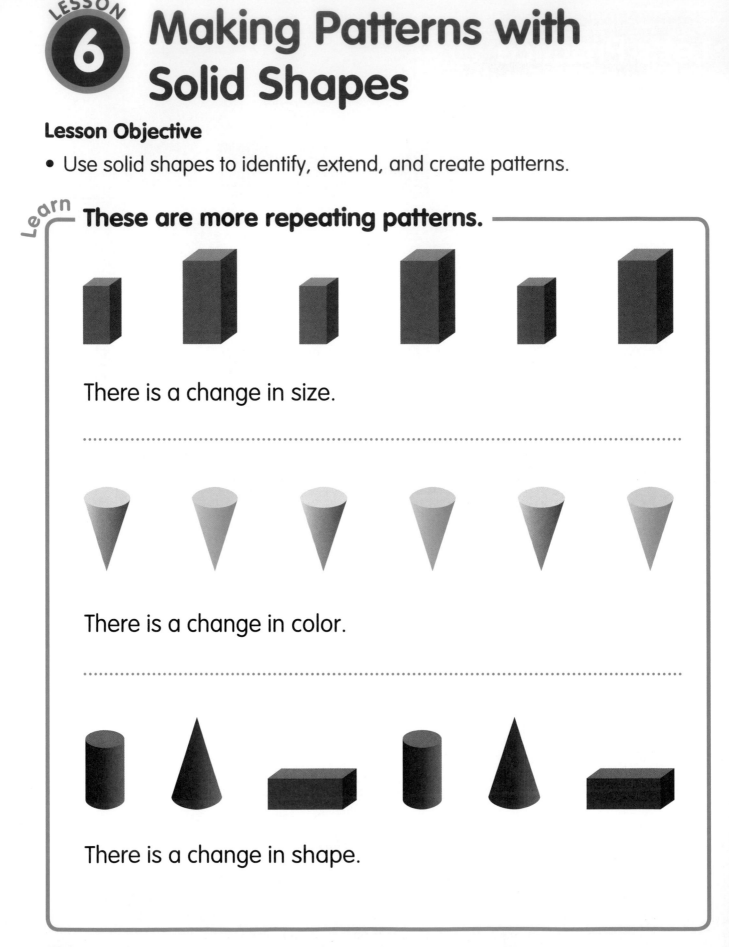

# LESSON 6 Making Patterns with Solid Shapes

## Lesson Objective

• Use solid shapes to identify, extend, and create patterns.

**Learn** **These are more repeating patterns.**

There is a change in size.

There is a change in color.

There is a change in shape.

# Guided Practice

## Complete the patterns.

**1**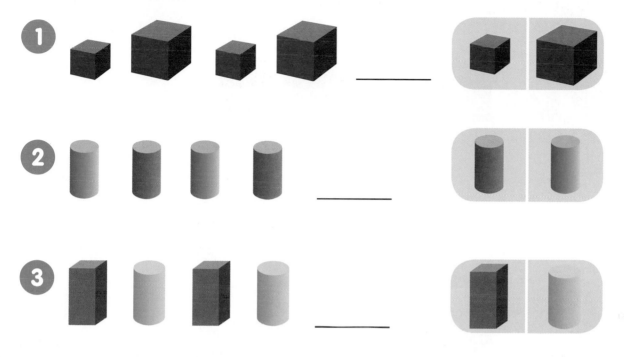

**2**

**3**

## Hands-On Activity

**WORK IN PAIRS**

**Use** .

Make your own pattern.
Ask your classmate to show what comes next.

### Example

# Let's Practice

## Complete the patterns.

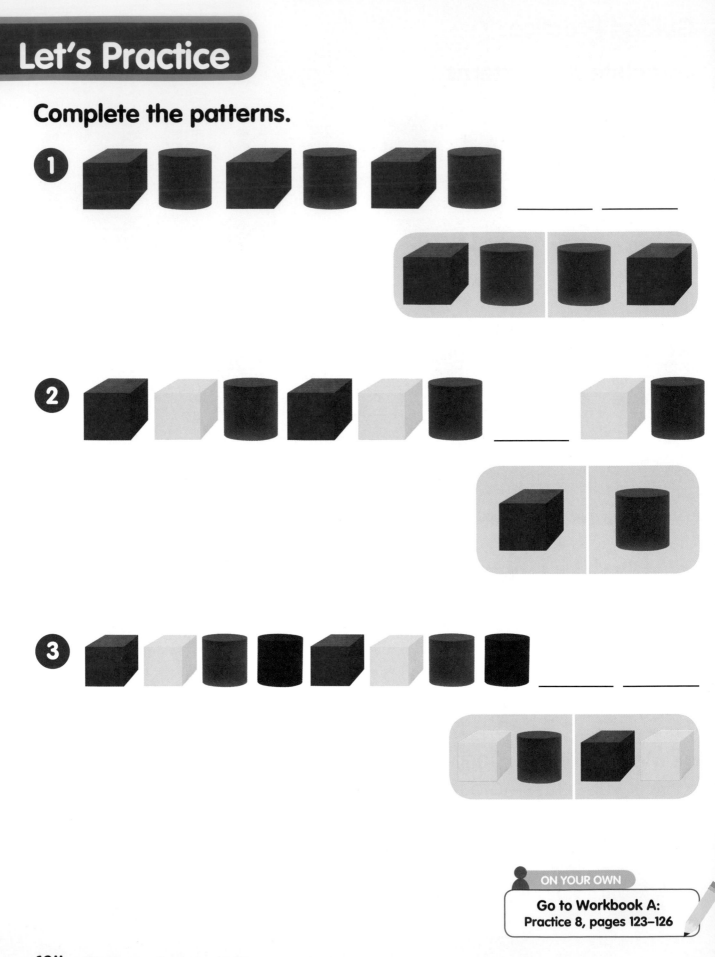

1 _____  _____

2 _____

3 _____  _____

ON YOUR OWN

Go to Workbook A:
Practice 8, pages 123–126

**PROBLEM SOLVING**

1 How are these shapes sorted?

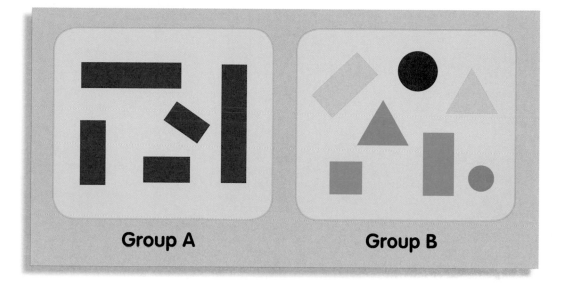

Group A                    Group B

2 What comes next in this pattern?

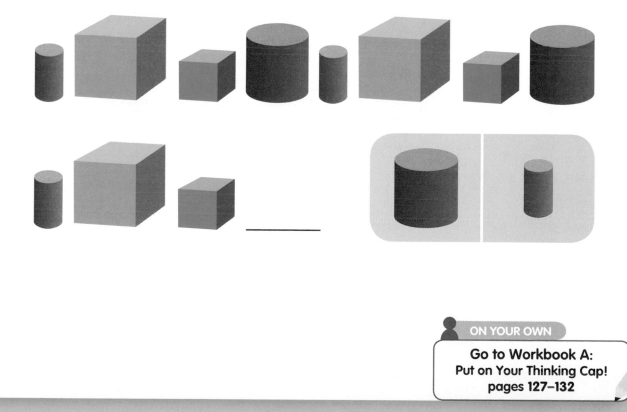

ON YOUR OWN

**Go to Workbook A:
Put on Your Thinking Cap!
pages 127–132**

# Chapter Wrap Up

**You have learned...**

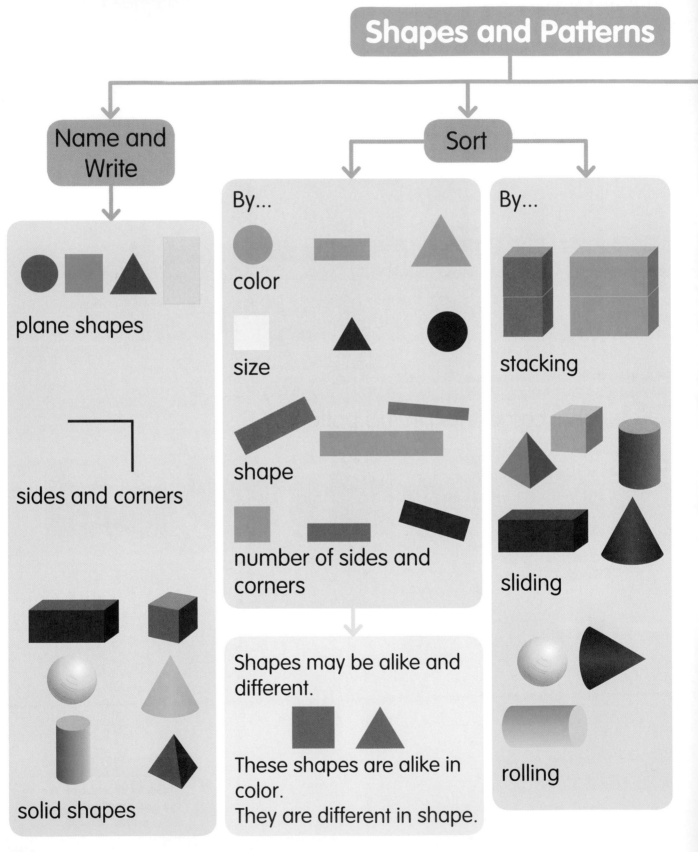

**Shapes and Patterns**

**Name and Write**

plane shapes

sides and corners

solid shapes

**Sort**

By...

color

size

shape

number of sides and corners

Shapes may be alike and different.

These shapes are alike in color.
They are different in shape.

By...

stacking

sliding

rolling

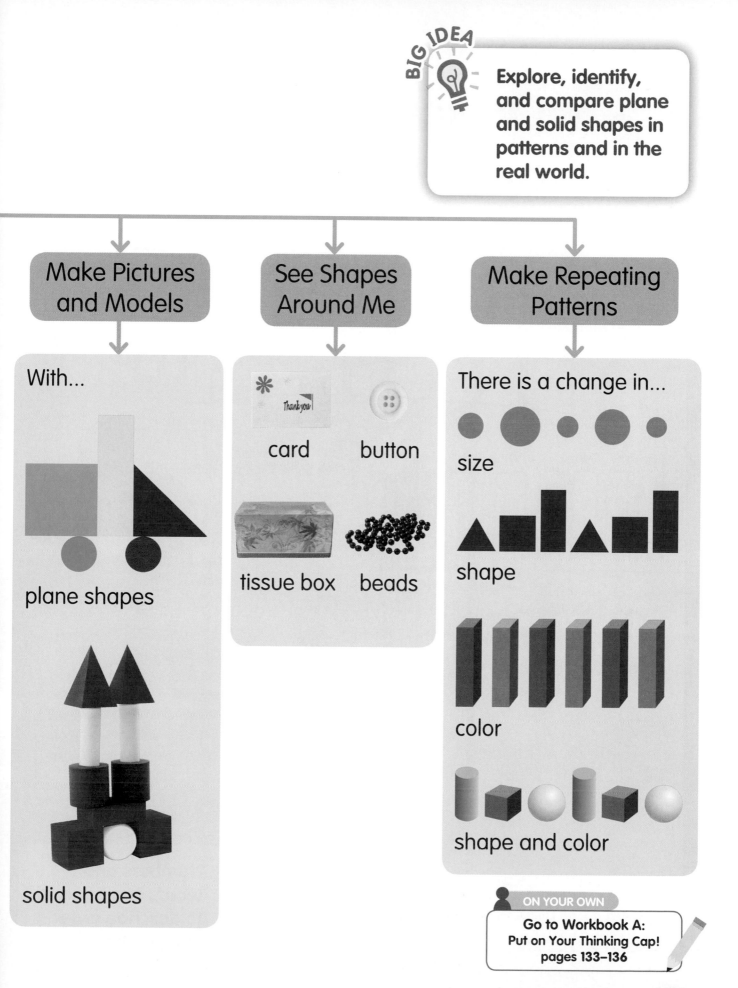

Explore, identify, and compare plane and solid shapes in patterns and in the real world.

## Make Pictures and Models

With...

plane shapes

solid shapes

## See Shapes Around Me

card        button

*Thank you*

tissue box      beads

## Make Repeating Patterns

There is a change in...

size

shape

color

shape and color

ON YOUR OWN

Go to Workbook A:
Put on Your Thinking Cap!
pages 133–136

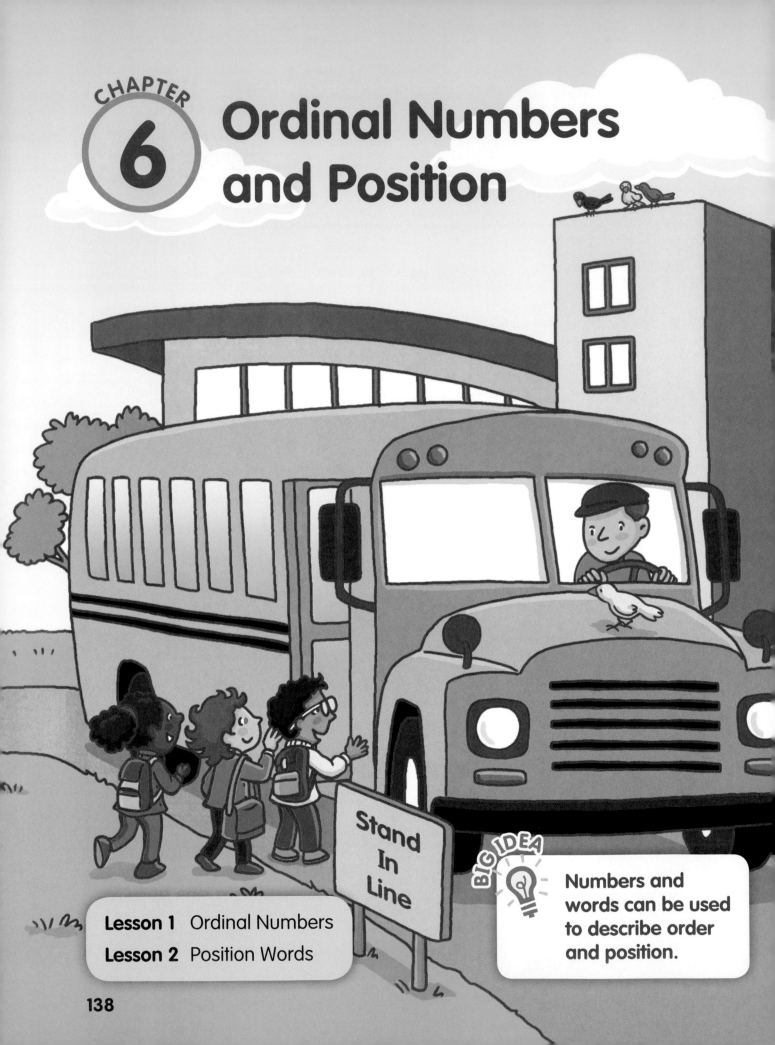

# CHAPTER 6

# Ordinal Numbers and Position

**Lesson 1** Ordinal Numbers

**Lesson 2** Position Words

Stand In Line

**BIG IDEA**

Numbers and words can be used to describe order and position.

# Recall Prior Knowledge

**Position numbers and words**

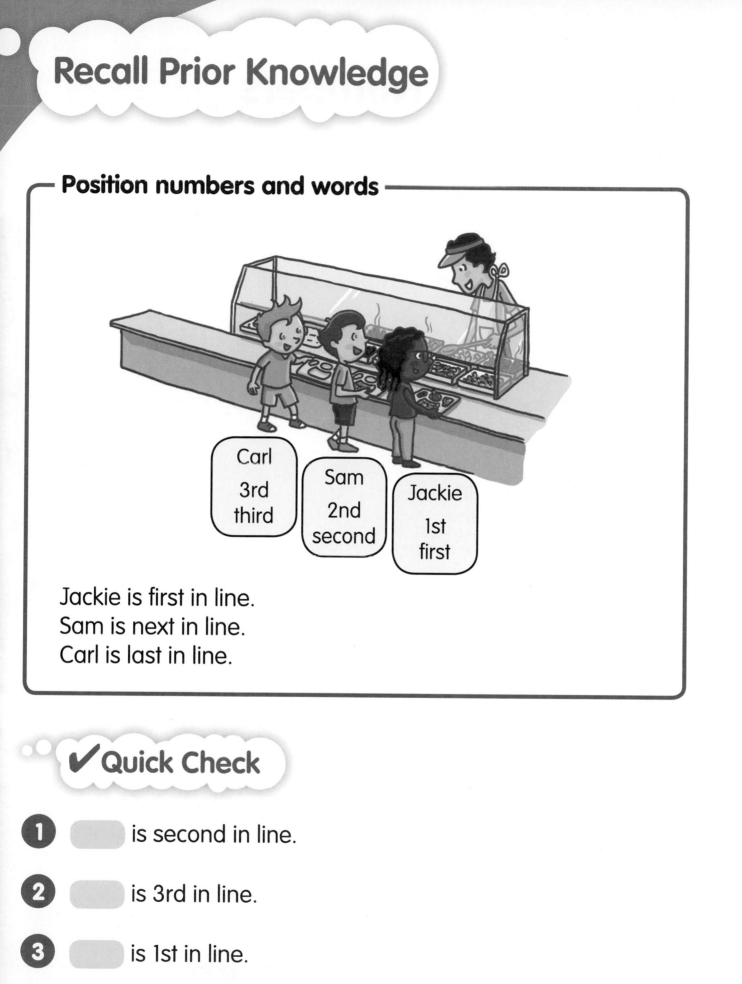

Carl
3rd
third

Sam
2nd
second

Jackie
1st
first

Jackie is first in line.
Sam is next in line.
Carl is last in line.

## ✔ Quick Check

**1** _____ is second in line.

**2** _____ is 3rd in line.

**3** _____ is 1st in line.

# LESSON
# 1  Ordinal Numbers

**Lesson Objective**

• Use ordinal numbers.

**Learn** You can use ordinal numbers to tell order.

Hippo
**3rd**
**third**

Flipper
**1st**
**first**

Alice
**5th**
**fifth**

Wally
**2nd**
**second**

Ben
**4th**
**fourth**

## Vocabulary

| first | second | third | fourth | fifth |
|-------|--------|-------|--------|-------|
| sixth | seventh | eighth | ninth | tenth |
| last | | | | |

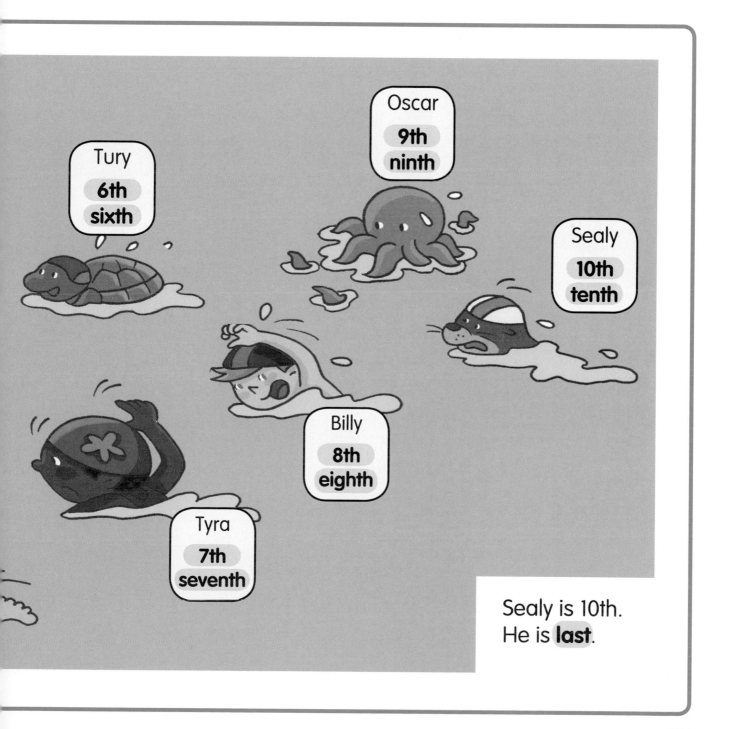

Sealy is 10th.
He is **last**.

## Guided Practice

**Look at the picture.
Answer the questions.**

Greg

Kyle

Jason

**1** How many children are climbing the wall?

**2** Who is 1st?

**3** Who is 2nd?

**4** Who is 6th?

**5** Who is 4th?

**6** In which position is Ally?

**7** In which position is Zack?

**8** Who is last?

# Let's Practice

## Look at the picture.
## Answer the questions.

**1** Is anyone at home on the 1st floor?

**2** On which floor is the cat?

**3** On which floor is the dog sleeping?

**4** On which floor is a man washing his hair?

**5** On which floor is the goldfish?

**6** What is on the 10th floor?

**7** What is the man on the ninth floor doing?

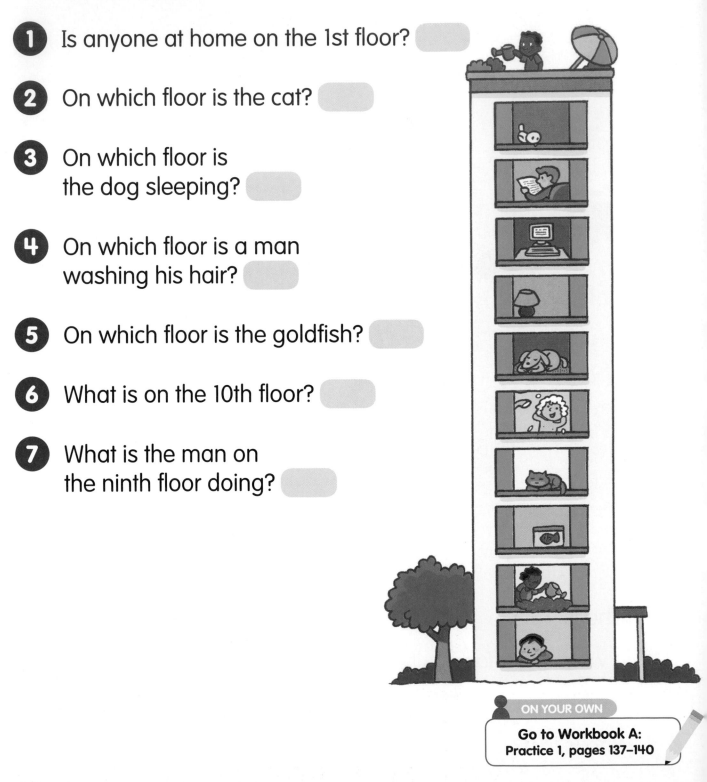

**ON YOUR OWN**

**Go to Workbook A:**
**Practice 1, pages 137–140**

# LESSON 2 Position Words

## Lesson Objective

- Use position words to name relative positions.

**Learn** **You can use position words to tell order and position.**

Alan is **before** Ben.
Chris is **after** Ben.
Ben is **between** Alan and Chris.

## Guided Practice

**Name the positions of Demi and Evan using these words.**

1.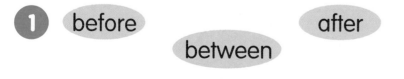
before        after
between

LEFT RIGHT

The T-shirt is first on the **left**.
The pants are second from the left.

The T-shirt is fifth from the **right**.
It is also last from the right.

The towel is third from the left.
It is also third from the right.

The dress is **next to** the towel.
The dress is also next to the skirt.

The pants are between the T-shirt and the towel.

# Guided Practice

## Answer the questions.

Raj  Megan  Lin  Dylan  Mr. Smith  Jorge

LEFT                                    RIGHT

**2** Who is first on the right? ⬭

**3** Who is second from the left? ⬭

**4** Who is last from the left? ⬭

**5** Who is next to Mr. Smith? ⬭

Who is between Dylan and Jorge?

 Hands-On Activity

**WORKING TOGETHER**

## Carry out these activities.

**1** Your teacher will choose ten children.
They should stand in a row facing the class.

Your teacher will ask the rest of you where each person is in the row.

Then take turns talking to your partner.
Talk about where each person is in the row.
Use these words:

| 1st | 2nd | 3rd | 4th | 5th | 6th | 7th | 8th | 9th | 10th |
|-----|-----|-----|-----|-----|-----|-----|-----|-----|------|
|  | left |  | right |  | last |  | next to |  |  |

**2** Put some school supplies in a row on your table.
Take turns with your partner.
Talk about where each thing is in the row.

WORKING TOGETHER **Game**

# Find it First!

Players: 3
You need:
- 10
- 10

**How to play:** Use only 1, 2, or 3 fingers to count.

**STEP 1** Players 1 and 2 put their in a row.

**STEP 2** Player 3 calls out an ordinal position.

9th from the left!

**STEP 3** The first player to grab the correct from his or her own row scores 1 point.

**STEP 4** Put the back. Player 3 then calls out another ordinal position. The first player to score 5 points wins.

**STEP 5** Take turns calling out and playing.

## Let's Practice

**Look at the picture.**
**Complete the sentences.**

1. The black mouse is before the brown mouse.
   The white mouse is [ ] the brown mouse.

2. The brown mouse is [ ] the black mouse and the white mouse.

3. The peanut butter is second from the [ ].

4. The cheese is [ ] on the right.

5. The apple is [ ] the peanut butter.

6. The potato is third from the [ ] and the [ ].

ON YOUR OWN

**Go to Workbook A:**
**Practice 2, pages 141–144**

# You can use the picture to learn more position words.

Jasmine is **under** the table.

Shenice is **above** Pedro.
Pedro is **below** Shenice.

Danny is **behind** the curtains.
Jacob is **in front of** the curtains.

## Guided Practice

**Look at the picture.**
**Find the missing position words.**

| under | above | below | behind | in front of |

**6** Tom is ⬜ Sue.

**7** Sue is ⬜ Tom.

**8** The toys are ⬜ the books.

**9** The books are ⬜ the toys.

**10** The ball is ⬜ the shelf.

## You can use the picture to learn more position words.

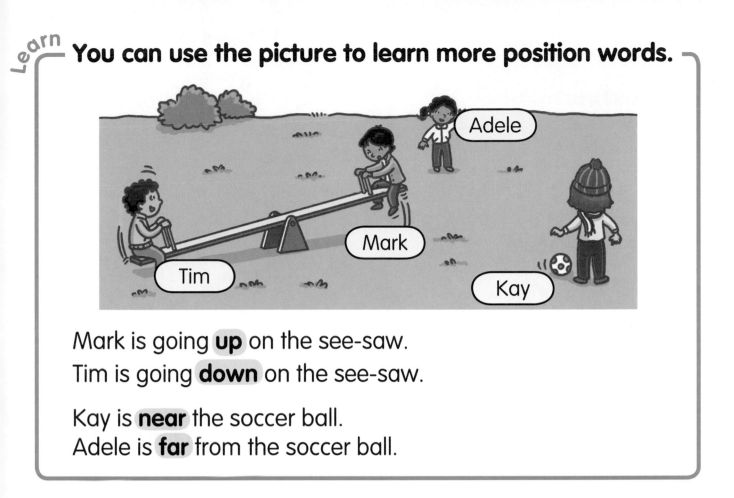

Mark is going **up** on the see-saw.
Tim is going **down** on the see-saw.

Kay is **near** the soccer ball.
Adele is **far** from the soccer ball.

## Guided Practice

### Look at the picture.
### Find the missing position words.

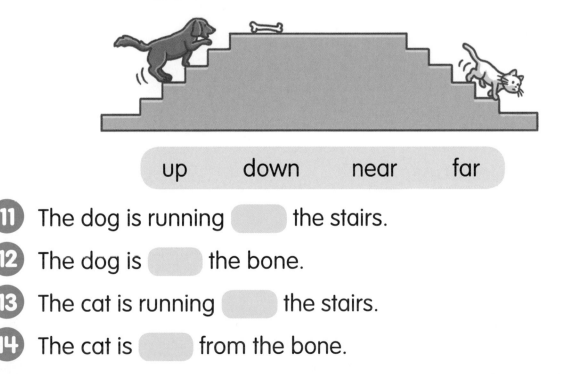

up     down     near     far

**11** The dog is running ⬚ the stairs.

**12** The dog is ⬚ the bone.

**13** The cat is running ⬚ the stairs.

**14** The cat is ⬚ from the bone.

# Let's Practice

Short Sally

Quick Quentin

Tall Tom

Funny Fred

Tiny Tim

LEFT

## Look at the picture.
## Answer the questions.

**1** Who is below Short Sally?

**2** Who is in front of Tapping Tina?

**3** Who is above Tall Tom?

**4** Who is under Bashful Betty's hat?

Mini Monkey

Hairy Harry

Tapping Tina

Bashful Betty

Sleeping Sam

RIGHT

**5** Who is behind Sleeping Sam?

**6** Who is sliding down the pole?

**7** Who is climbing up the ladder?

**8** Who is near the ball?

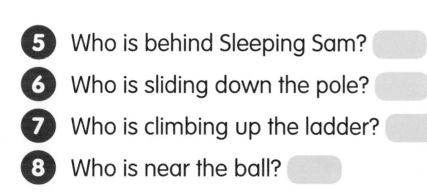

ON YOUR OWN

**Go to Workbook A:**
**Practice 3, pages 145–146**

# Let's Explore!

**Use nine** **and one** .

**STEP 1** Mix the .
Then arrange the in a row.

**STEP 2** Write the answer to each of these questions.
What is the position of the from the left?
What is the position of the from the right?

| Position of from the Left | Position of from the Right | ☐ + ☐ |
|:---:|:---:|:---:|
| ☐ | ☐ | ☐ |
| ☐ | ☐ | ☐ |
| ☐ | ☐ | ☐ |
| ☐ | ☐ | ☐ |

Repeat **STEP 1** and **STEP 2** to complete the chart.

The total number of is 10.

The answer in the ☐ is always ☐ more than the total number of .

# Math Journal

## Look around your classroom. Complete the sentences.

**1** The books on the shelf are near the ▢.

**2** My backpack is ▢ my table.

**3** ▢ sits behind me.

**4** The ▢ is far from me.

**5** ▢ sits to the left of me.

## CRITICAL THINKING SKILLS
# Put On Your Thinking Cap!

**PROBLEM SOLVING**

## Write the names in the correct order.

**1** Annie Ant, Billy Beetle and Lizzy Lizard are in a line.
Annie Ant is last.
Billy Beetle is not 2nd.

▢        ▢        ▢

first

Who is between 1st and 3rd?
How do you know?

**2** Tanya plants 4 flowers in a row.
The orchid is not 2nd from the left.
The daisy is between the rose and the sunflower.
The sunflower is 1st on the right.

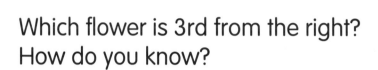

LEFT                                                    RIGHT

Which flower is 3rd from the right?
How do you know?

**3** Joshua counts the number of children in his group.
Nick is the 4th person from the right.
He is also the 2nd person from the left.
How many people are there in his group?

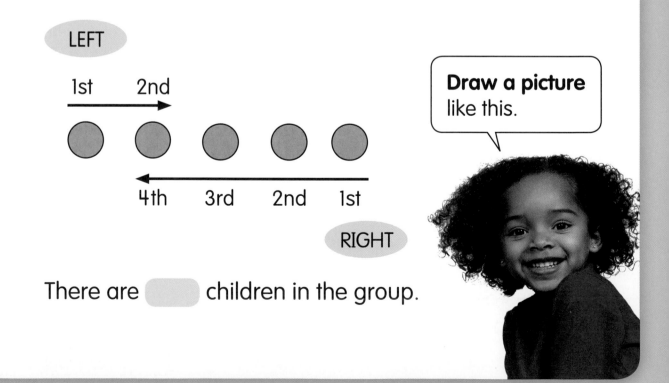

**Draw a picture** like this.

There are ⬜ children in the group.

**4** Beth arranges 10 beads in a row.
There is only one red bead.
The red bead is placed 6th from the right.
If Beth counts from the left, in what position
is the red bead?

**Draw a picture** or **act it out**.

ON YOUR OWN

Go to Workbook A:
Put on Your Thinking Cap!
pages 147–150

# Chapter Wrap Up
## You have learned...

**Ordinal Numbers and Position**

Use ordinal and position words to talk about where things are

Hippo
3rd
third

Tury
6th
sixth

Billy
8th
eighth

Flipper
1st
first

Alice
5th
fifth

Wally
2nd
second

Ben
4th
fourth

Tyra
7th
seventh

Wally is after Flipper.
Wally is before Hippo.
Wally is between Flipper and Hippo.
Sealy is last.

The ⬡ is first on the left.
The ⬡ is first on the right.

BIG IDEA

Numbers and words can be used to describe order and position.

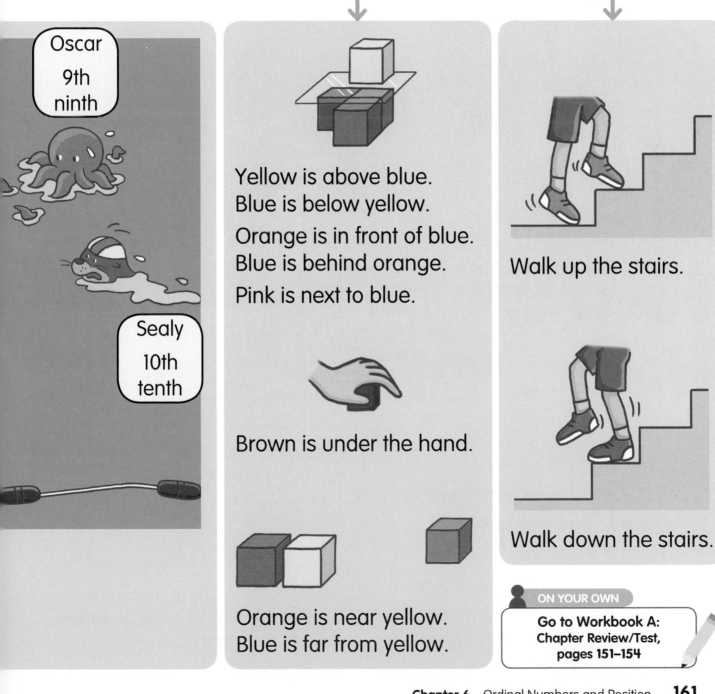

Oscar
9th
ninth

Sealy
10th
tenth

Yellow is above blue.
Blue is below yellow.

Orange is in front of blue.
Blue is behind orange.

Pink is next to blue.

Brown is under the hand.

Orange is near yellow.
Blue is far from yellow.

Walk up the stairs.

Walk down the stairs.

ON YOUR OWN

Go to Workbook A:
Chapter Review/Test,
pages 151–154

# CHAPTER 7 Numbers to 20

I'm 10 years old!

I'm 3 years old!

How many candles are there in all?

**BIG IDEA**

Count, compare, and order numbers to 20.

# Recall Prior Knowledge

## Counting

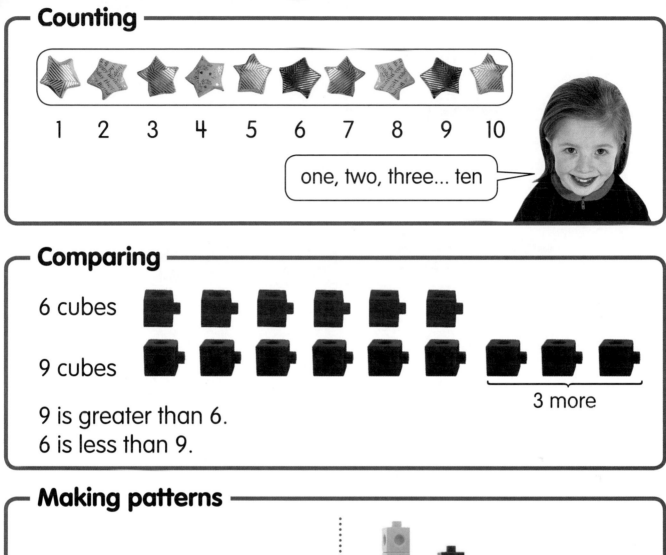

1  2  3  4  5  6  7  8  9  10

one, two, three... ten

## Comparing

6 cubes

9 cubes

3 more

9 is greater than 6.
6 is less than 9.

## Making patterns

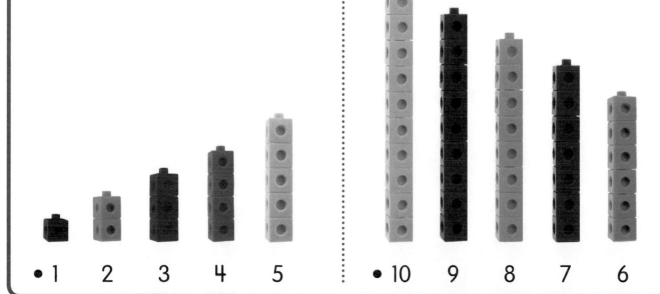

•1  2  3  4  5    •10  9  8  7  6

## Count.

**1** Count from 1 to 10.

**2** How many  are there?
Write the number and word. ⬚ ⬚

## Find the missing numbers.

**3**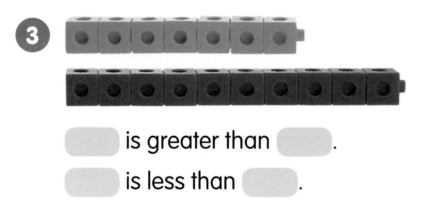

⬚ is greater than ⬚.

⬚ is less than ⬚.

## Complete the number patterns.

**4**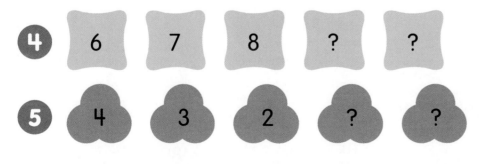

| 6 | 7 | 8 | ? | ? |

**5**

| 4 | 3 | 2 | ? | ? |

# Counting to 20

## Lesson Objectives

- Count on from 10 to 20.
- Read and write 11 to 20 in numbers and words.

**Vocabulary**

| | |
|---|---|
| eleven | twelve |
| thirteen | fourteen |
| fifteen | sixteen |
| seventeen | eighteen |
| nineteen | twenty |

*Learn* **You can count on from 10.**

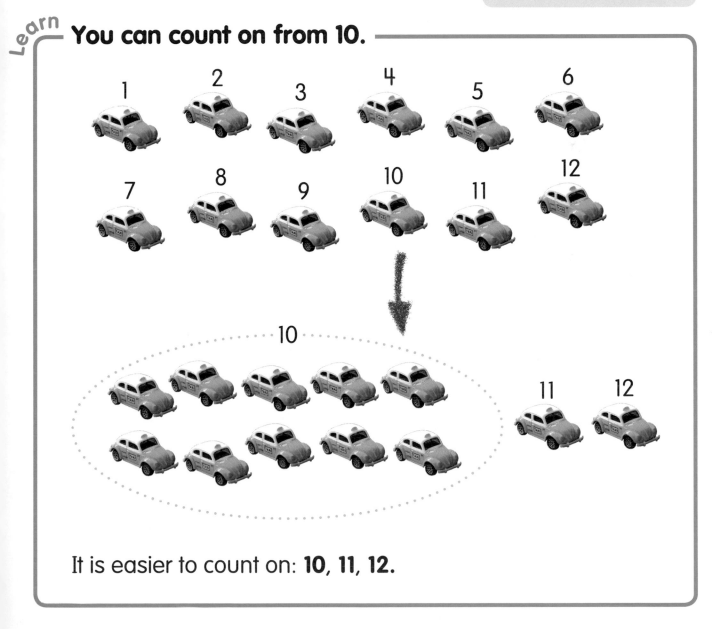

It is easier to count on: **10, 11, 12.**

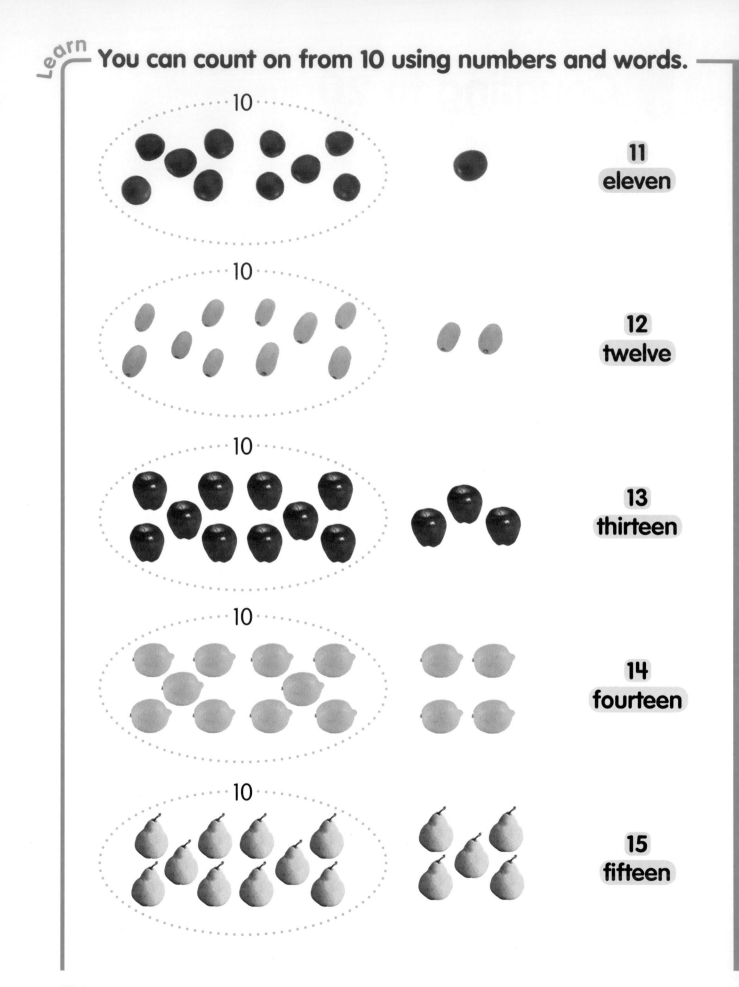

10

**11**
eleven

10

**12**
twelve

10

**13**
thirteen

10

**14**
fourteen

10

**15**
fifteen

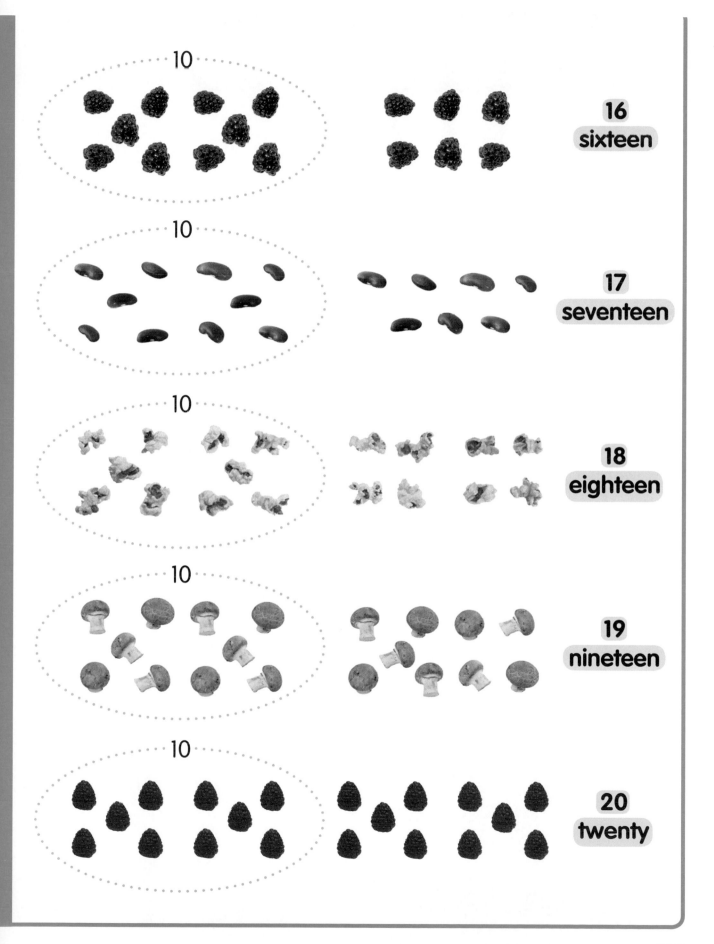

10

**16**
sixteen

10

**17**
seventeen

10

**18**
eighteen

10

**19**
nineteen

10

**20**
twenty

# You can first make a ten. Then count on.

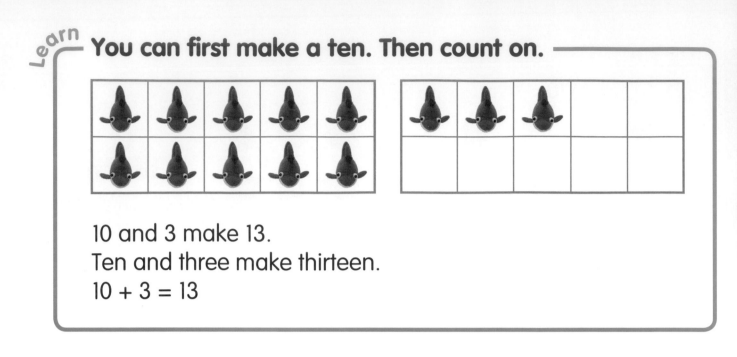

10 and 3 make 13.
Ten and three make thirteen.
10 + 3 = 13

## Guided Practice

**Make a ten.**
**Then count on.**

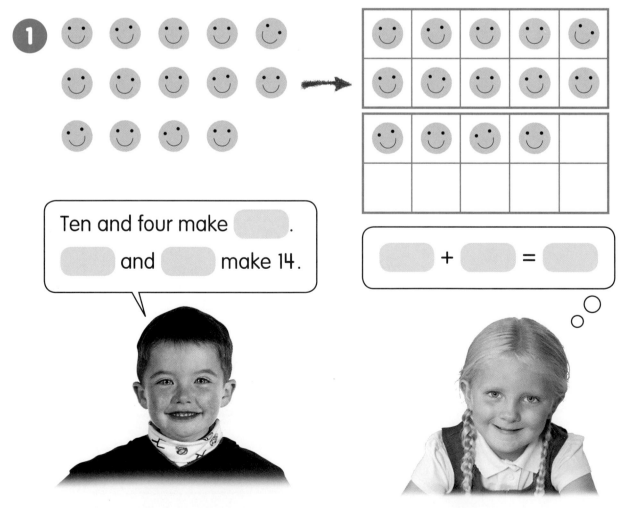

1

Ten and four make ____.

____ and ____ make 14.

____ + ____ = ____

# Roll the Number Cube!

**Players: 4**
**You need:**
- one number cube
- base ten blocks

**STEP 1** Roll the number cube.
Then take this number of 🔲.

6!

**STEP 2** Each player take turns to roll the number cube and take 🔲.

**STEP 3** On your next turn, roll the number cube again.
Then take this number of 🔲.
If you have 10 🔲, trade them for one ▬▬▬▬▬.

6 + 4 = 10!

The first player to get 2 ▬▬▬▬▬ wins!

## Guided Practice

**Find the missing numbers.**

**2** 10 and 7 make [  ] .  10 + 7 = [  ]

**3** 10 and 10 make [  ] .  10 + 10 = [  ]

## Let's Practice

**Make a ten.**
**Then count on.**

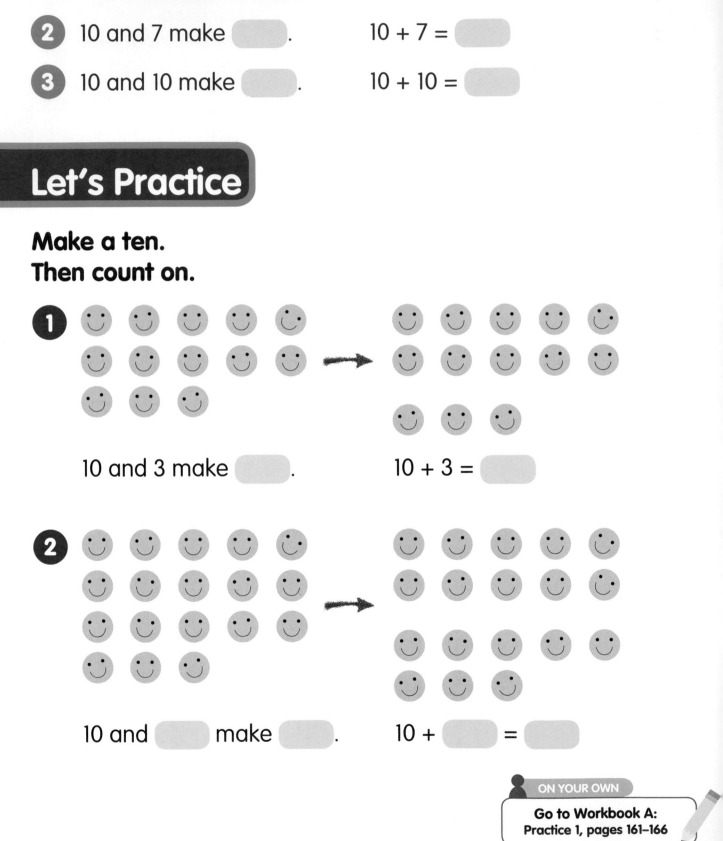

**1**

10 and 3 make [  ] .  10 + 3 = [  ]

**2**

10 and [  ] make [  ] .  10 + [  ] = [  ]

ON YOUR OWN

**Go to Workbook A:**
**Practice 1, pages 161–166**

# Place Value

**Lesson Objectives**

- Use a place-value chart to show numbers up to 20.
- Show objects up to 20 as tens and ones.

**Learn** You can use place value to show numbers to 20.

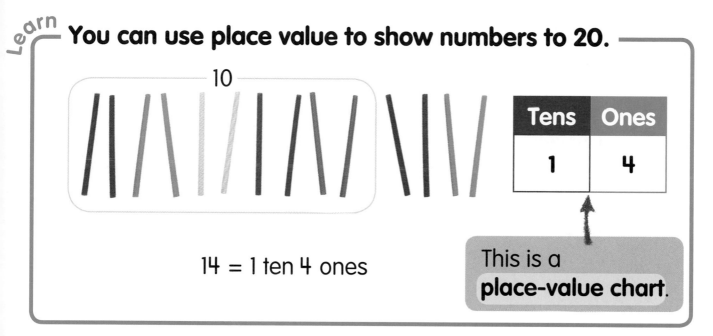

10

14 = 1 ten 4 ones

| Tens | Ones |
|------|------|
| 1 | 4 |

This is a **place-value chart**.

## Guided Practice

**Use place value to find the missing numbers.**

**1**

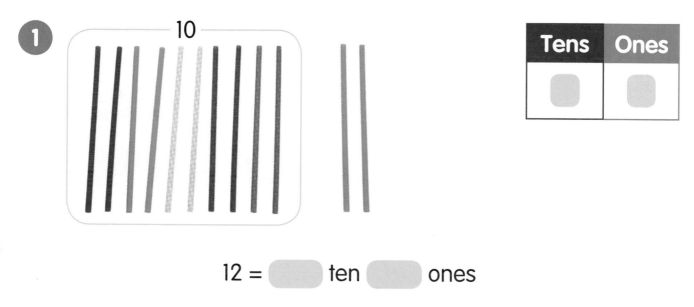

10

| Tens | Ones |
|------|------|
|      |      |

12 = _____ ten _____ ones

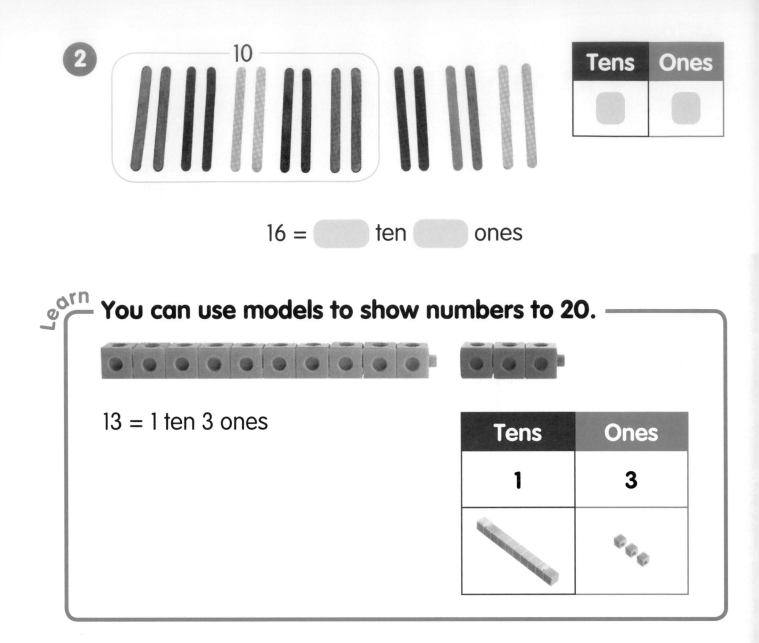

**2**

10

| Tens | Ones |
|------|------|
|      |      |

16 = ⬜ ten ⬜ ones

## You can use models to show numbers to 20.

13 = 1 ten 3 ones

| Tens | Ones |
|------|------|
| 1    | 3    |

## Guided Practice

### Find the correct place-value chart for the number.

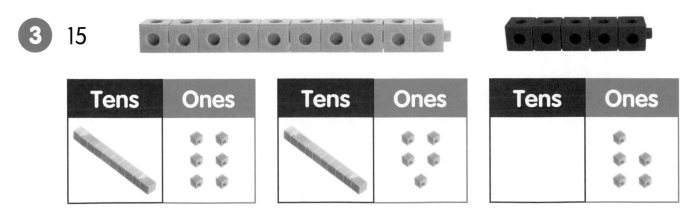

**3**  15

| Tens | Ones |
|------|------|
|      |      |

| Tens | Ones |
|------|------|
|      |      |

| Tens | Ones |
|------|------|
|      |      |

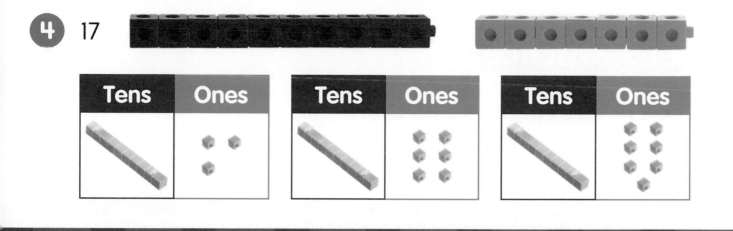

**4** 17

| Tens | Ones |
|------|------|
| | • • • |

| Tens | Ones |
|------|------|
| | ⬚⬚ ⬚⬚ ⬚⬚ |

| Tens | Ones |
|------|------|
| | ⬚⬚ ⬚⬚ ⬚ |

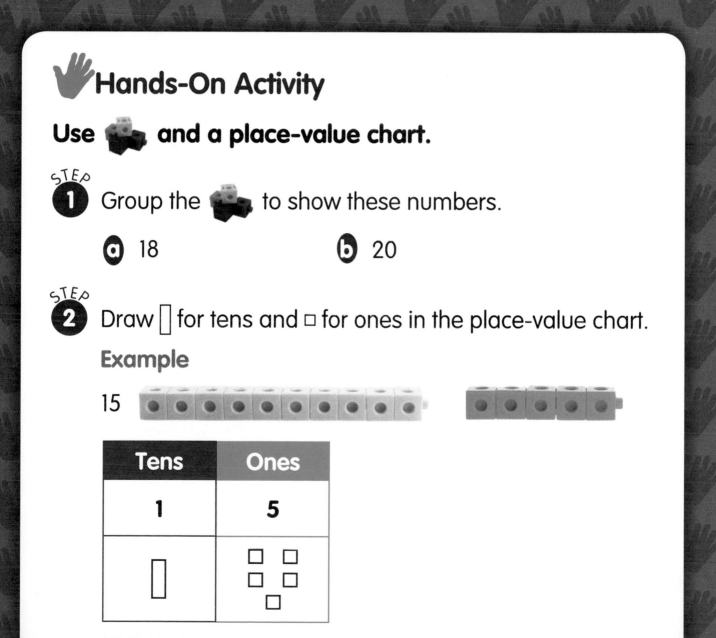

# ✋ Hands-On Activity

Use 🧊 and a place-value chart.

**STEP 1** Group the 🧊 to show these numbers.

**ⓐ** 18                    **ⓑ** 20

**STEP 2** Draw ▯ for tens and □ for ones in the place-value chart.

**Example**

15

| Tens | Ones |
|------|------|
| **1** | **5** |
| ▯ | □ □ <br> □ □ <br> □ |

Look at each place-value chart.
What is the number shown?

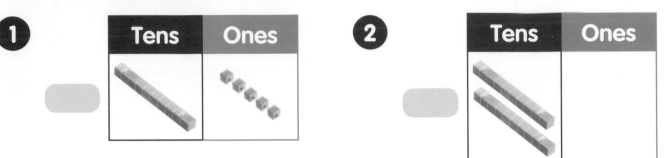

**1**

| Tens | Ones |
|------|------|

**2**

| Tens | Ones |
|------|------|

Show the number.
Draw ▯ for tens and □ for ones.

**3**

14

| Tens | Ones |
|------|------|

**4**

17

| Tens | Ones |
|------|------|

Find the missing numbers.

**5**  11 = ⬭ ten ⬭ one

**6**  10 = ⬭ ten ⬭ ones

**7**  16 = ⬭ ten ⬭ ones

**8**  18 = ⬭ ten ⬭ ones

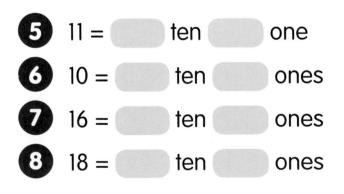

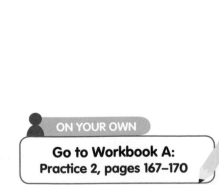

ON YOUR OWN

Go to Workbook A:
Practice 2, pages 167–170

# LESSON 3 Comparing Numbers

## Lesson Objective

• Compare numbers to 20.

**Vocabulary**
greatest
least

**Learn** Compare sets and numbers.

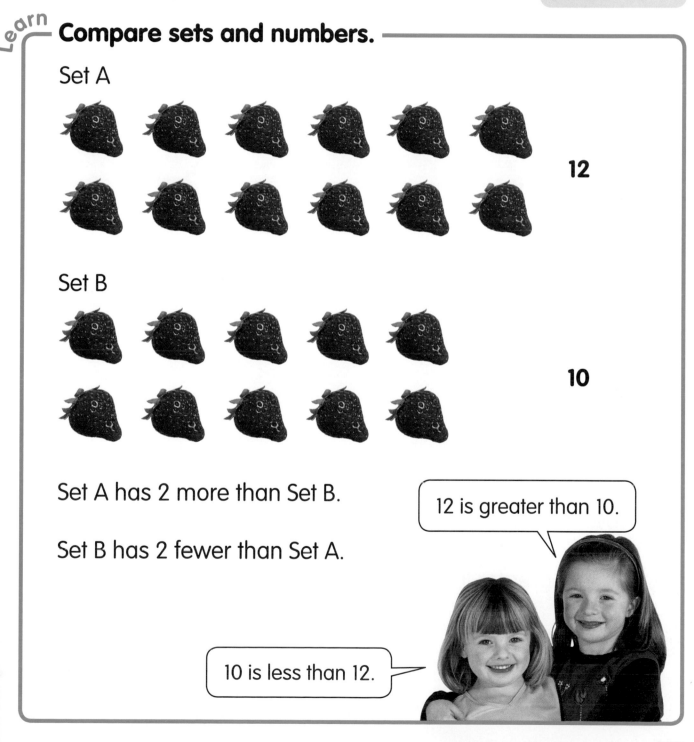

Set A

12

Set B

10

Set A has 2 more than Set B.

Set B has 2 fewer than Set A.

12 is greater than 10.

10 is less than 12.

# Guided Practice

## Count.
## Then answer the questions.

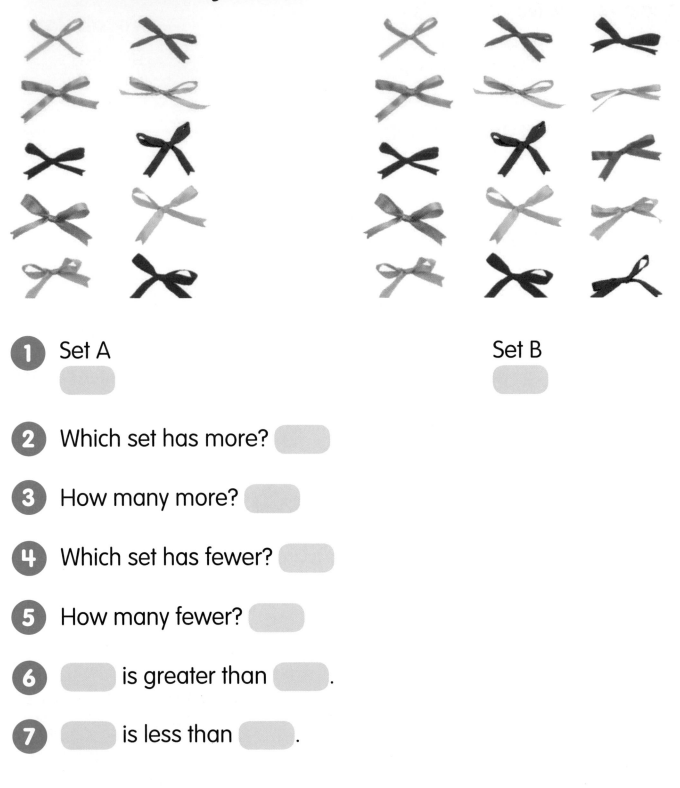

1  Set A
   [ ]

   Set B
   [ ]

2  Which set has more? [ ]

3  How many more? [ ]

4  Which set has fewer? [ ]

5  How many fewer? [ ]

6  [ ] is greater than [ ].

7  [ ] is less than [ ].

# You can use place value to find how much greater or how much less.

Compare 13 and 15.
Which number is greater?
How much greater is the number?

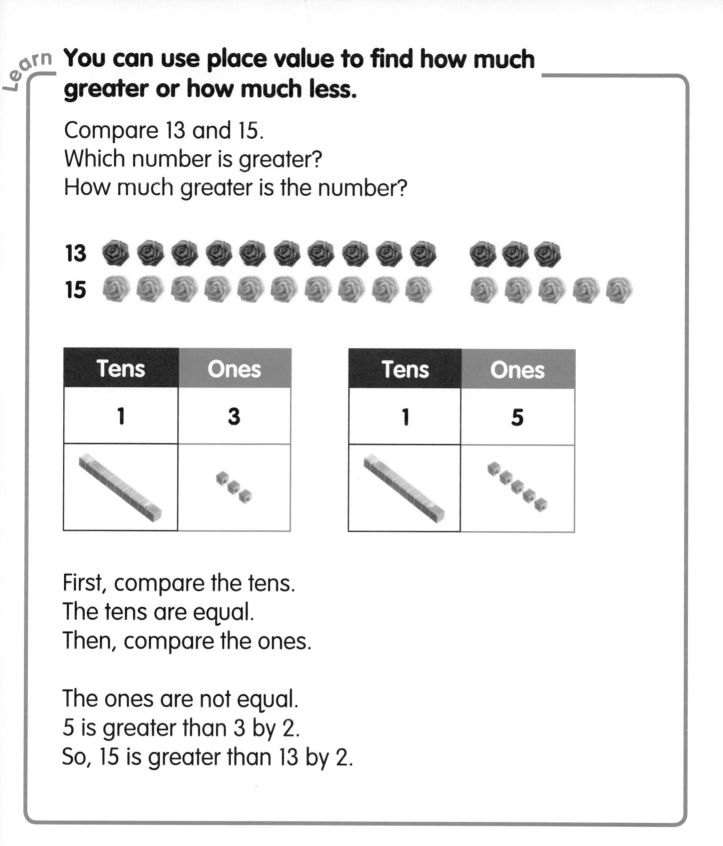

First, compare the tens.
The tens are equal.
Then, compare the ones.

The ones are not equal.
5 is greater than 3 by 2.
So, 15 is greater than 13 by 2.

## Compare the numbers.
## Use place value to help you.

**8** Which number is greater?
How much greater?

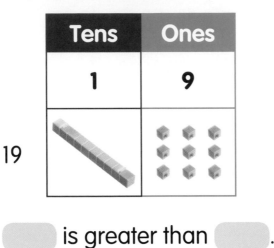

19

| Tens | Ones |
|:---:|:---:|
| 1 | 9 |

17

| Tens | Ones |
|:---:|:---:|
| 1 | 7 |

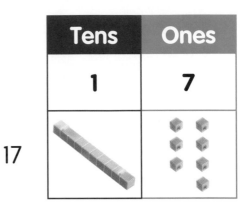

⬭ is greater than ⬭.

⬭ is greater than ⬭ by ⬭.

**9** Which number is less?
How much less?

16

| Tens | Ones |
|:---:|:---:|
| 1 | 6 |

12

| Tens | Ones |
|:---:|:---:|
| 1 | 2 |

⬭ is less than ⬭.

⬭ is less than ⬭ by ⬭.

**You can use place value to compare three numbers.**

Compare 14, 11 and 16.

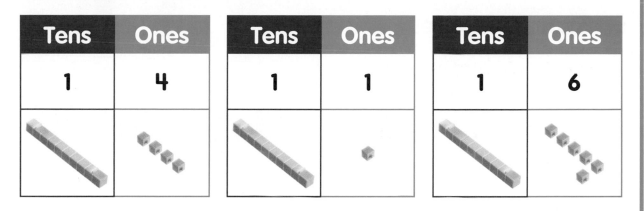

| Tens | Ones |
|------|------|
| 1 | 4 |

| Tens | Ones |
|------|------|
| 1 | 1 |

| Tens | Ones |
|------|------|
| 1 | 6 |

The tens are all equal.
So, compare the ones.

4 is greater than 1.
6 is greater than 4.

16 is the **greatest** number.
11 is the **least** number.

## Guided Practice

**Compare the numbers.
Use place value to help you.**

**10** Which is the greatest?
Which is the least?

10  17  12

| Tens | Ones |
|------|------|
|      |      |
|      |      |

_____ is the greatest number.

_____ is the least number.

## Count and compare.

 **1** Which set has more?

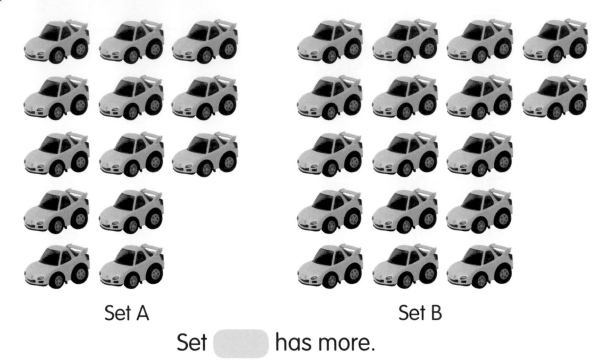

Set A                    Set B

Set [ ] has more.

**2** Which set has fewer?

Set A                    Set B

Set [ ] has fewer.

## Which number is greater?
## How much greater?

**3**   9   or   5

          is greater.

It is greater by       .

## Which number is less?
## How much less?

**4**   19   or   10

          is less.

It is less by       .

## Compare these numbers.

**5**   12   18   14

Which is the least?      

Which is the greatest?      

**6**   11   20   10

Which is the least?      

Which is the greatest?      

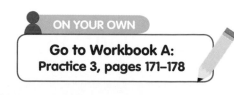

**ON YOUR OWN**

**Go to Workbook A:
Practice 3, pages 171–178**

# Let's Explore!

Use .
Look at these numbers.

11    15    12

**STEP 1** Make a number train for the greatest number. Name it Train G.

**STEP 2** Make a number train for the least number. Name it Train L.

**STEP 3** Take some 🟦 from Train G to give to Train L. Make both trains have the same number of 🟦.

How many 🟦 must you take from Train G?

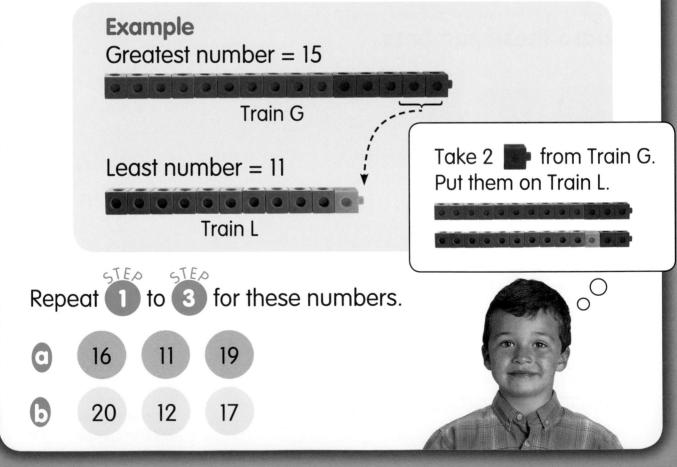

**Example**
Greatest number = 15

Train G

Least number = 11

Train L

Take 2 🟦 from Train G.
Put them on Train L.

Repeat **STEP 1** to **STEP 3** for these numbers.

**a**   16   11   19

**b**   20   12   17

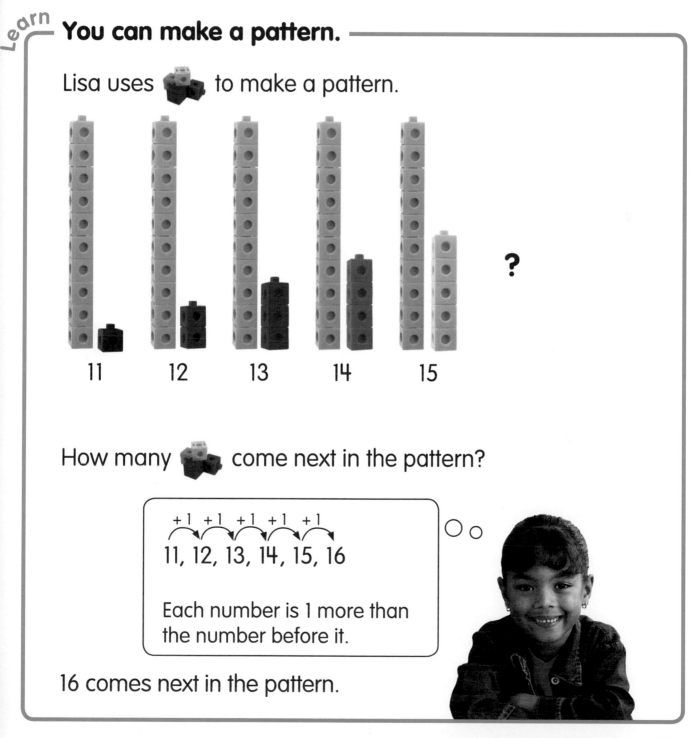

# LESSON 4
# Making Patterns and Ordering Numbers

**Lesson Objective**

- Order numbers by making number patterns.

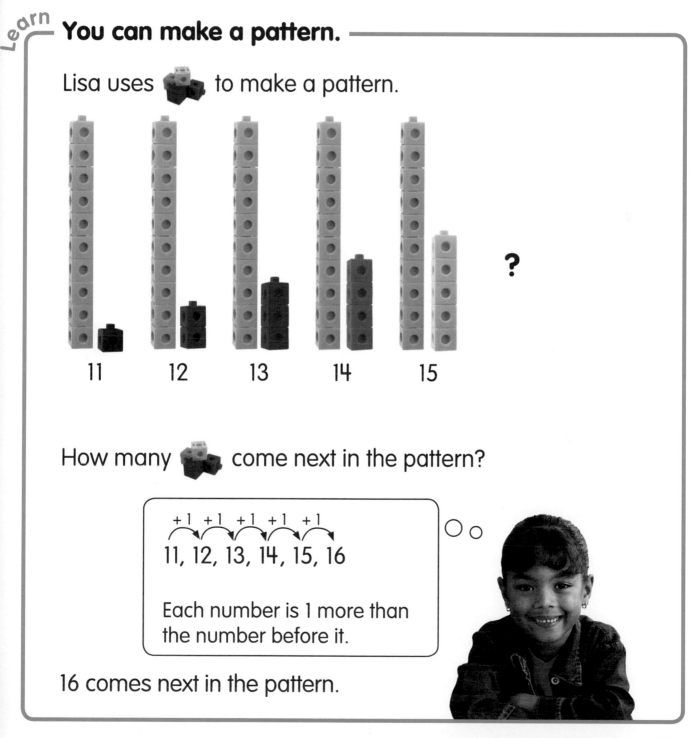

**Vocabulary**
order

## Learn  You can make a pattern.

Lisa uses ▨ to make a pattern.

11    12    13    14    15    **?**

How many ▨ come next in the pattern?

+1 +1 +1 +1 +1
11, 12, 13, 14, 15, 16

Each number is 1 more than the number before it.

16 comes next in the pattern.

## Guided Practice

### Complete the patterns.

**1** Jenny uses beads to make a pattern.

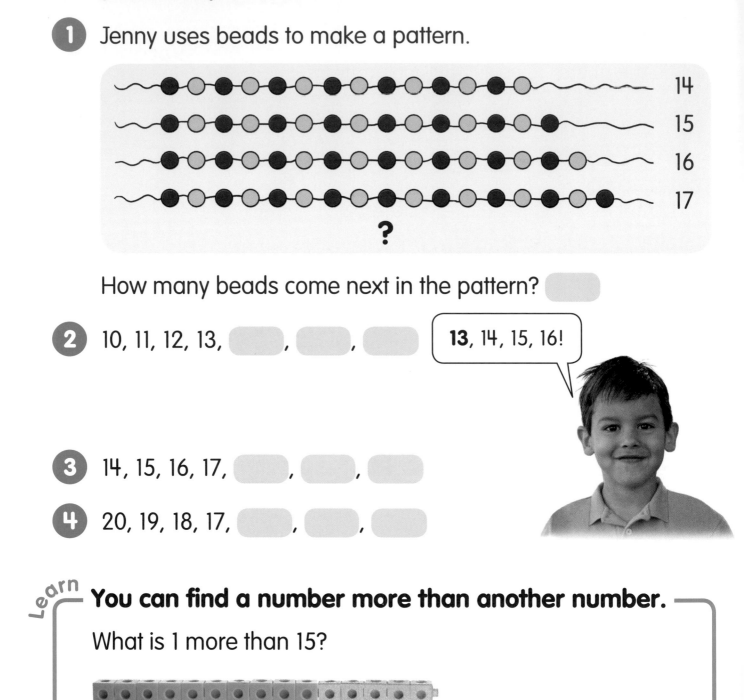

14
15
16
17

?

How many beads come next in the pattern? [ ]

**2** 10, 11, 12, 13, [ ], [ ], [ ]

> **13**, 14, 15, 16!

**3** 14, 15, 16, 17, [ ], [ ], [ ]

**4** 20, 19, 18, 17, [ ], [ ], [ ]

### Learn You can find a number more than another number.

What is 1 more than 15?

↓ 1 more

1 more than 15 is 16.

## Guided Practice

### Solve.

**5** What is 2 more than 17?

2 more

2 more than 17 is ⬭.

## Learn

## You can find a number less than another number.

What is 1 less than 16?

1 less

1 less than 16 is 15.

## Guided Practice

### Solve.

**6** What is 2 less than 20?

2 less

2 less than 20 is ⬭.

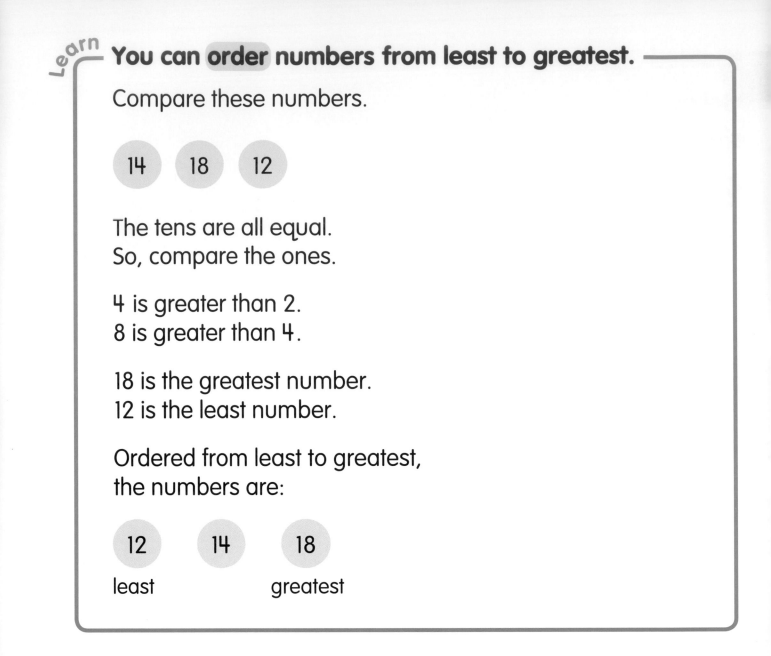

**Learn** **You can order numbers from least to greatest.**

Compare these numbers.

14  18  12

The tens are all equal.
So, compare the ones.

4 is greater than 2.
8 is greater than 4.

18 is the greatest number.
12 is the least number.

Ordered from least to greatest,
the numbers are:

12  14  18

least      greatest

## Guided Practice

**Order the numbers.**

**7** from greatest to least

20  2  13

**8** from least to greatest

8  10  18

# Let's Practice

**Find the missing numbers.**

**1**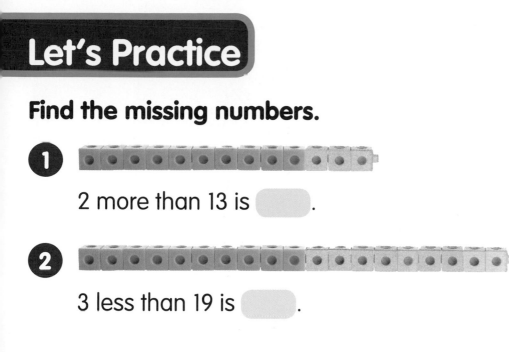

2 more than 13 is [ ].

**2**

3 less than 19 is [ ].

**Find the missing numbers.**
**Use the picture to help you.**

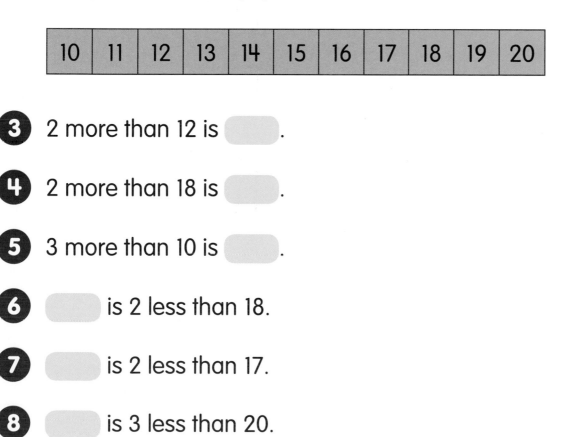

| 10 | 11 | 12 | 13 | 14 | 15 | 16 | 17 | 18 | 19 | 20 |
|----|----|----|----|----|----|----|----|----|----|----|

**3** 2 more than 12 is [ ].

**4** 2 more than 18 is [ ].

**5** 3 more than 10 is [ ].

**6** [ ] is 2 less than 18.

**7** [ ] is 2 less than 17.

**8** [ ] is 3 less than 20.

## Complete the patterns.

**9** 11, 12, 13, [＿＿], 15, 16

**10** 17, 16, 15, [＿＿], [＿＿], 12, 11

**11** 7, 9, [＿＿], 13, 15, [＿＿], 19

**12** [＿＿], 18, 16, [＿＿], [＿＿], 10, 8

## Order the numbers from greatest to least.

**13** ( 11 ) ( 9 ) ( 18 ) ( 15 )

## Order the numbers from least to greatest.

**14** [ 20 ] [ 6 ] [ 12 ] [ 16 ]

ON YOUR OWN

**Go to Workbook A:
Practice 4, pages 179–181**

**PROBLEM SOLVING**

# Find the two missing numbers in the pattern.
# Then put the cards in order.

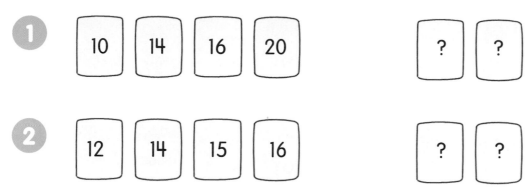

1. | 10 | 14 | 16 | 20 |        | ? | ? |

2. | 12 | 14 | 15 | 16 |        | ? | ? |

There is more than one correct answer for Question 2.

**ON YOUR OWN**

**Go to Workbook A:
Put on Your Thinking Cap!
pages 183–186**

# Chapter Wrap Up

**You have learned...**

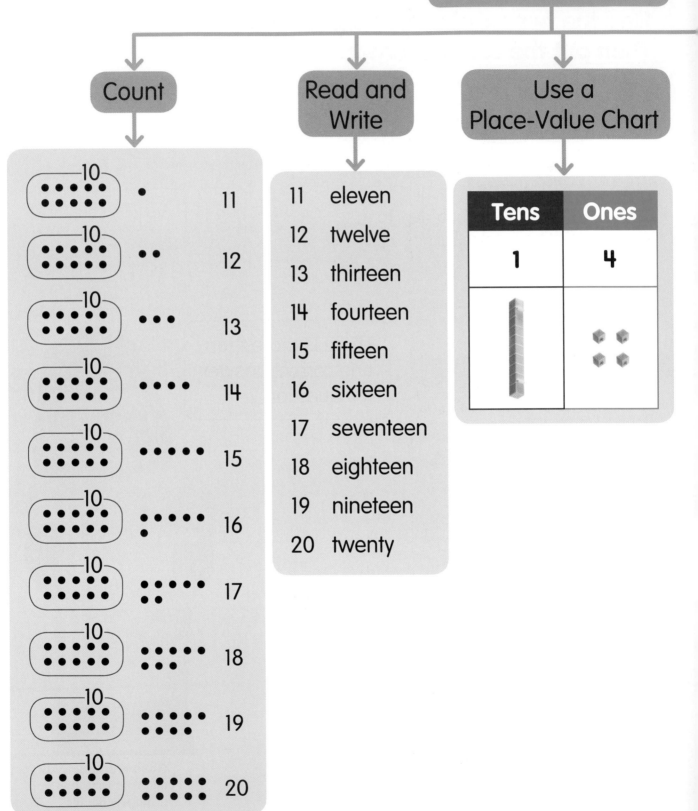

Numbers to 20

**Count**

**Read and Write**

| 11 | eleven |
| 12 | twelve |
| 13 | thirteen |
| 14 | fourteen |
| 15 | fifteen |
| 16 | sixteen |
| 17 | seventeen |
| 18 | eighteen |
| 19 | nineteen |
| 20 | twenty |

**Use a Place-Value Chart**

| Tens | Ones |
|------|------|
| 1 | 4 |

Compare

Make Patterns

Order

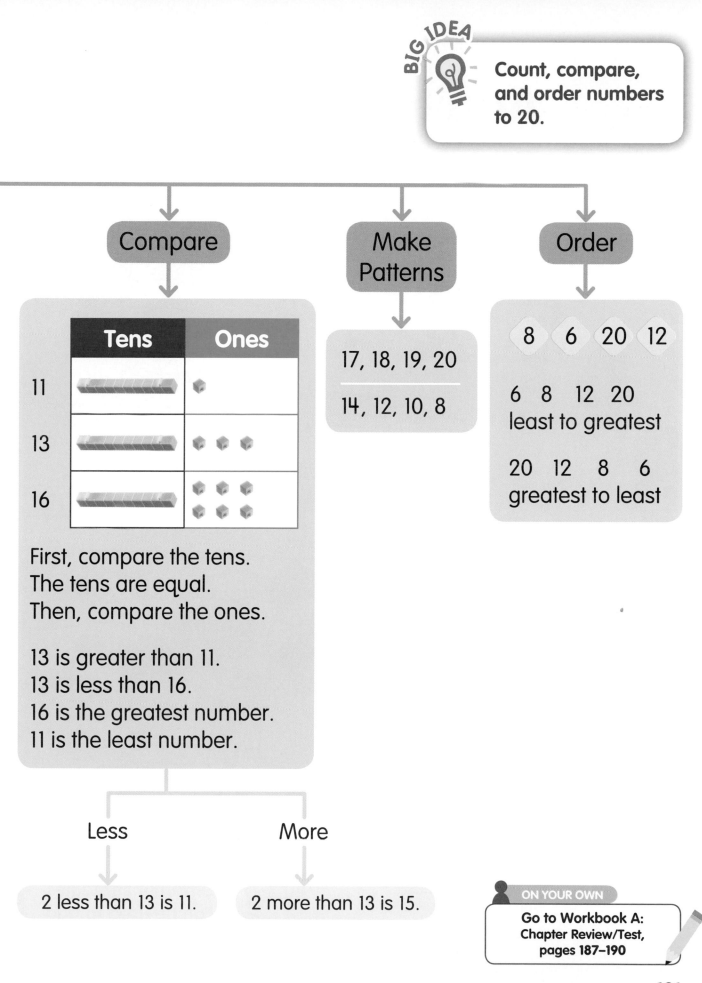

| Tens | Ones |
|------|------|
| 11 | |
| 13 | |
| 16 | |

First, compare the tens.
The tens are equal.
Then, compare the ones.

13 is greater than 11.
13 is less than 16.
16 is the greatest number.
11 is the least number.

17, 18, 19, 20

14, 12, 10, 8

8   6   20   12

6   8   12   20
least to greatest

20   12   8   6
greatest to least

Less

More

2 less than 13 is 11.

2 more than 13 is 15.

ON YOUR OWN

Go to Workbook A:
Chapter Review/Test,
pages 187–190

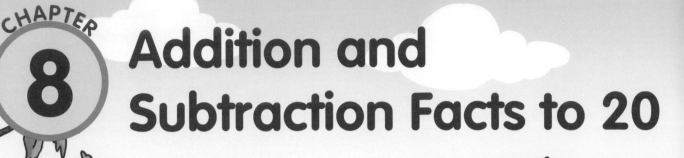

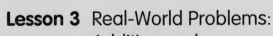

**BIG IDEA**

Different strategies can be used to add and subtract.

# Recall Prior Knowledge

## Using fact families to solve number sentences

1 + 3 = 4
3 + 1 = 4
4 − 1 = 3
4 − 3 = 1

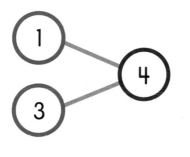

? − 1 = 3

1 + 3 = 4 is the related addition fact.
So, 4 − 1 = 3.

3 + ? = 4

4 − 3 = 1 is the related subtraction fact.
So, 3 + 1 = 4.

## Adding and subtracting 0

3 + 0 = 3
3 − 0 = 3

## Addition facts

10 and 2 make 12.
12 is 10 and 2.
10 + 2 = 12

## Comparing numbers

15 is 2 more than 13.

14 is 3 less than 17.

**Make a fact family.**

**1**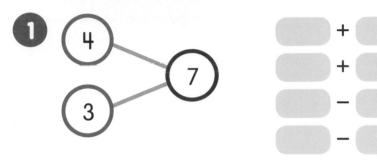

⬜ + ⬜ = ⬜

⬜ + ⬜ = ⬜

⬜ − ⬜ = ⬜

⬜ − ⬜ = ⬜

**Complete the number sentences.**
**Use related facts.**

**2** 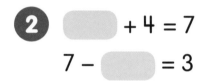 ⬜ + 4 = 7

7 − ⬜ = 3

**Solve.**

**3** 9 + 1 = 10

1 + ⬜ = 10

**4** 5 + 0 = ⬜

**5** 5 − ⬜ = 5

**6** 10 and 4 make ⬜ .

14 is ⬜ and 4.

10 + ⬜ = 14

**7** ⬜ is 3 more than 15.

**8** 5 less than 20 is ⬜ .

# 1 Ways to Add

**Lesson Objective**

• Use different strategies to add 1- and 2-digit numbers.

**Vocabulary**

group    doubles fact

same    doubles plus one

## Learn

### You can add by making a 10.

Gus has 8 cherries.
Ava gives him 6 more.

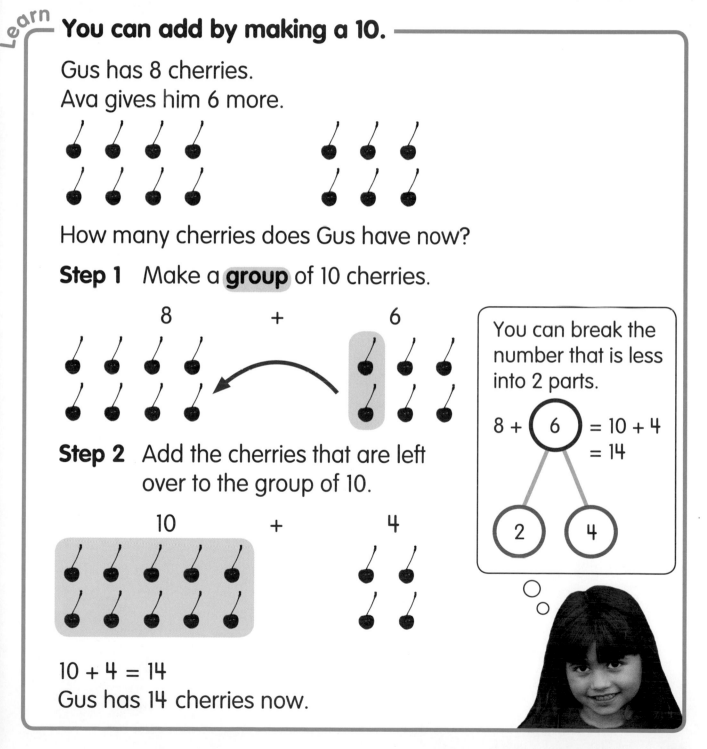

How many cherries does Gus have now?

**Step 1**  Make a **group** of 10 cherries.

8          +          6

You can break the number that is less into 2 parts.

$8 + 6 = 10 + 4$
$= 14$

8 + ⑥

2        4

**Step 2**  Add the cherries that are left over to the group of 10.

10          +          4

$10 + 4 = 14$
Gus has 14 cherries now.

# Hands-On Activity

Use 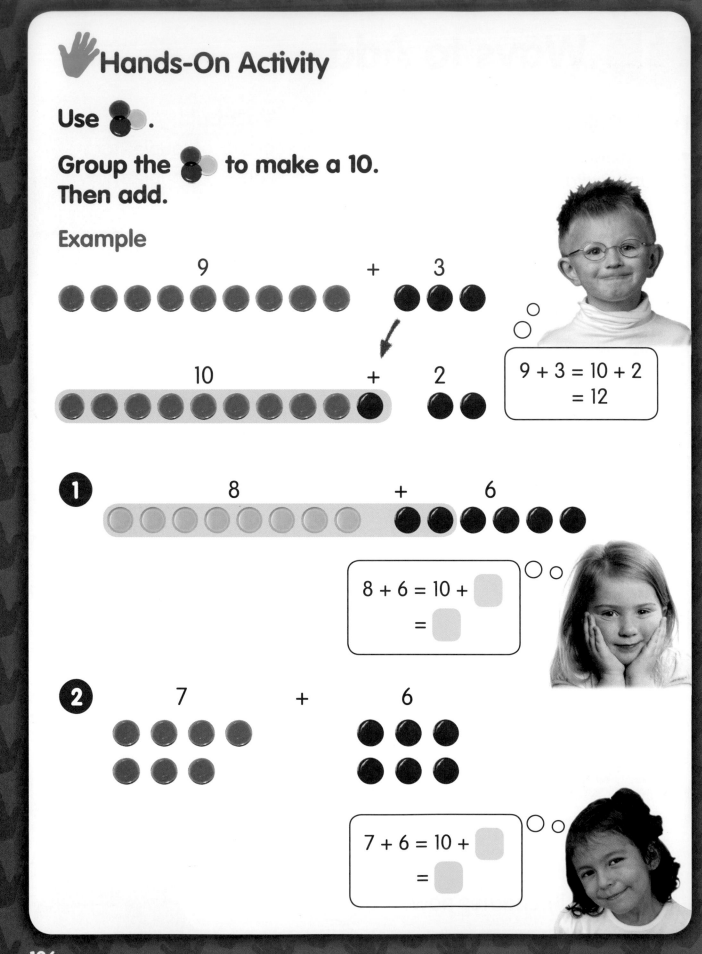.

Group the to make a 10.
Then add.

**Example**

9     +    3

10     +    2

9 + 3 = 10 + 2
      = 12

**1**     8     +    6

8 + 6 = 10 + ⬜
     = ⬜

**2**     7     +    6

7 + 6 = 10 + ⬜
     = ⬜

## Guided Practice

**Make a 10.**
**Then add.**
**Use number bonds to help you.**

**1** 9 + 5 = [ ]

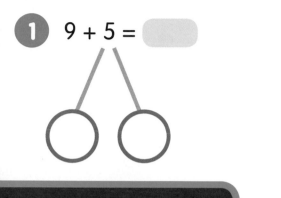

**2** 8 + 7 = [ ]

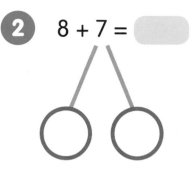

# Let's Practice

**Make a 10.**
**Then add.**

**1** 9 + 4 = [ ]

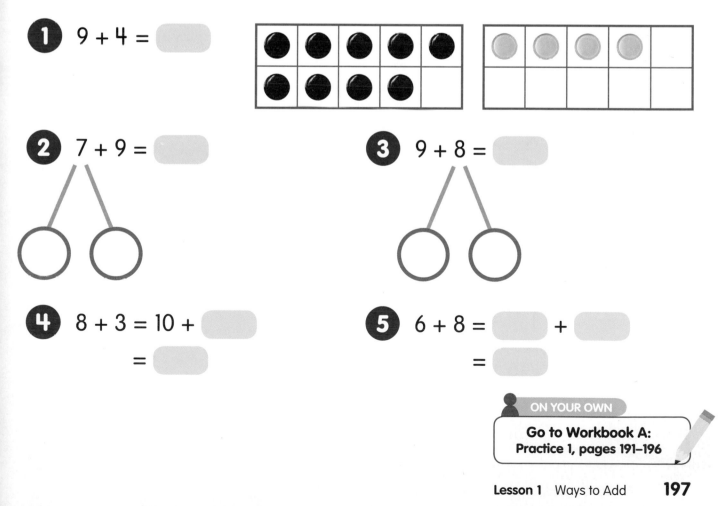

**2** 7 + 9 = [ ]

**3** 9 + 8 = [ ]

**4** 8 + 3 = 10 + [ ]
     = [ ]

**5** 6 + 8 = [ ] + [ ]
     = [ ]

**ON YOUR OWN**

Go to Workbook A:
Practice 1, pages 191–196

## You can add by grouping into a 10 and ones.

Paul has 16 dinosaurs.

His sister gives him 3 more dinosaurs.

How many dinosaurs does Paul have now?

**Step 1**  Group 16 into a 10 and ones.

$16 = 10 + 6$

$16 + 3 = ?$

10    6

$16 + 3 = ?$

**Step 2**  Add the ones.

$6 + 3 = 9$

**Step 3**  Add the 10 and ones.

$10 + 9 = 19$

So, $16 + 3 = 19$.

Paul has 19 dinosaurs now.

## Guided Practice

**Group into a 10 and ones.
Then add.**

**3**   13 + 3 = [ ]

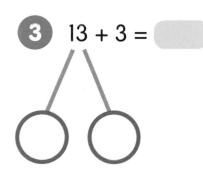

**4**   12 + 7 = [ ]

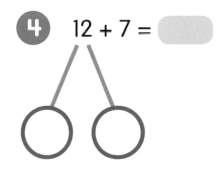

## Let's Practice

**Group into a 10 and ones.
Then add.**

**1**   11 + 7 = [ ]

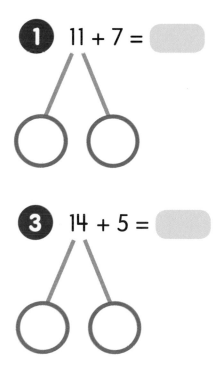

**2**   4 + 13 = [ ]

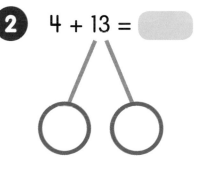

**3**   14 + 5 = [ ]

**4**   2 + 17 = [ ]

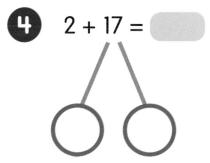

**ON YOUR OWN**

**Go to Workbook A:
Practice 2, pages 197–198**

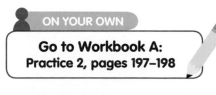

# You can use doubles facts to add.

This is a **doubles fact**.

$$2 + 2 = 4$$

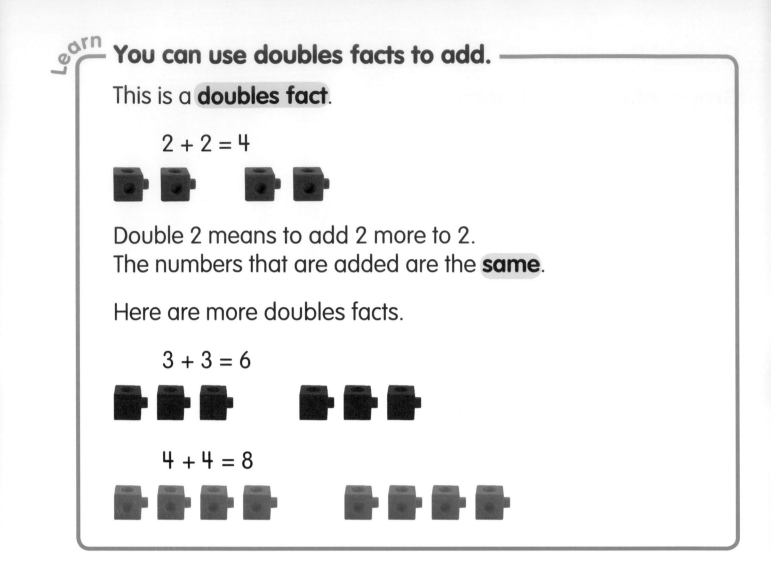

Double 2 means to add 2 more to 2.
The numbers that are added are the **same**.

Here are more doubles facts.

$$3 + 3 = 6$$

$$4 + 4 = 8$$

## Guided Practice

### Solve.

**5** Which is the doubles fact?

$$1 + 1 = 2 \qquad \text{or} \qquad 10 + 1 = 11$$

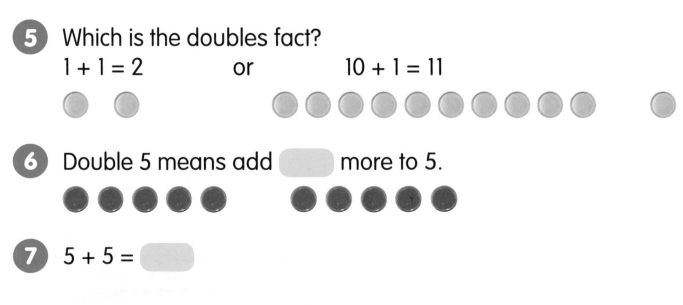

**6** Double 5 means add _____ more to 5.

**7** $5 + 5 = $ _____

# You can use doubles plus one facts to add.

2 + 2 = 4 is a doubles fact.

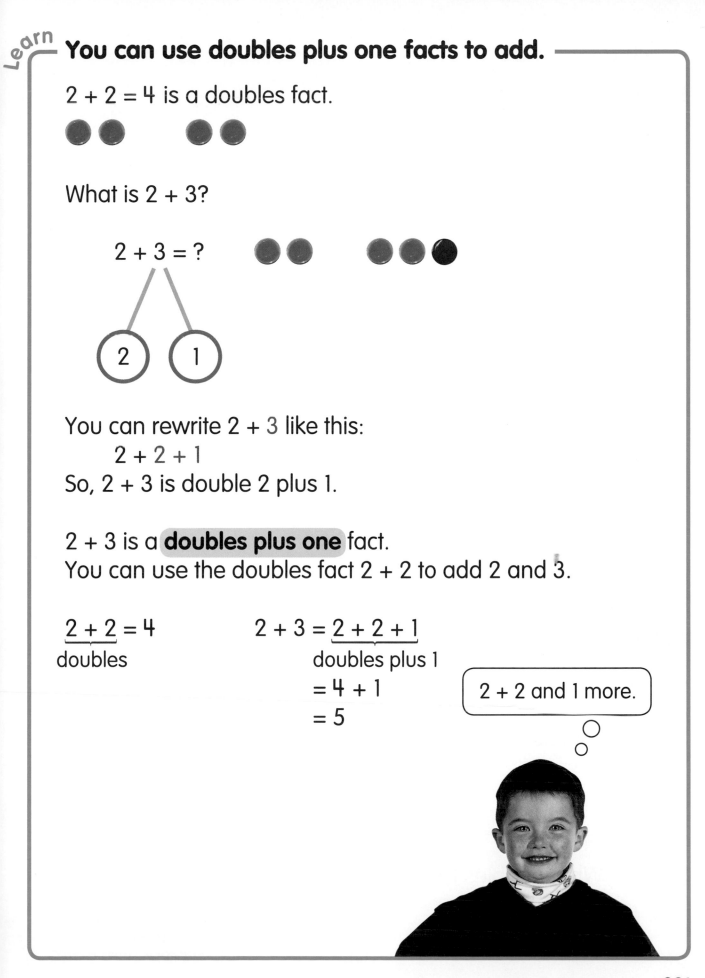

What is 2 + 3?

2 + 3 = ?

2     1

You can rewrite 2 + 3 like this:
    2 + 2 + 1
So, 2 + 3 is double 2 plus 1.

2 + 3 is a **doubles plus one** fact.
You can use the doubles fact 2 + 2 to add 2 and 3.

$\underline{2 + 2} = 4$
doubles

$2 + 3 = \underline{2 + 2 + 1}$
    doubles plus 1
    = 4 + 1
    = 5

2 + 2 and 1 more.

## Guided Practice

**Solve.**

**8** Which are the doubles facts?
Which are the doubles plus one facts?

$4 + 4 = 8$      $4 + 5 = 9$      $8 + 7 = 15$      $7 + 7 = 14$

**9** $5 + 6 = ?$

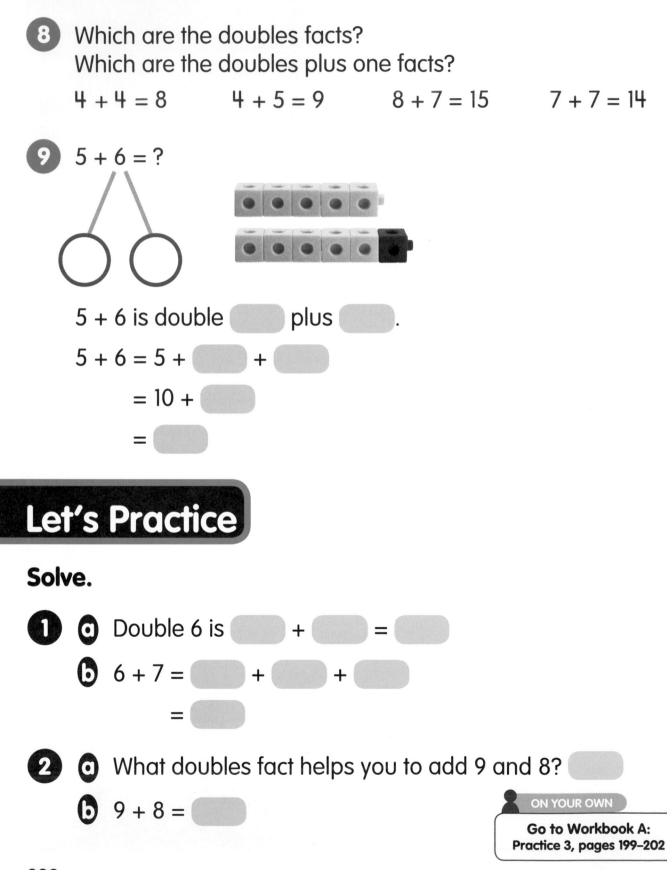

$5 + 6$ is double ⬭ plus ⬭.

$5 + 6 = 5 +$ ⬭ $+$ ⬭

       $= 10 +$ ⬭

       $=$ ⬭

## Let's Practice

**Solve.**

**1 ⓐ** Double 6 is ⬭ $+$ ⬭ $=$ ⬭

   **ⓑ** $6 + 7 =$ ⬭ $+$ ⬭ $+$ ⬭

           $=$ ⬭

**2 ⓐ** What doubles fact helps you to add 9 and 8? ⬭

   **ⓑ** $9 + 8 =$ ⬭

ON YOUR OWN

Go to Workbook A:
Practice 3, pages 199–202

# LESSON 2 Ways to Subtract

## Lesson Objective

• Subtract a 1-digit from a 2-digit number with and without grouping.

**Learn** **You can subtract by grouping into a 10 and ones.**

Ray has 17 toy cars.
He gives away 3 toy cars.
How many cars does he have left?

**Step 1** Group 17 into a 10 and ones.
17 = 10 + 7

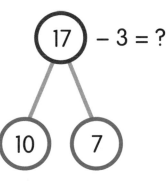

17 − 3 = ?

17 − 3 = ?

**Step 2** Subtract the ones.
7 − 3 = 4

**Step 3** Add the 10 and the ones.
10 + 4 = 14

So, 17 − 3 = 14.

Ray has 14 toy cars left.

## Guided Practice

**Group the numbers into a 10 and ones.**
**Then subtract.**

**1** 17 − 5 = ⬭

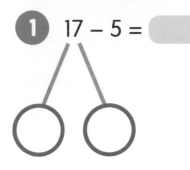

**2** 18 − 3 = ⬭

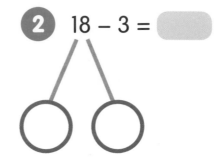

**Solve the riddle.**
**Subtract, then write the letter on the correct line.**

**3** 13 − 3 = ◯ **T**

15 − 3 = ◯ **H**

16 − 1 = ◯ **E**

17 − 0 = ◯ **U**

17 − 6 = ◯ **S**

18 − 5 = ◯ **W**

19 − 3 = ◯ **I**

18 − 4 = ◯ **O**

### Where does the President of the United States live?

THE

___ ___ ___ ___ ___
13    12    16    10    15

___ ___ ___ ___ ___
12    14    17    11    15

# You can subtract by grouping into a 10 and ones.

Shawn makes 12 stars.
He gives 7 to Gina.
How many stars does Shawn have left?

**Step 1**   Group 12 into a 10 and ones.
$$12 = 10 + 2$$

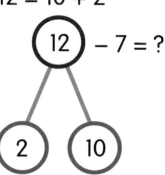

$$12 - 7 = ?$$

**Step 2**   You cannot subtract 7 from 2.
So, subtract 7 from 10.
$$10 - 7 = 3$$

**Step 3**   Add the ones.
$$2 + 3 = 5$$

So, $12 - 7 = 5$.

Shawn has 5 stars left.

Group the numbers into a 10 and ones.
Then subtract.

**4**  11 – 3 = [ ]

**5**  13 – 6 = [ ]

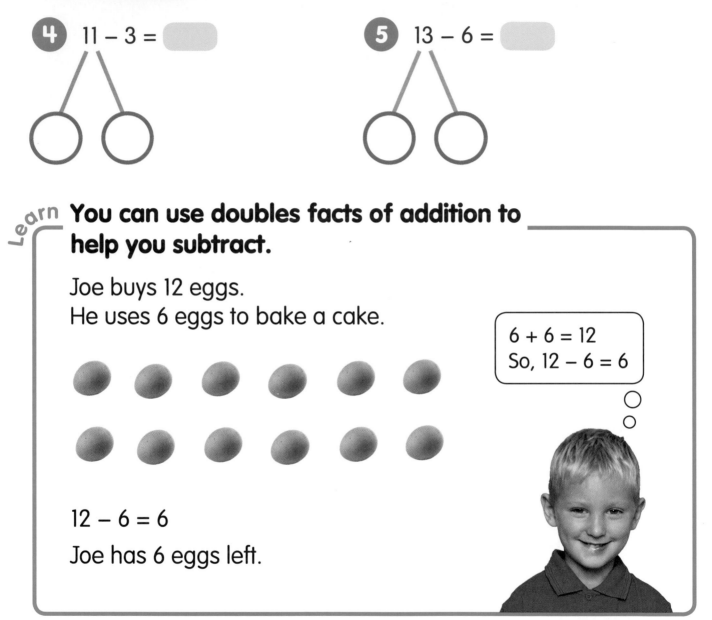

**Learn**  You can use doubles facts of addition to help you subtract.

Joe buys 12 eggs.
He uses 6 eggs to bake a cake.

6 + 6 = 12
So, 12 – 6 = 6

12 – 6 = 6
Joe has 6 eggs left.

## Guided Practice

**Solve.**

**6**  10 – 5 = [ ]

**7**  14 – 7 = [ ]

# Spin and Subtract!

Players: 3

You need:
- 2 spinners (A and B)

## How to play:

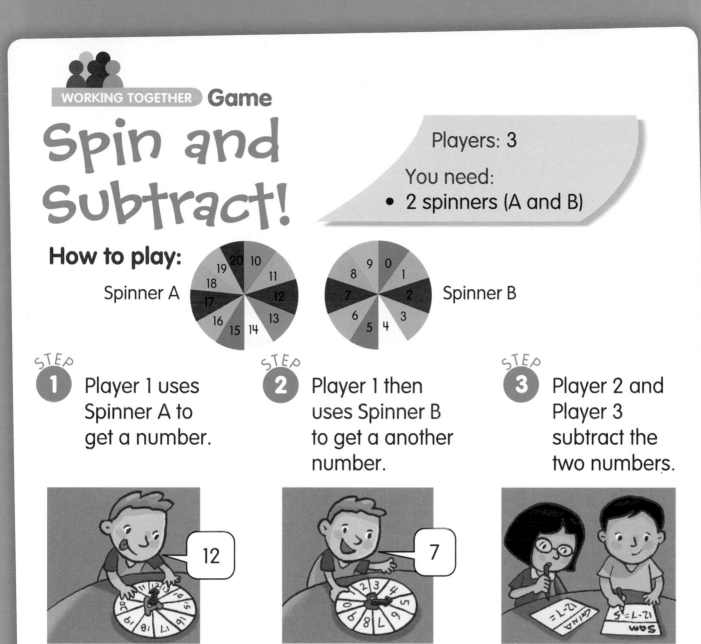

Spinner A

Spinner B

**STEP 1** Player 1 uses Spinner A to get a number.

12

**STEP 2** Player 1 then uses Spinner B to get a another number.

7

**STEP 3** Player 2 and Player 3 subtract the two numbers.

**STEP 4** The player who gets the right subtraction sentence first gets 1 point. Take turns spinning the spinner.

12 – 7 = 5

The player who gets the most points after six rounds wins!

# Let's Practice

**Subtract.**
**You can use number bonds to help you.**

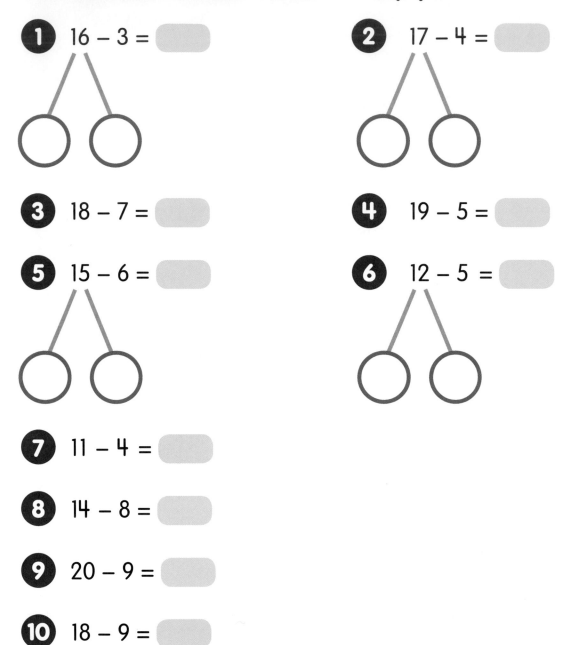

**1** 16 − 3 = 

**2** 17 − 4 = 

**3** 18 − 7 = 

**4** 19 − 5 = 

**5** 15 − 6 = 

**6** 12 − 5 = 

**7** 11 − 4 = 

**8** 14 − 8 = 

**9** 20 − 9 = 

**10** 18 − 9 = 

ON YOUR OWN

**Go to Workbook A:**
**Practice 4, pages 203–210**

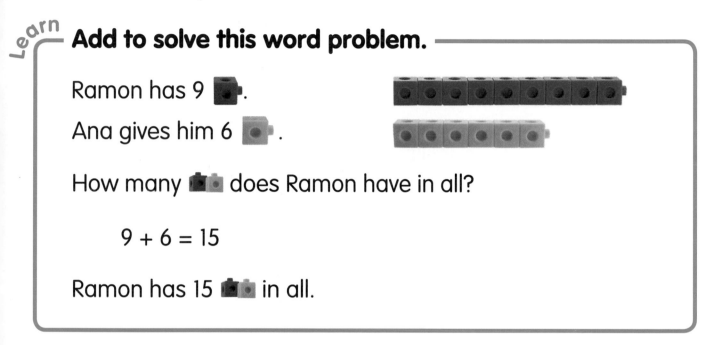

# LESSON 3 Real-World Problems: Addition and Subtraction Facts

**Lesson Objective**

• Solve real-world problems.

*Learn* ── **Add to solve this word problem.** ──────

Ramon has 9 ⬛.

Ana gives him 6 ⬜.

How many ⬛⬜ does Ramon have in all?

$$9 + 6 = 15$$

Ramon has 15 ⬛⬜ in all.

## Guided Practice

**Solve.**

**1** Lin makes 6 pasta rings.
Kate makes 6 pasta rings.
How many pasta rings do they
make in all?

⬭ ⬭ ⬭ = ⬭

They make ⬭ pasta rings in all.

## Subtract to solve this word problem.

Ali has 16 clay shells.
He gives Mani 5 clay shells.
How many clay shells does Ali have left?

$$16 - 5 = 11$$

Ali has 11 clay shells left.

## Guided Practice

**Solve.**

**2** George has 11 paper clips.
3 paper clips are blue.
The rest are red.
How many paper clips are red?

⬭ ⬤ ⬭ = ⬭

⬭ paper clips are red.

# Let's Practice

**Solve.**

**1** Terry picks 8 tomatoes.
Nan picks 8 tomatoes.
How many tomatoes do Terry
and Nan have in all?

⬭ ⬤ ⬭ = ⬭

They have ⬭ tomatoes in all.

**2** Pam makes 14 paper flowers.
9 are blue.
How many are pink?

[  ]  [  ]  [  ] = [  ]

[  ] flowers are pink.

**3** Walter finds 15 leaves.
His brother gives him 4 more leaves.
How many leaves does Walter have in all?

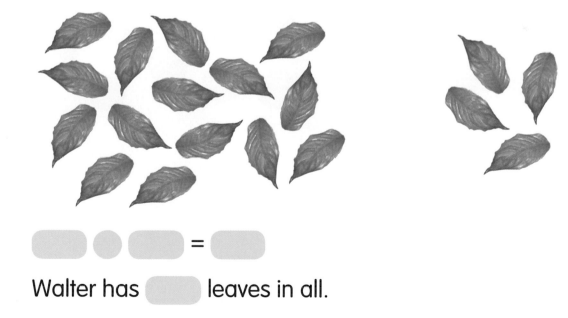

[  ]  [  ]  [  ] = [  ]

Walter has [  ] leaves in all.

**4** Junie gives away 8 oranges.
She has 9 oranges left.
How many oranges did she have at first?

What is the doubles fact?

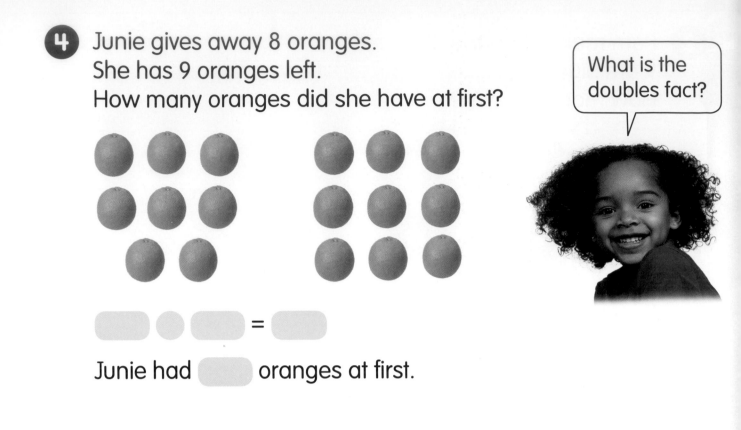

[ ] ● [ ] = [ ]

Junie had [ ] oranges at first.


**5** Tim has 16 marbles.
He loses some and has 8 marbles left.
How many marbles does he lose?

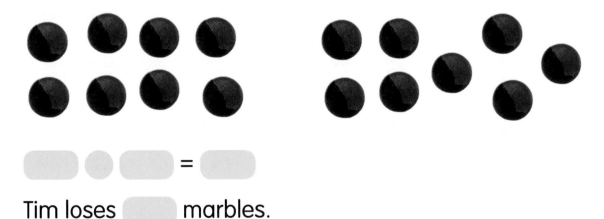

[ ] ● [ ] = [ ]

Tim loses [ ] marbles.

**ON YOUR OWN**

**Go to Workbook A:**
**Practice 5, pages 211–212**

# READING AND WRITING MATH
# Math Journal

**Look at the people around you.**
**Write an addition or subtraction story about them.**
**Use a number bond to help you.**

Example

There are 12 children in my class.
3 children have blonde hair.
The rest have brown hair.
How many children have brown hair?

12 − 3 =

2    10

_____ children have brown hair.

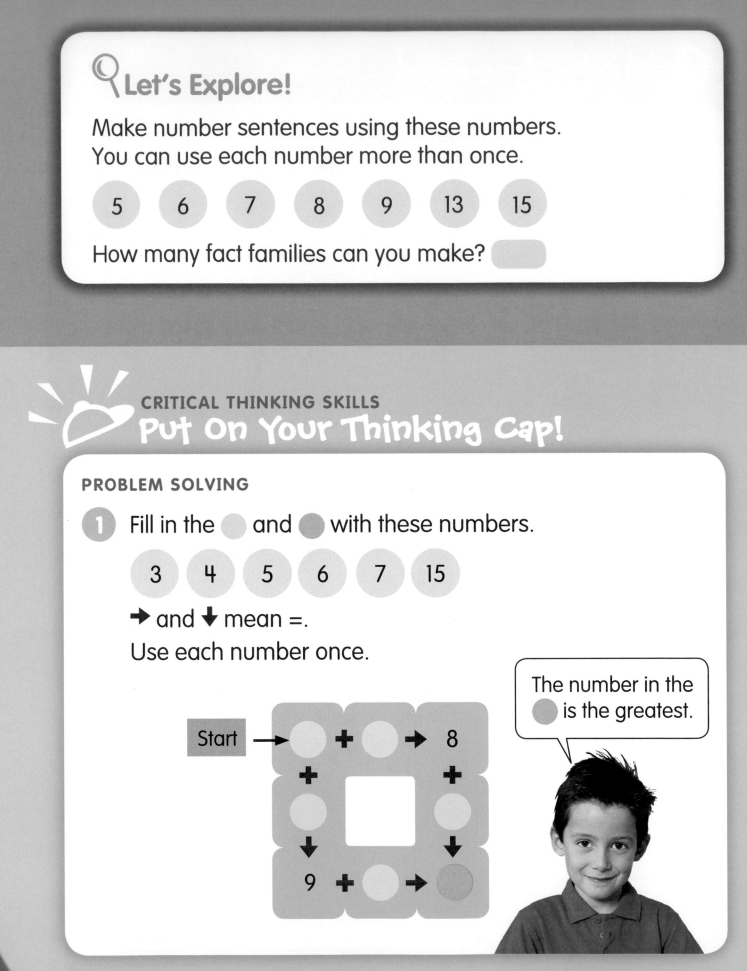

## Let's Explore!

Make number sentences using these numbers.
You can use each number more than once.

5   6   7   8   9   13   15

How many fact families can you make?

## CRITICAL THINKING SKILLS
# Put On Your Thinking Cap!

**PROBLEM SOLVING**

1   Fill in the ⬤ and ⬤ with these numbers.

3   4   5   6   7   15

→ and ↓ mean =.
Use each number once.

The number in the ⬤ is the greatest.

Start →  ⬤  +  ⬤  →  8

+ ▢ +

⬤ ⬤

↓ ↓

9  +  ⬤  →  ⬤

**PROBLEM SOLVING**

2 Fill in the ⬤ and ⬤ with these numbers.

3   4   6   7   8   17

→ and ↓ mean =.
Use each number once.

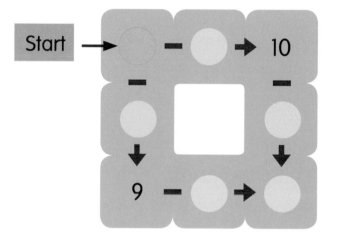

ON YOUR OWN

**Go to Workbook A:
Put on Your Thinking Cap!
pages 213–216**

# Chapter Wrap Up
**You have learned...**

## Addition and Subtraction Facts to 20

to add by making a 10.

$8 + 5 = 10 + 3$
$\qquad = 13$

$8 + 5$

$8 + 2 = 10$

$8 + 5 = 10 + 3$
$\qquad = 13$

to add by grouping into a 10 and ones.

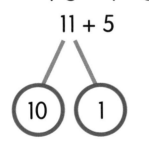

$11 + 5$

$5 + 1 = 6$

$11 + 5 = 10 + 6$
$\qquad = 16$

to add using doubles facts.

$3 + 3 = 6$ is a doubles fact.
The numbers that are added are the same.

to add using doubles plus one.

$3 + 4$ is $3 + 3$ plus 1
$3 + 4 = 3 + 3 + 1$
$\qquad = 7$

to subtract by grouping into a 10 and ones.

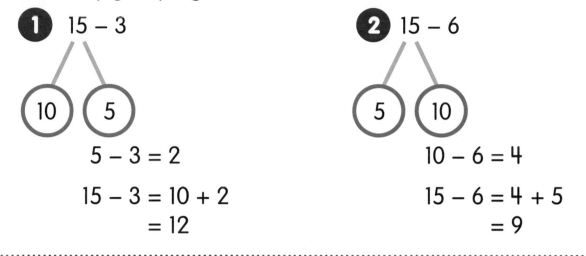

**1** 15 − 3

10   5

5 − 3 = 2

15 − 3 = 10 + 2

= 12

**2** 15 − 6

5   10

10 − 6 = 4

15 − 6 = 4 + 5

= 9

to subtract using doubles facts.

7 + 7 = 14

So, 14 − 7 = 7.

to add or subtract to solve real-world problems.

**1** Joy has 8 tadpoles.
Ben gives her 5 more tadpoles.
How many tadpoles does she have now?

8 + 5 = 13

Joy has 13 tadpoles now.

**2** Con has 18 marbles.
He gives Pete 9 marbles.
How many marbles does Con have left?

18 − 9 = 9

Con has 9 marbles left.

ON YOUR OWN

Go to Workbook A:
Chapter Review/Test,
pages 217–218

# CHAPTER
# 9 Length

## BIG IDEA

Compare the height and length of things. Measure with non-standard units to find length.

# Recall Prior Knowledge

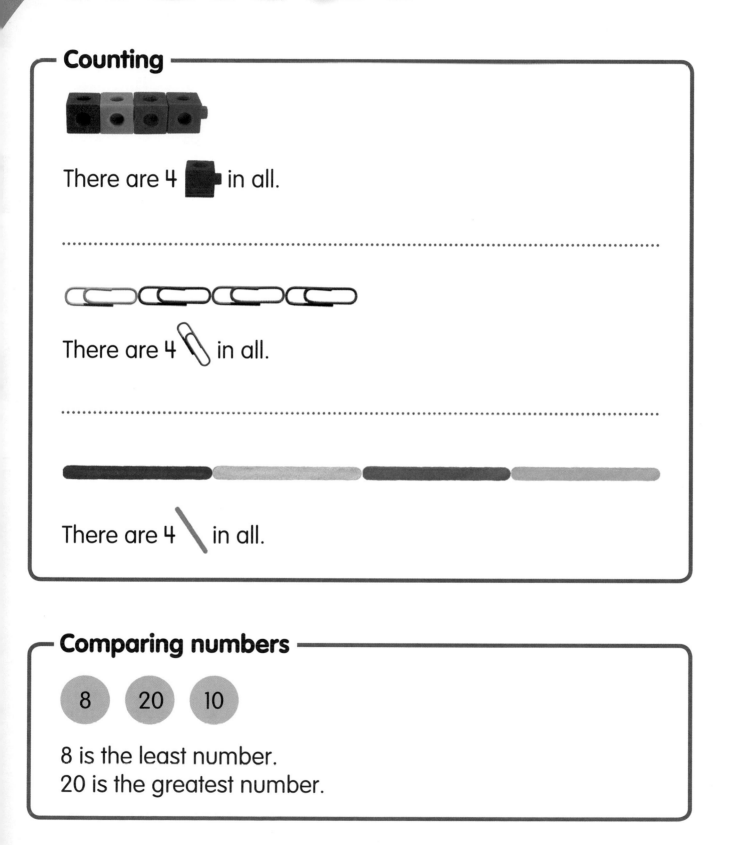

## Counting

There are 4 ⬛ in all.

There are 4 📎 in all.

There are 4 ╲ in all.

## Comparing numbers

( 8 )  ( 20 )  ( 10 )

8 is the least number.
20 is the greatest number.

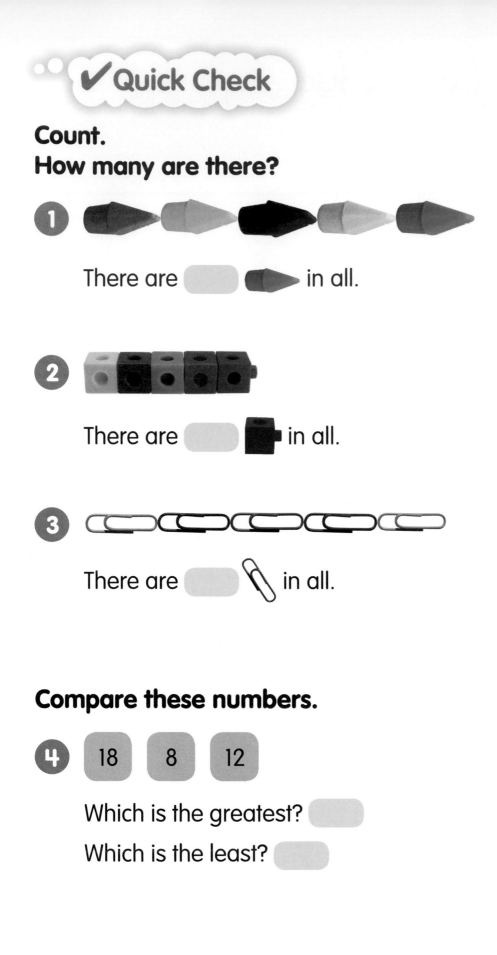

## ✔ Quick Check

## Count.
## How many are there?

**1** There are ⬜ ◀ in all.

**2** There are ⬜ ◼ in all.

**3** There are ⬜ ⌇ in all.

## Compare these numbers.

**4** 18    8    12

Which is the greatest? ⬜

Which is the least? ⬜

# Comparing Two Things

## Lesson Objective

- Compare two lengths using the terms tall/taller, long/longer, and short/shorter.

**Vocabulary**

| tall | taller |
| --- | --- |
| short | shorter |
| long | longer |

**Learn** You can compare the height of people.

I am **tall**.

I am **taller**.

I am **short**.

I am **shorter**.

## Guided Practice

**Look at your desk and your teacher's desk.
Answer the questions.**

**1** Which is taller?

**2** Which is shorter?

**You can compare the length of things.**

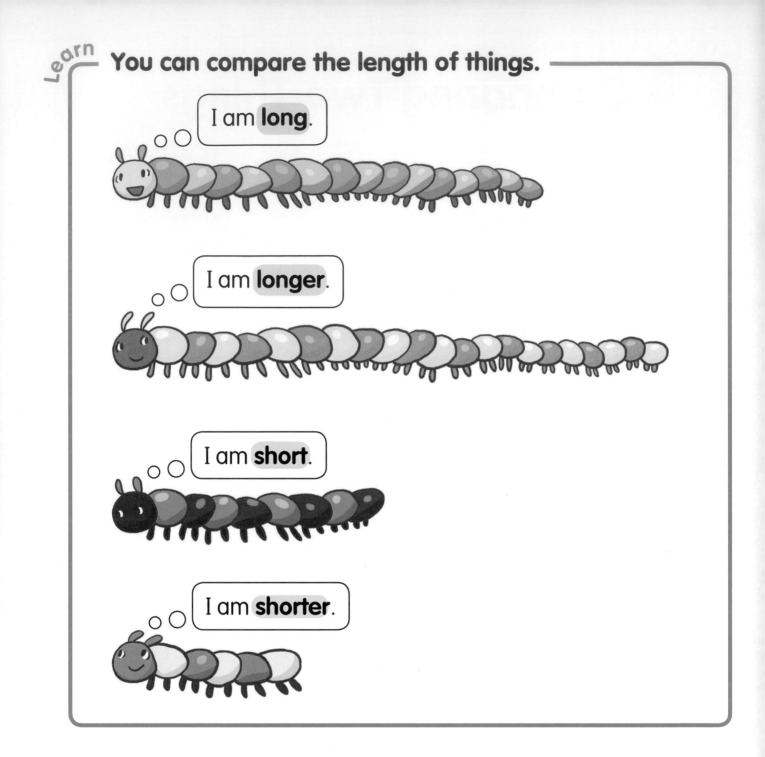

I am **long**.

I am **longer**.

I am **short**.

I am **shorter**.

## Guided Practice

**Look at your pencil and your friend's pencil.
Answer the questions.**

**3** Whose pencil is longer?

**4** Whose pencil is shorter?

# 🖐 Hands-On Activity

Use 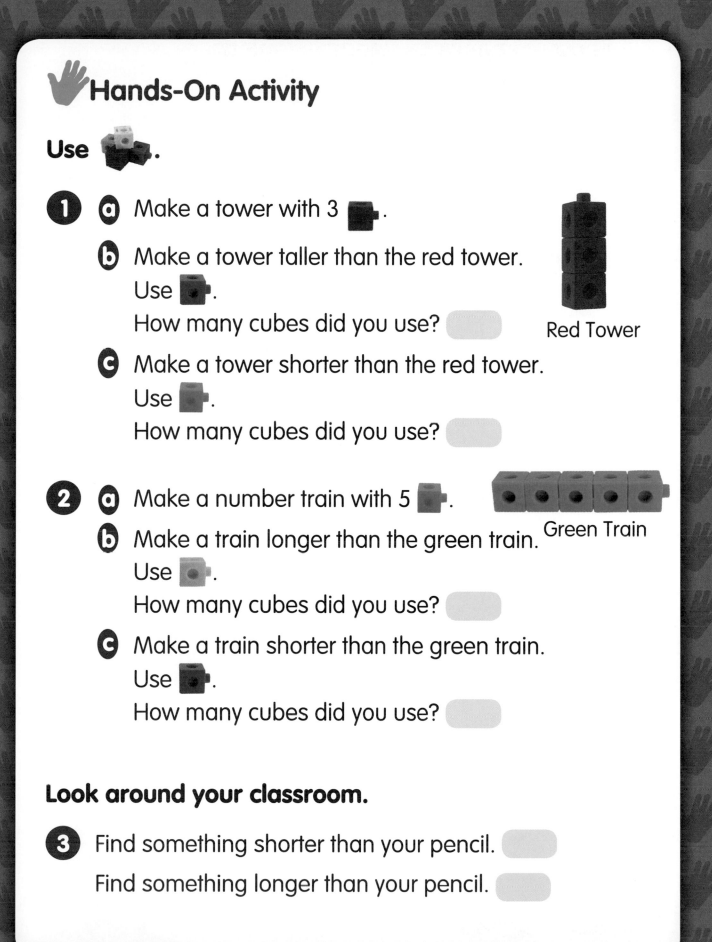.

**1** **ⓐ** Make a tower with 3 🔲.

**ⓑ** Make a tower taller than the red tower.
Use 🔲.
How many cubes did you use? ▢

Red Tower

**ⓒ** Make a tower shorter than the red tower.
Use 🔲.
How many cubes did you use? ▢

**2** **ⓐ** Make a number train with 5 🔲.

Green Train

**ⓑ** Make a train longer than the green train.
Use 🔲.
How many cubes did you use? ▢

**ⓒ** Make a train shorter than the green train.
Use 🔲.
How many cubes did you use? ▢

## Look around your classroom.

**3** Find something shorter than your pencil. ▢

Find something longer than your pencil. ▢

WORK IN PAIRS

Papa Cat and Little Cat are sewing!
Talk about this picture with a friend.
Use these words.

tall    taller

long    longer

short    shorter

Little Cat's tail is long.
Papa Cat's tail is longer.

**Look at the pictures.**
**Solve.**

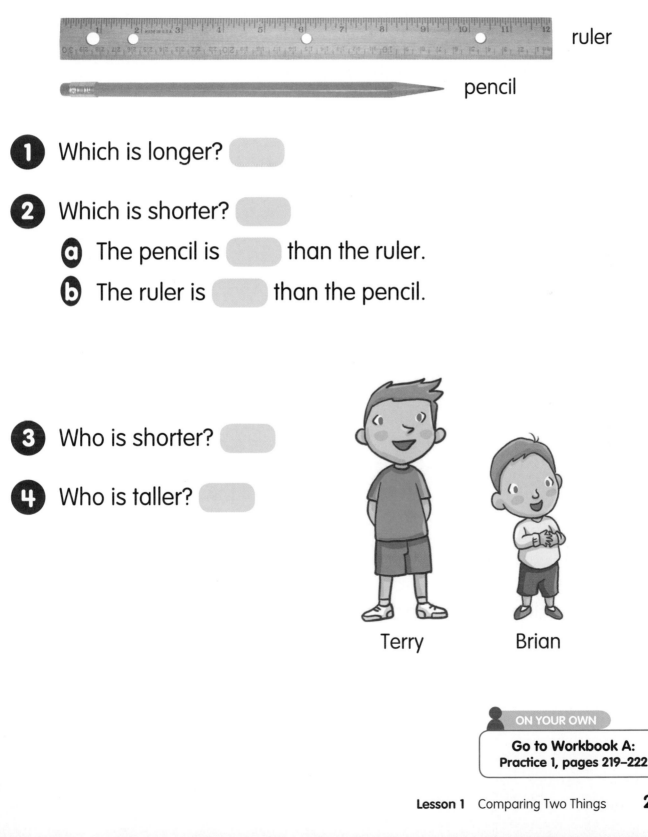

ruler

pencil

**1** Which is longer?

**2** Which is shorter?

**a** The pencil is ⬚ than the ruler.

**b** The ruler is ⬚ than the pencil.

**3** Who is shorter?

**4** Who is taller?

Terry     Brian

**ON YOUR OWN**

**Go to Workbook A:**
**Practice 1, pages 219–222**

# Comparing More Than Two Things

## Lesson Objectives

- Compare two lengths by comparing each with a third length.

- Compare more than two lengths using the terms tallest, longest, and shortest.

Learn **You can compare the height of more than two people.**

Chris   Brandon   Annie

Chris is taller than Brandon.
Brandon is taller than Annie.
So, Chris is taller than Annie.

## Guided Practice

**Fill in the blanks.**

**1**

The red scarf is longer than the blue scarf.

The blue scarf is longer than the [    ] scarf.

So, the red scarf is longer than the [    ] scarf.

*Learn* **You can compare the height and length of more than two people or things.**

Annie          Brandon          Chris

Chris is the **tallest**.
Annie is the **shortest**.

Annie has the **longest** scarf.
Brandon has the **shortest** scarf.

## Guided Practice

**Look at the picture.
Answer the questions.**

Pablo and Erin see some animals in the zoo.

**2** Which is the tallest animal? _____

**3** Which is the shortest animal? _____

**4** Which is the longest animal? _____

**5** Which is the shortest animal? _____

**Hands-On Activity**

**Use** .

**STEP 1** Make four towers like this.
Then place them in order.
You may start with the tallest
or the shortest tower.

**STEP 2** Make a tower taller than the tallest tower.

**STEP 3** Make a tower shorter than the shortest tower.

**Look around your classroom.
Find these things.**

**1** the longest thing ⬜

**2** the tallest thing ⬜

**3** the shortest thing ⬜

**Rearrange the letters to solve.**

T E H   S T A U T E   F O   L I E B R T Y

Which is the longest word? ⬜

# Let's Practice

**Compare.**
**Answer the questions.**

Lee    Tania    Will

**1** Who is taller, Lee or Will?

**2** Who is taller, Tania or Will?

**3** Is Tania taller than Lee?

**4** Who is the tallest?

**5** Who is the shortest?

ON YOUR OWN

**Go to Workbook A:**
**Practice 2, pages 223–227**

# 3 Using a Start Line

**Lesson Objective**

• Use a common starting point when comparing lengths.

**Vocabulary**
start line

**Learn** **You can compare the length of things with a start line.**

Which fish is longest?

Now, can you tell which fish is the longest?

Start Line

The blue fish is longest.

Putting things at a **start line** helps you to see which is the longest.

## Hands-On Activity

Use 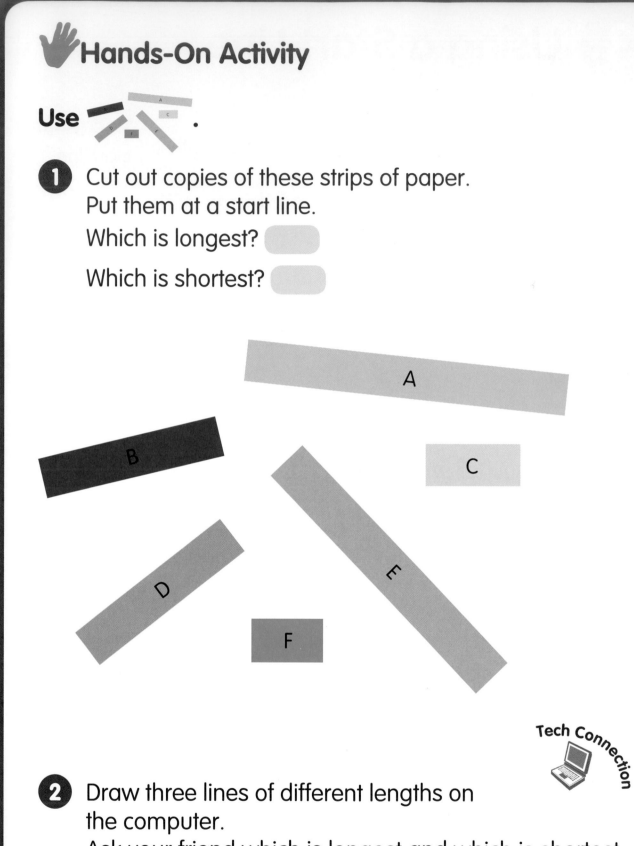 .

**1** Cut out copies of these strips of paper.
Put them at a start line.

Which is longest? ◯

Which is shortest? ◯

**2** Draw three lines of different lengths on
the computer.
Ask your friend which is longest and which is shortest.

Tech Connection

**Solve.**

A

**1** **ⓐ** Which ribbon is longer than Ribbon A?
Name it Ribbon B.

**ⓑ** Which ribbon is shorter than Ribbon A?
Name it Ribbon C.

**ⓒ** Which ribbon is the longest?
Which ribbon is the shortest?

**2** **ⓐ** Which is the tallest building?

**ⓑ** Which is the shortest building?

**ⓒ** Which building is as tall as Building Q?

P    Q    R    S    T

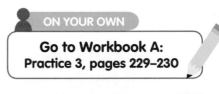

ON YOUR OWN

**Go to Workbook A:**
**Practice 3, pages 229–230**

# Measuring Things

**LESSON 4**

## Lesson Objectives

- Measure lengths using non-standard units.

- Understand that using different non-standard units may give different measurements for the same item.

**Learn** — **You can measure length with objects.**

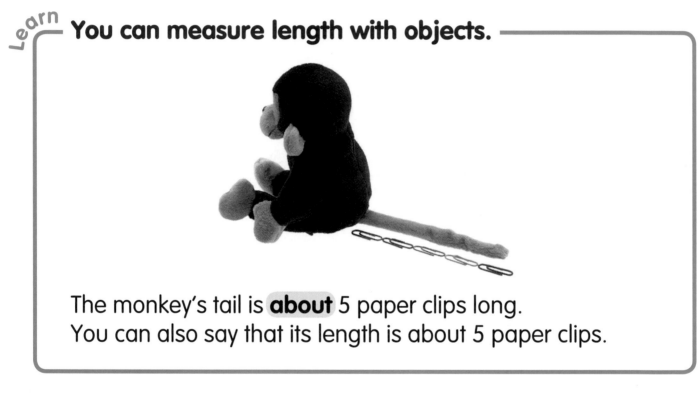

The monkey's tail is **about** 5 paper clips long.
You can also say that its length is about 5 paper clips.

## Guided Practice

**Complete.**

1

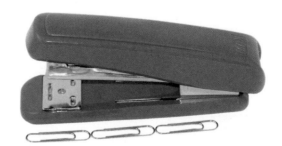

The stapler is about ⬜ paper clips long.

**2**

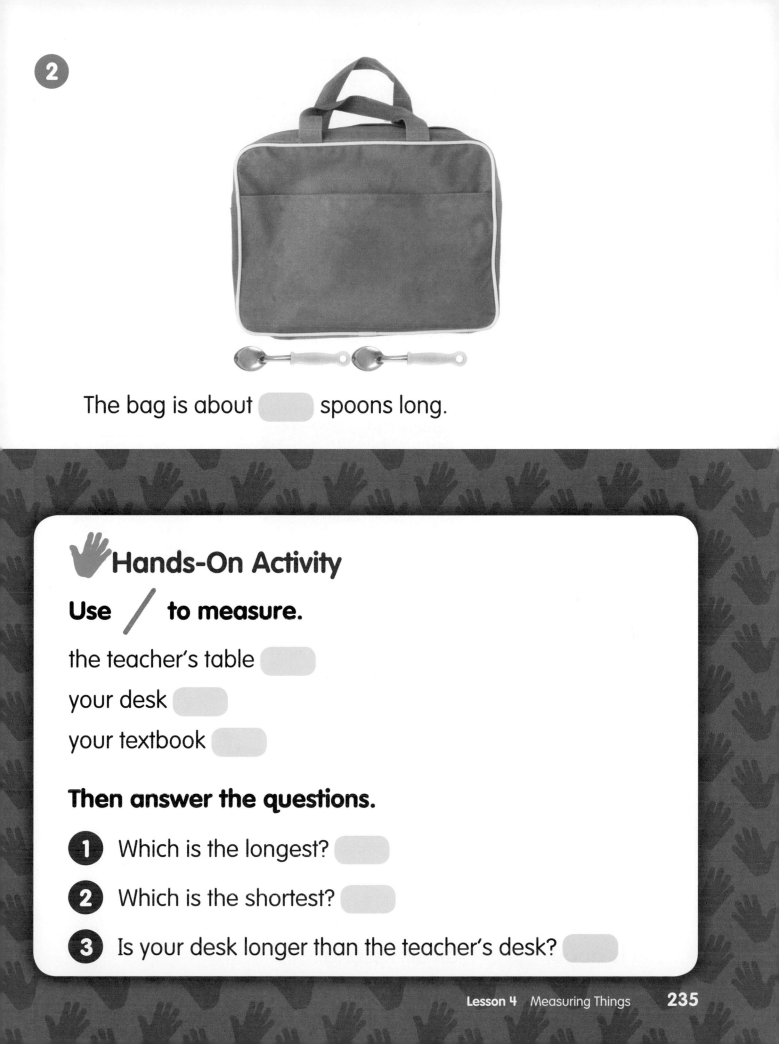

The bag is about ( ) spoons long.

## 🖐 Hands-On Activity

**Use  /  to measure.**

the teacher's table ( )

your desk ( )

your textbook ( )

**Then answer the questions.**

**1** Which is the longest? ( )

**2** Which is the shortest? ( )

**3** Is your desk longer than the teacher's desk? ( )

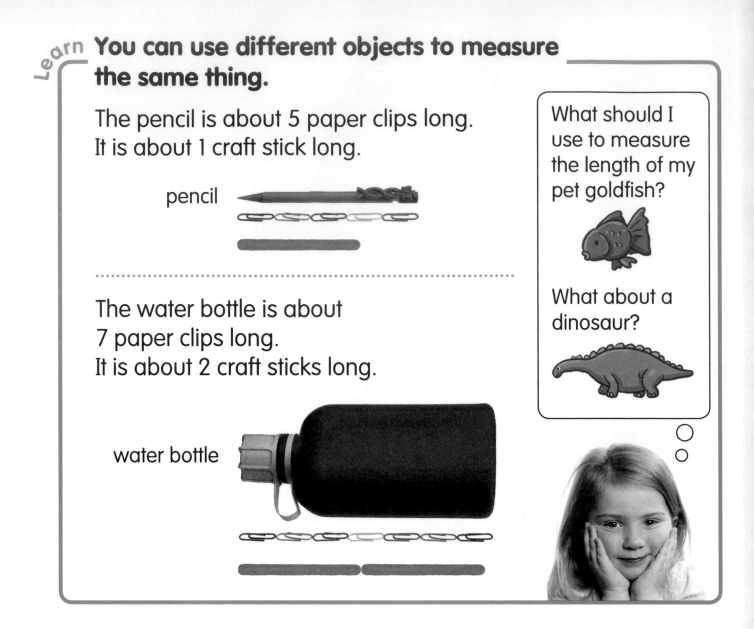

# Learn You can use different objects to measure the same thing.

The pencil is about 5 paper clips long.
It is about 1 craft stick long.

pencil

The water bottle is about
7 paper clips long.
It is about 2 craft sticks long.

water bottle

What should I use to measure the length of my pet goldfish?

What about a dinosaur?

## Guided Practice

## Complete.

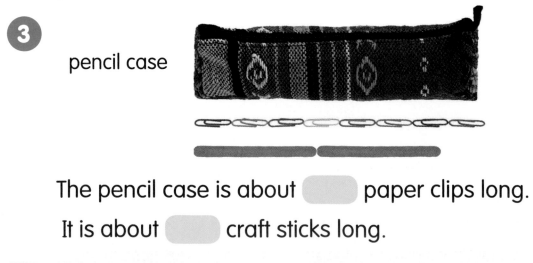

(3) pencil case

The pencil case is about [ ] paper clips long.

It is about [ ] craft sticks long.

 # Hands-On Activity

**Use** ⬜ .

**STEP 1** Cut out some strips of paper.

**STEP 2** Partners use these strips to measure the length of each other's forearm.

My forearm is about ⬭ strips of paper long.

**STEP 3** Trace your foot on a piece of paper.

**STEP 4** Use the strips of paper to measure the length of your foot.

My foot is about ⬭ strips of paper long.

# Hands-On Activity

**Use** 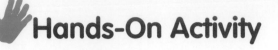 **and** ✏️ .

**STEP 1** Guess how many paper clips long each strip is.

**STEP 2** Then check by placing paper clips along the strips.
How many of your guesses are correct?

Which strips have the same length?
Which is the longest strip?
Which is the shortest strip?

**STEP 3** Put the strips in order from longest to shortest.

# Let's Practice

**Look at the picture.**
**Answer the questions.**

**1**

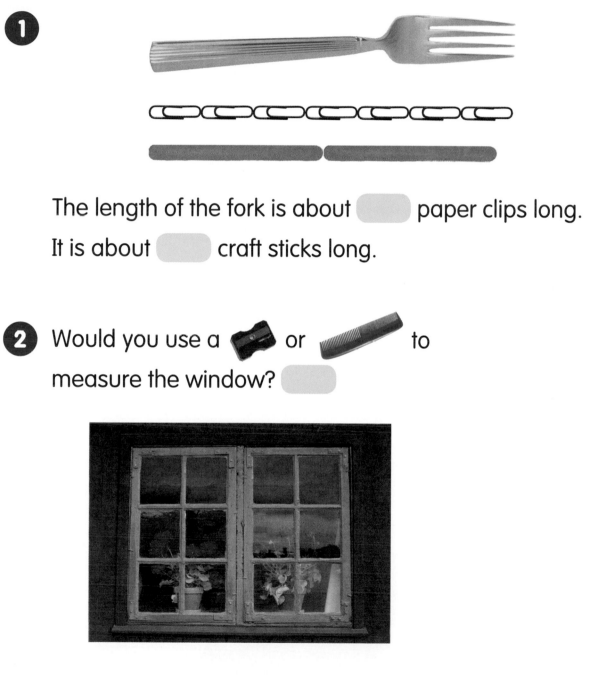

The length of the fork is about ⬭ paper clips long.

It is about ⬭ craft sticks long.

**2** Would you use a 🔲 or 🔲 to measure the window? ⬭

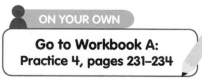

ON YOUR OWN

Go to Workbook A:
Practice 4, pages 231–234

## LESSON 5 Finding Length in Units

### Lesson Objectives

- Use the term "unit" to describe length.
- Count measurement units in a group of ten and ones.

**Vocabulary**
unit

**Learn** You can measure length with units.

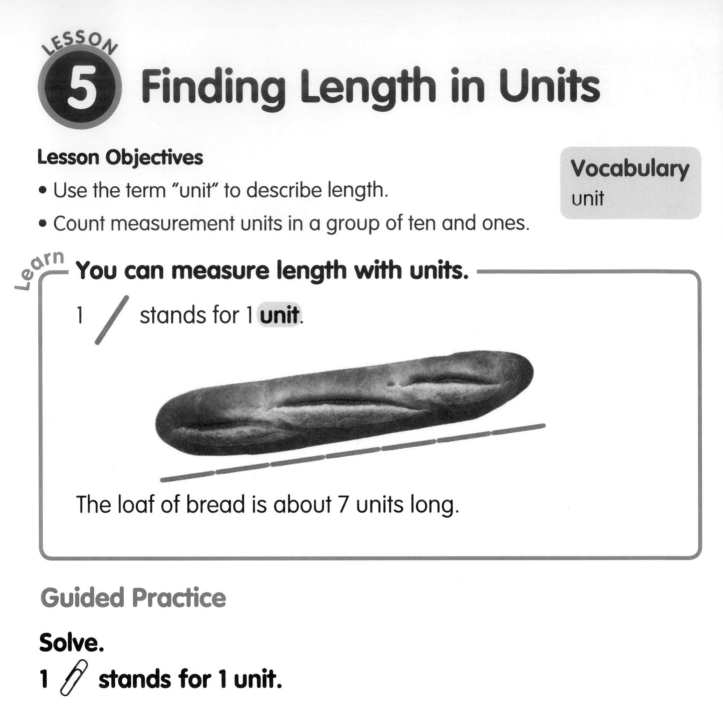

1 / stands for 1 **unit**.

The loaf of bread is about 7 units long.

## Guided Practice

**Solve.**

1 ⧄ stands for 1 unit.

**1**

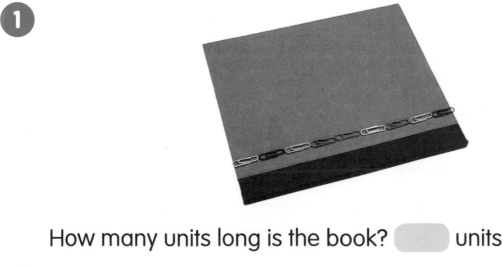

How many units long is the book? ⬭ units

## You can measure length with units.

1 / stands for 1 unit.

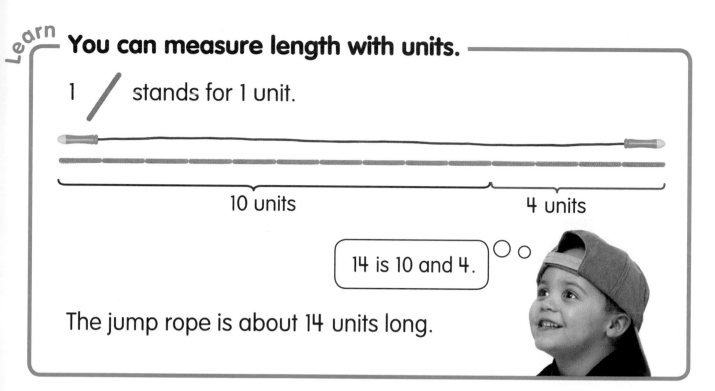

10 units          4 units

14 is 10 and 4.

The jump rope is about 14 units long.

## Guided Practice

CIRCUS
SHOW

Show time: 7–9 P.M.
June 1–5

**Solve.**

1 / **stands for 1 unit.**

2 How many units long is the poster?

⬜ units

⬜ is 10 and ⬜ .

# Look at the picture.
# Then answer the questions.
# Each ☐ stands for 1 unit.

**3** How long is the towel rack? ▢ units

**4** How tall is the shower? ▢ units

▢ is 10 and ▢ .

**5** How tall is the boy? ▢ units

▢ is ▢ and ▢ .

**6** Is the brush longer than the mirror? ▢

**7** Which is shorter, the brush or the towel rack? ▢

# ✋ Hands-On Activity

Use 📎 and ╱ to measure these things in your classroom.

| | 📎 stands for 1 unit | ╱ stands for 1 unit |
|---|---|---|
| computer screen | ⬜ | ⬜ |
| pencil case | ⬜ | ⬜ |
| doorway | ⬜ | ⬜ |
| lunch box | ⬜ | ⬜ |
| tissue box | ⬜ | ⬜ |

Look at the two measurements for the computer screen.

Does it take more 📎 or ╱ to measure its length? ⬜

Is this also true for the other things that you measured? ⬜

Why do you think this is so? ⬜

**Use** 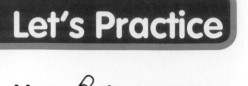 **to measure.**
**1** 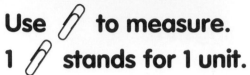 **stands for 1 unit.**

The picture shows Chris's house, his school, and the playground.

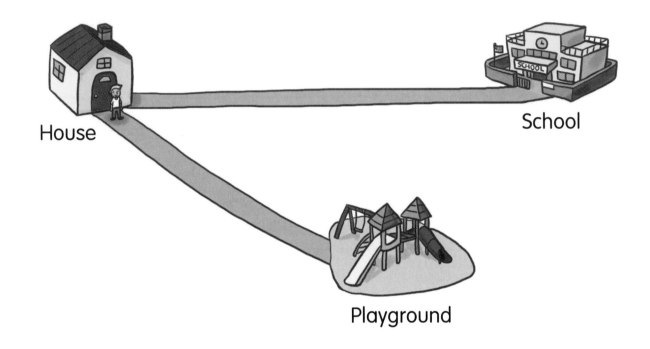

House

School

Playground

**1** The sidewalk from Chris's house to school is about [ ] units long.

**2** The sidewalk from Chris's house to the playground is about [ ] units long.

# Solve.

Snails A, B, and C crawl along the lines.

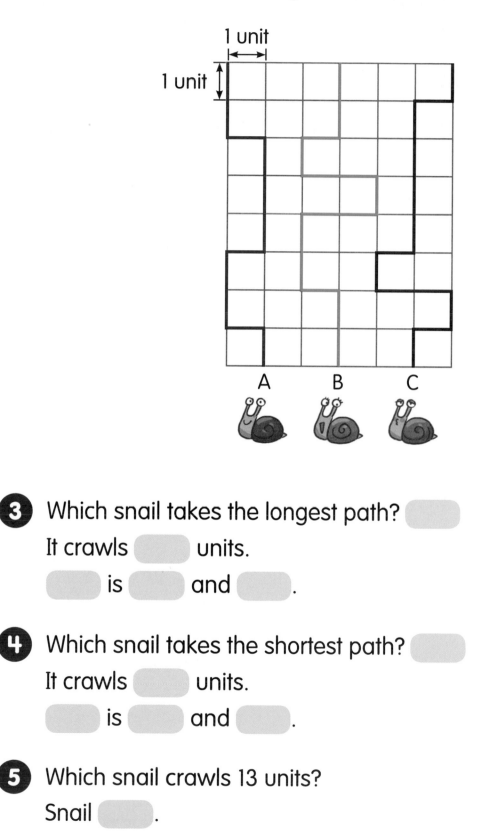

**3** Which snail takes the longest path? ⬜

It crawls ⬜ units.

⬜ is ⬜ and ⬜ .

**4** Which snail takes the shortest path? ⬜

It crawls ⬜ units.

⬜ is ⬜ and ⬜ .

**5** Which snail crawls 13 units?

Snail ⬜ .

**6** 1 ☐ stands for 1 unit.

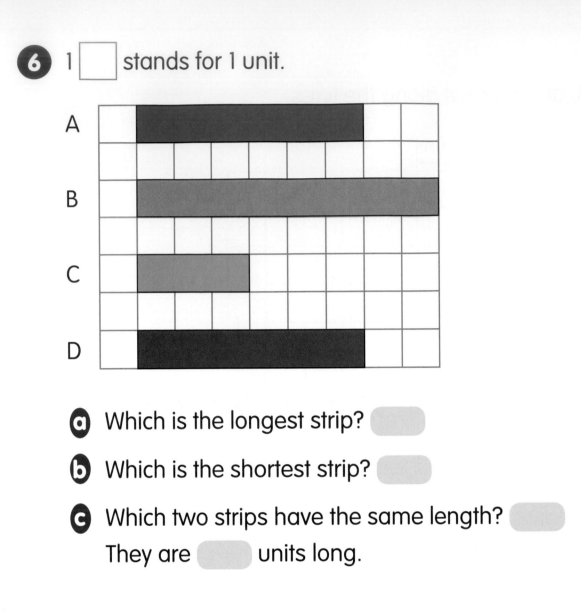

**ⓐ** Which is the longest strip? ▢

**ⓑ** Which is the shortest strip? ▢

**ⓒ** Which two strips have the same length? ▢
They are ▢ units long.

ON YOUR OWN

**Go to Workbook A:**
**Practice 5, pages 235–238**

**PROBLEM SOLVING**

1 Look at the loaf of bread and the book.

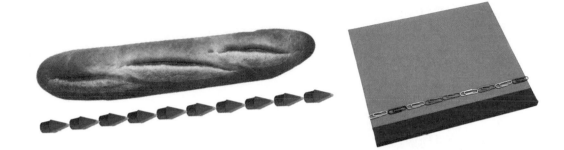

Can you say that the book is longer than the loaf of bread?
Why?

2

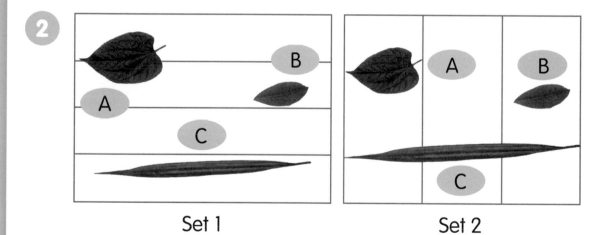

Set 1                                    Set 2

You want to find out how long the leaves are.
Which set of lines will you use?
Why?

ON YOUR OWN

**Go to Workbook A:
Put on Your Thinking Cap!
pages 239–242**

# Chapter Wrap Up

**You have learned...**

to compare two things.

tall          taller                    short        shorter

long                              longer

........................................................................................................

to compare more than two things.

Ally          Ben          Carlo

Ally is taller than Ben.
Ben is taller than Carlo.
So, Ally is also taller
than Carlo.

Ally is the tallest.
Carlo is the shortest.

to use a start line.

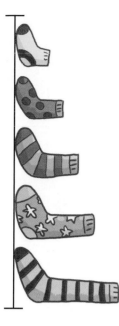

**BIG IDEA**

Compare the height and length of things. Measure with non-standard units to find length.

to use objects to measure.

The dog is about 10 socks long.
It is about 1 scarf long.

to use units to measure.

1 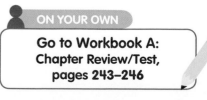 stands for 1 unit.
The cat is 2 units long.

**ON YOUR OWN**

Go to Workbook A:
Chapter Review/Test,
pages 243–246

# Glossary

## A

- **above**

  Pip is above Boo.

- **add**

  Put together two or more parts to make a whole.

  $$2 + 3 = 5$$

  part    part    whole

- **addition sentence**

  $2 + 5 = 7$ is an addition sentence.

- **addition story**

  Mary picks 4 cherries.
  June picks 5 cherries.

  $$4 + 5 = 9$$

  They pick 9 cherries in all.

- **after**

  Boo is after Wink.

- **alike**

  These shapes are circles. They are alike because they are all the same shape.

# B

- **before**

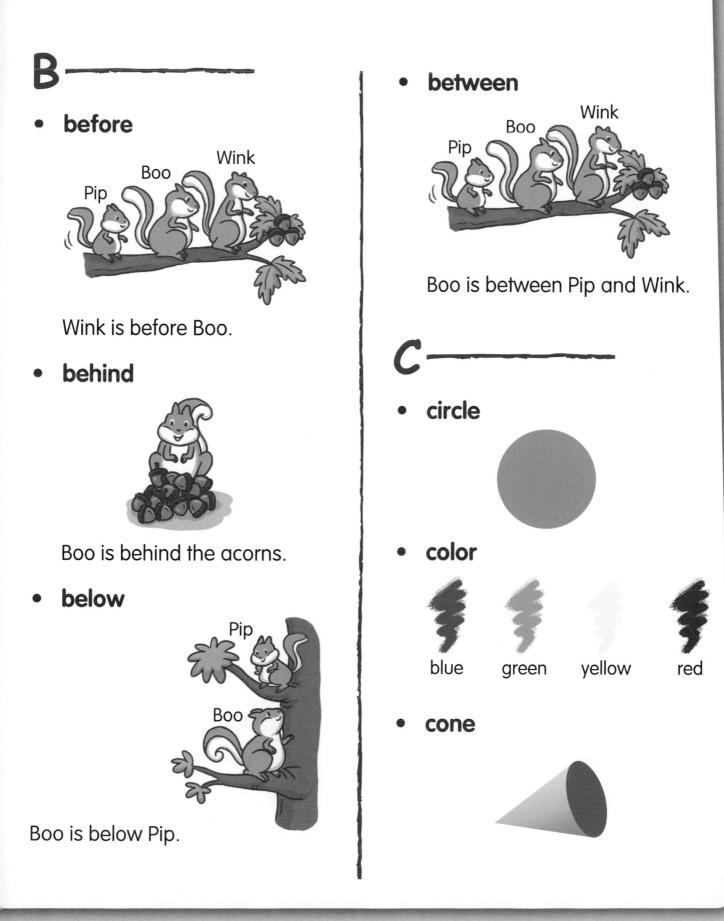

Pip | Boo | Wink

Wink is before Boo.

- **behind**

Boo is behind the acorns.

- **below**

Pip

Boo

Boo is below Pip.

- **between**

Boo | Wink

Pip

Boo is between Pip and Wink.

# C

- **circle**

- **color**

blue    green    yellow    red

- **cone**

- **corner**

  A corner is where two sides meet.

  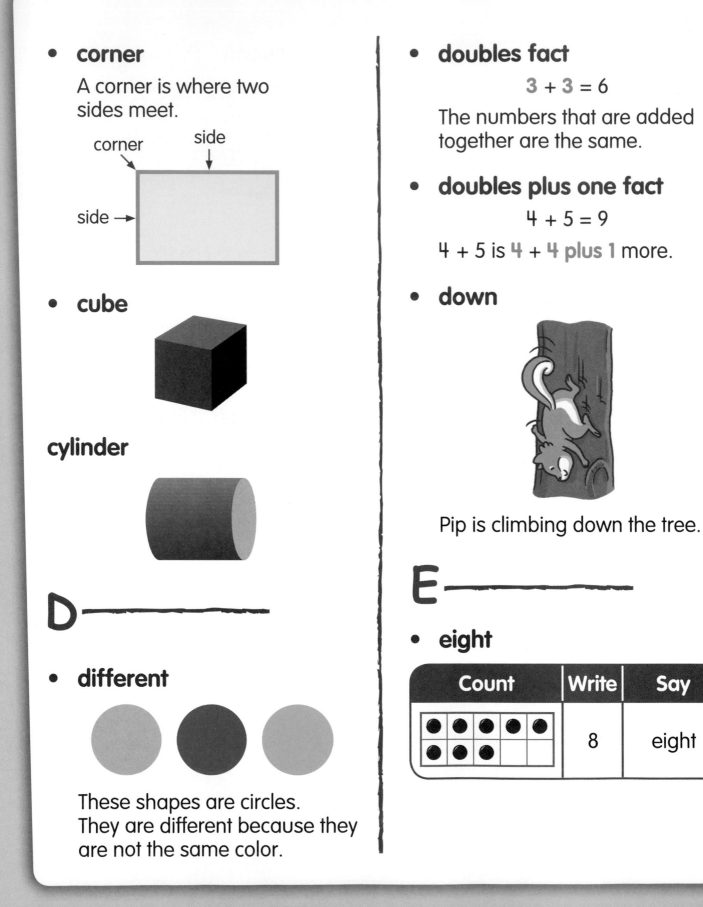

  corner    side

  side →

- **cube**

- **cylinder**

# D

- **different**

  These shapes are circles. They are different because they are not the same color.

- **doubles fact**

  $$3 + 3 = 6$$

  The numbers that are added together are the same.

- **doubles plus one fact**

  $$4 + 5 = 9$$

  4 + 5 is 4 + 4 plus 1 more.

- **down**

  Pip is climbing down the tree.

# E

- **eight**

  | Count | Write | Say |
  |---|---|---|
  | | 8 | eight |

## eighteen

| Count | Write | Say |
|-------|-------|-----|
| ●●●●● ●●●●● ●●●●● ●●● | 18 | eighteen |

## eighth

Free Acorns!

## eleven

| Count | Write | Say |
|-------|-------|-----|
| ●●●●● ●●●●● ● | 11 | eleven |

## equal

Having the same amount or number.

3 is the same as 2 + 1

$$3 = 3$$

equal sign

## F

## fact family

A group of addition and subtraction sentences that have the same parts and whole.

| | |
|---|---|
| 3 + 5 = 8 | 8 − 5 = 3 |
| 5 + 3 = 8 | 8 − 3 = 5 |

## far

Wink

Pip

Wink is far from the acorn.

- **fewer than**

There are fewer ⭐ than ❤.

- **fifteen**

| Count | Write | Say |
|---|---|---|
| (dots) | 15 | fifteen |

- **fifth**

- **first**

- **five**

| Count | Write | Say |
|---|---|---|
| ●●●●● | 5 | five |

- **four**

| Count | Write | Say |
|---|---|---|
| ●●●● | 4 | four |

- **fourteen**

| Count | Write | Say |
|---|---|---|
| (dots) | 14 | fourteen |

- **fourth**

# G

- **greater than**

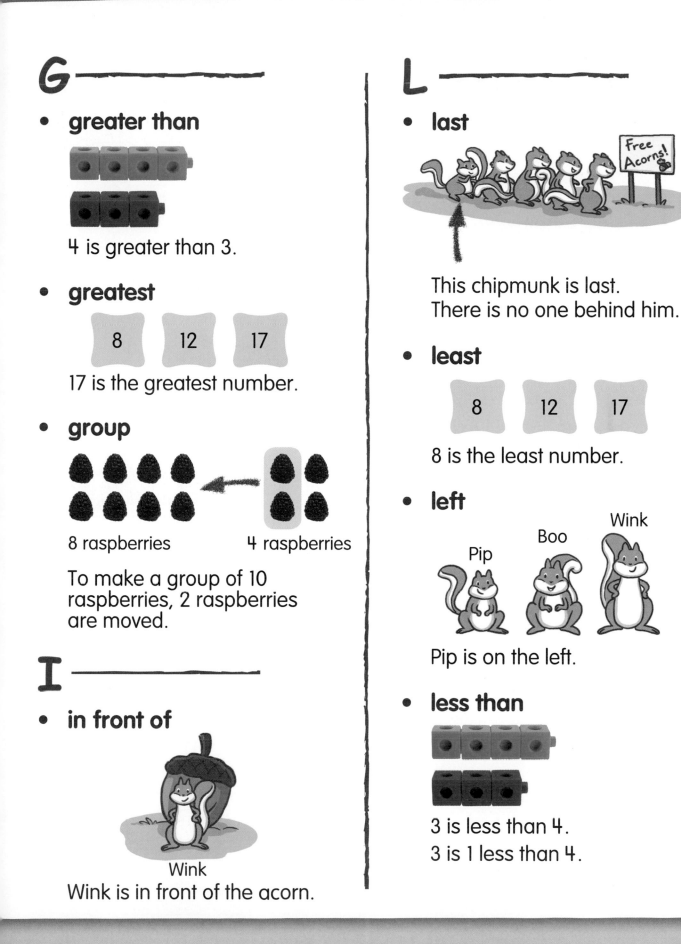

4 is greater than 3.

- **greatest**

8   12   17

17 is the greatest number.

- **group**

8 raspberries   4 raspberries

To make a group of 10 raspberries, 2 raspberries are moved.

# I

- **in front of**

Wink

Wink is in front of the acorn.

# L

- **last**

Free Acorns!

This chipmunk is last.
There is no one behind him.

- **least**

8   12   17

8 is the least number.

- **left**

Pip   Boo   Wink

Pip is on the left.

- **less than**

3 is less than 4.
3 is 1 less than 4.

- **long, longer, longest**

long

longer

longest

## M

- **minus**

  To subtract.

  $$8 - 1 = 7$$

  minus sign

- **more than**

  There are more ⭐ than ♥.

  There is 1 more ⭐ than ♥.

## N

- **near**

Wink

Pip

Pip is near the acorn.

- **next to**

Pip   Boo   Wink

Boo is next to Pip.
Boo is also next to Wink.

- **nine**

| Count | Write | Say |
|---|---|---|
| ●●●●● ●●●●○ | 9 | nine |

- **nineteen**

| Count | Write | Say |
|-------|-------|-----|
|  | 19 | nineteen |

- **ninth**

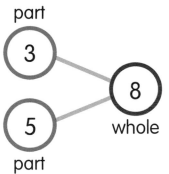

- **number bond**

part
3
8  whole
5
part

A number bond shows parts and the whole.

Parts make up a whole.

You can use a number bond to help you add or subtract.

- **number words**

zero            eight
sixteen         twenty

- **numbers**

0      1      16      20

O ——————————

- **one**

| Count | Write | Say |
|-------|-------|-----|
| • | 1 | one |

- **order**

You can order numbers from least to greatest or greatest to least.

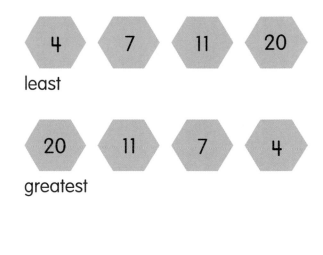

4      7      11      20
least

20      11      7      4
greatest

## P

- **part**

  See **number bond**.

- **pattern**

  number patterns
  - 2, 4, 6, 8, 10
  - 20, 19, 18, 17, 16

  a shape pattern

  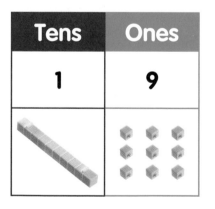

- **place-value chart**

  A place-value chart shows how many tens and ones are in a number.

  In the number 19, there is 1 ten and 9 ones.

  | Tens | Ones |
  |:----:|:----:|
  | 1 | 9 |

- **plus**

  To add.

  $$10 + 1 = 11$$

  ↑ plus sign

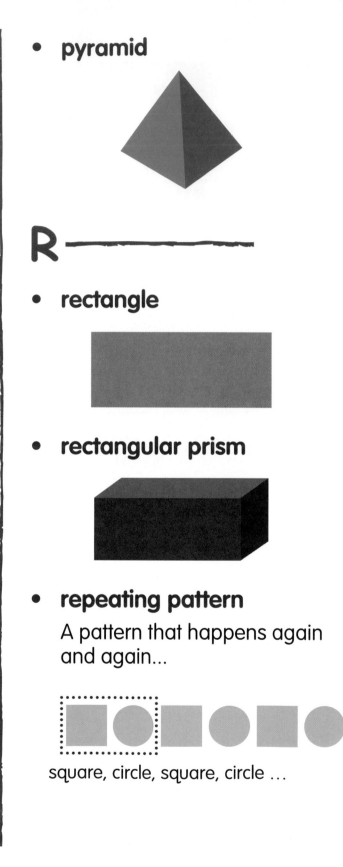

- **pyramid**

## R

- **rectangle**

- **rectangular prism**

- **repeating pattern**

  A pattern that happens again and again...

  square, circle, square, circle ...

- **right**

Wink is on the right.

- **roll**

S ———————

- **same**

4 stars

4 hearts

same number

same color        same shape

- **second**

- **seven**

| Count | Write | Say |
|---|---|---|
| ●●●●●<br>●● | 7 | seven |

- **seventeen**

| Count | Write | Say |
|---|---|---|
| ●●●●●<br>●●●●●<br>●●●●●<br>●● | 17 | seventeen |

- **seventh**

- **shape**

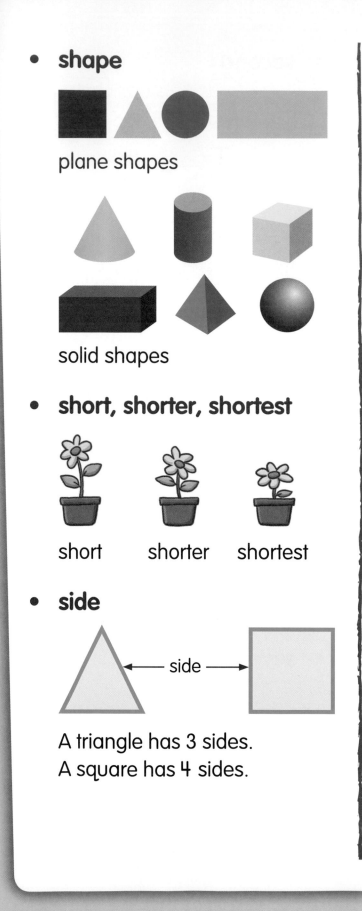

plane shapes

solid shapes

- **short, shorter, shortest**

short        shorter        shortest

- **side**

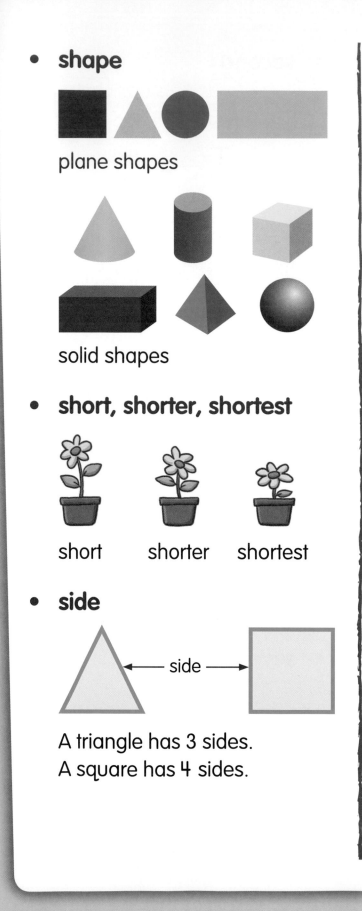

side

A triangle has 3 sides.
A square has 4 sides.

- **six**

| Count | Write | Say |
|---|---|---|
| | 6 | six |

- **sixteen**

| Count | Write | Say |
|---|---|---|
| | 16 | sixteen |

- **sixth**

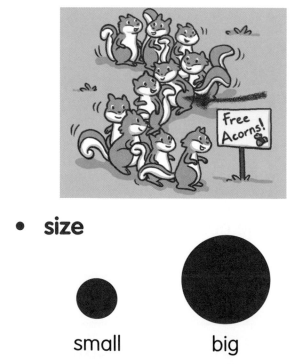

- **size**

small        big

## slide

## sphere

## square

## stack

## start line

You can use a start line to compare the length of things.

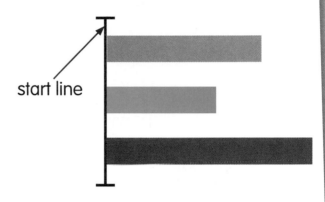

start line

## subtract

Take away one part from the whole to find the other part.

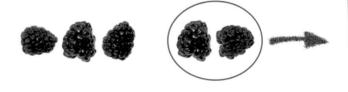

$$5 - 2 = 3$$

whole   part   part

## subtraction sentence

$7 - 3 = 4$ is a subtraction sentence.

- **subtraction story**

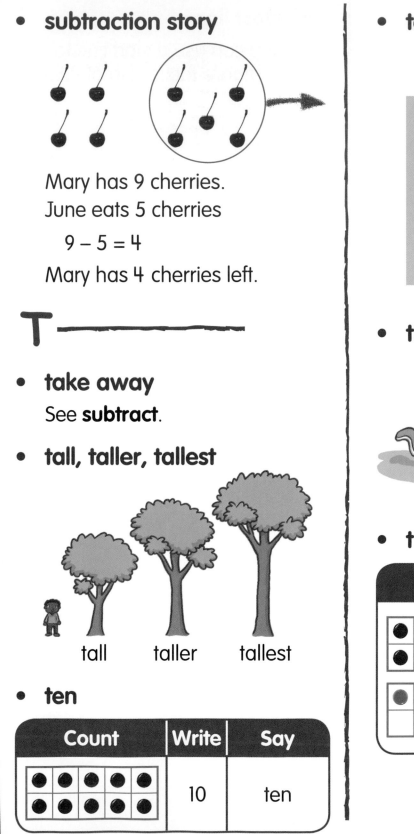

Mary has 9 cherries.
June eats 5 cherries

$9 - 5 = 4$

Mary has 4 cherries left.

## T

- **take away**
  See **subtract**.

- **tall, taller, tallest**

| tall | taller | tallest |

- **ten**

| Count | Write | Say |
|---|---|---|
| ● ● ● ● ●<br>● ● ● ● ● | 10 | ten |

- **tenth**

- **third**

- **thirteen**

| Count | Write | Say |
|---|---|---|
| ● ● ● ● ●<br>● ● ● ● ●<br>● ● ● | 13 | thirteen |

- **three**

| Count | Write | Say |
|---|---|---|
| ● ● ● | 3 | three |

- **triangle**

- **twelve**

| Count | Write | Say |
|---|---|---|
| ● ● ● ● ●<br>● ● ● ● ●<br>● ● | 12 | twelve |

- **twenty**

| Count | Write | Say |
|---|---|---|
| ● ● ● ● ●<br>● ● ● ● ●<br>● ● ● ● ●<br>● ● ● ● ● | 20 | twenty |

- **two**

| Count | Write | Say |
|---|---|---|
| ● ● | 2 | two |

# U

- **under**

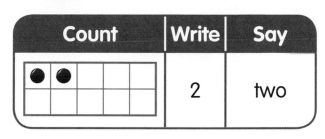

Pip

Pip is under the leaf.

- **unit**

Units are used to measure things.

 can be used to measure.

1  stands for 1 unit.

The pencil is 6 units long.

- **up**

Pip is climbing up the tree.

- **whole**
  See **number bond**.

- **zero**

| Count | Write | Say |
|-------|-------|-----|
|       | 0 | zero |

# Index

Pages listed in regular type refer to Student Book A.
Pages listed in blue type refer to Student Book B.
Pages in *italic* type refer to Workbook (WB) A.
Pages listed in *blue italic type* refer to WorkBook (WB) B.
Pages in **boldface** type show where a term is introduced.

less, **16**, 17, 19, 24–27, 36, 61, 69–70, 72–73, 178, 181, 185, 187, 191, *2, 4, 56, 66–69, 71, 73–79, 174, 187–193, 195–199, 203; WB 12, 17, 20, 38, 90, 174–176, 180, 183–184; WB 51–54, 57, 60, 95, 143–144, 146–148, 180–181*

more, **13**, 14–15, 19, 23–27, **44**, 45, 47, 58, 175–176, 180, 183–185, 187, 191, 195, 198, 200–201, 211, 217, *54, 66–67, 70–74, 77, 79, 174, 188–191, 195–196, 198–199, 203; WB 8–9, 11, 20, 37, 59, 62, 90, 171–172, 180, 182, 183–184, 248; WB 51–52, 54, 58, 60, 95, 113, 143, 151, 180, 255*

number line, 187, 188, 190–191, 195–196; *WB 143, 151, 180, 260*

numbers, 4–5, 27, 165–167, 190–191, *54, 66–69, 74, 79, 174–175, 187–188; WB 12, 17, 20, 38, 90, 174–176, 180, 183–184; WB 51, 53–54, 57, 60*

ones, *54, 68, 174, 193*

one-to-one correspondence, 13

same, **13**, 18; *WB 7–10, 12, 20, 37, 217*

sets, **175**, 176, 180, *72, 198; WB 188, 248; WB 52, 180*

tens, *54, 67, 174, 192–193*

weight, *See* Weight

Computers, 118, 130, 232

Communication
    Math Journal, 26, 34, 157, 213, *74, 200, 253; WB 54, 78, 125–126, 182; WB 16, 38, 124, 238*

Cone, *See* Geometry

Congruent shapes, *See* Geometry

Connecting cubes, *See* Manipulatives

Corner, *See* Geometry

Connecting cubes, *See* Manipulatives

Counting
    0 to 10, 4–7, 9, 11–12, 27, *53; WB 1–6, 7–11, 35, 253; WB 45, 135–136, 177*
    11 to 20, 165–168, 170, 190, *53; WB 161–165, 187–188, 247, 255; WB 45, 135–136, 177*

    *21 to 40, 51–60, 63, 173–175; WB 45–47, 49–50, 139–141, 177–79*
    *41 to 100, 63, 177–178, 182–183, 200; WB 135–136, 138–141, 177–179*
    counting tape, **66,** *70–71, 187*
    estimate, **180**, 183; *WB 138, 151–152, 178*
    back, *See* Ones, Patterns, *and* Subtraction
    making a ten, **168**, 169–170, *53, 58, 61, 173, 175, 177–180, 183; WB 45–50, 58–59, 135–136, 138–141, 177, 259*
    money, *See* Money
    on, *See* Addition, Ones, Money, Patterns, *and* Subtraction
    place value, **171**, 172–184, *177–179, 190–191, 53, 63, 173–174, 184–186, 192–193, 203; WB 49–50, 142*

Counters, *See* Manipulatives

Counting tape, *See* Counting

Cube, *See* Geometry

Cumulative Review, *See* Assessment

Cylinder, *See* Geometry

Data,
    collect/count, **30**, 36, 42, 50
    meaning of, **30**
    organize, **36**, 42
    show
        as picture graph, 31, 44; *WB 25–34, 90–91*
        in a bar graph, 42, 45, 51; *WB 37, 40, 42–44 , 91*
        in a tally chart, 42–43; *WB 35–37, 40, 43–44, 91*
        with pictures, 28; *WB 35–37*
    understand, 36, 38, 50; *WB 25–34, 39, 41*

Date, *See* Calendar

Days, *See* Calendar

Dimes, *See* Money

order, 276, 282; *WB 221*
    sort, *WB 221*
price, **260**, 270
save, 226–227
    savings, 226–227
subtract, 258, 284–287, 293; *WB 27, 232–236, 246*
    change, 284, 286–287; *WB 233–234, 237, 240, 252*
use
    buy, **258**, 259, 261, 267, 274–275, 279, 285–289,
        291; *WB 222–224, 230–231, 233–238,*
        *242–244, 246*
    pay, **267**, 273, 275, 280, 283; *WB 217, 226,*
        *234–235*
    spend, **287**, 288, 293; *WB 231, 234, 236, 246*
value, **259**, 261–263, 265–266, 271, 273–274, 278, 282,
    293; *WB 210–213, 215–216. 218–219, 225–226, 241,*
    *245, 251*
    equal/same, 271, 292; *WB 216, 251*
    greater, 261, 265–266
    greatest, 274, 276, 278–279; *WB 212*
    least, 282
    total, 278

Months, *See* Calendar

Morning, *See* Time

Multiplication, **240**,
    adding the same number, 241–246; *WB 185–190, 207*
    addition sentence, 241, 245, 255–256; *WB 207*
    concept of, **242**
    groups, 242–245; *WB 185–186, 247–250*
        count, 240; *WB 185–190, 247–250*
        each group, 242–243; *WB 185–186, 247*
    related to addition, 256
    repeated addition, 242, 256; *WB 185–186*

Night, *See* Time

Nickels, *See* Money

Non-standard units, *See* Length, Weight

Number bonds, **30**
    addition, 48–49, 52–55, 57–59, 62–63, 81–83, 85–86,
        89–92, 119–120, 130, 133–134, 137–138, 140, 146,
        149, 212; *WB 45–47*
    part-part-whole, **30**, 31–35, 37–38; *WB 21–34, 39–40*
    related to fact families, 85
    subtraction, 74–78, 82–83, 92–93; 103, 106–107, 114,
        116–117, 141–145, 149, 226

Number line, *See* Comparing

Number sentence, *See* Addition *and* Subtraction

Number train, *throughout. See for example* 16, 23–25, 30,
    35–36, 38, 84, 86–89, 123

Numbers, *See also* Patterns *and* Place value
    0 to 10, 4–5, 27, 52–53; *WB 45, 177–179*
    11 to 20, 165–170, 190, 53–56; *WB 161–190; WB 45, 177, 179*
    21 to 40, 52–79, 173–174, 176–179; *WB 45–47, 49–50,*
        *59–60, 135–137, 177–179*
    41 to 100, 176–179, 191, 202; *WB 135–137, 177–179*
    comparing
        greater than, *See* Comparing
        less than, *See* Comparing
        one-to-one correspondence, *See* Comparing
    number line, *See* Comparing
    ordering, 186–188, 191, 66, 70, 79, 174–175, 187, 194–195,
        199, 203; *WB 181, 189, 248, 256; WB 51, 53–54, 57,*
        *60, 95, 143, 145–146, 181, 259*
    ordinal, *See* Ordinal Numbers
    place value, *See* Place Value
    reading, 4–5, 166–168, 57, 79, 176; *WB 19, 36, 165–166*
    same, *See* Multiplication
    writing, 8, 57, 59, 62, 78, 176, 182, 189–191, 202; *WB 19,*
        *187, 247, 256; WB 93, 136, 177, 257, 259*

**O**

O'clock, *See* Time

Ones
  adding, *See* Addition
  and tens, 171–174, 177–179, 181, 191, *54, 59, 64–65, 81–82, 140, 173, 179; WB 161–170, 248; WB 49–50, 60, 94, 96, 99–100, 139–141, 177, 255, 259*
  counting back, 21–22, 25, 72–73, 92, 184, 188, *66, 188; WB 150*
  doubles plus one, *See* Addition
  greater, 193
  less, 24–25, 27, 66, 71, 73, 79, 188–191, 193, 195, 199,203; *WB 14, 16, 20, 38, 253; WB 50, 143*
  more, 23–25, 27; *WB 13, 16, 20, 38, 44*
  subtracting, *See* Subtraction

Operations, *See* Addition *and* Subtraction

Ordering
  coins, *See* Money
  events, *WB 149; WB 125*
  height, length, *See* Length
  numbers, *See* Numbers
  weight, *See* Weight

Ordinal numbers, **140**
  first to tenth, **140–141**, 142–150, 156–161; *WB 137–140, 142, 144, 147–151, 154, 158–159, 160, 255, 257; WB 259–60*

Organize data, *See* Data

**P**

Part-part-whole, *See* Addition, Number bonds, *and* Subtraction

Patterns
  numbers, **20**, 27, 183, 191
    completing, 23, 25, 188, 56, 70–71, 73–74, 79, 175; *WB 14–15, 38, 180, 188, 123, 248, 256; WB 55, 95, 146, 149–150, 181, 255*
      by adding or subtracting, 70–71, 73–74, 79
    creating, 22, 54, 200
    describing, 20, 183, 174
    extending, 20–23, 25, 184; *WB 13, 18, 179*
    rule, 201, 203; *WB 149–150*
  shapes, 129, 132, 137; *WB 117–126*
    completing, 131, 134; *WB 124, 157*
    creating, 130, 133; *WB 121–122, 150*
    describing, 129, 132
    extending, 130–131, 133–135; *WB 118–120,123, 136, 160*
    repeating pattern, **129**

Picture graphs, **27**; *WB 25*
  data,
    collect/count, **30,** 36
    meaning of, **30**
    organize, **36**
    show
      as picture graph, 31; *WB 25–34*
      with pictures, 28; *WB 35–37*
    understand, 36, 38, 50; *WB 25–34*
    draw make, 37; *WB 25, 30, 32*
    meaning of, **31**
    picture
      represent, **50**, 157–158, 160–161; *WB 110, 111*
    symbols, **31**, 36, 50, 90
    read, **50**; *WB 26, 32–34*
Place value, **171**, 190–191, 53–55, 63–65, 67–68, 78, 84, 86–92, 96–98, 100–101, 103–109, 112–113, 115, 117, 173–174, 184–186, 192–193, 205–206 209–212, 214, 216–217, 219 222–227, 230–232; *WB 167–170, 190, 259; WB 49–50, 63–64, 94, 142, 179*
  chart, **171**, 172–174, 177–179, 190–191, 36, 50, 53, 55, 65, 67–68, 78, 84,86–92, 96–98, 101, 103–109, 113, 115, 185, 192–193, 202, 205–206 209–212, 214, 216–217, 219 222–227, 230–232; *WB 168–171, 176–177, 187, 190, 248, 259; WB 49, 63–64, 87, 94, 179*
  comparing and ordering numbers, 177–179, 186, 188, 191, 67–68, 174, 192–193; *WB 171–178*

ones, 171–174, 190–191, *53–55, 63–65, 79, 173–174,*
*184–186, 192–193, 202; WB 167–170, 176 –177, 187,*
*190, 248, 259; WB 49–50, 94, 142*
tens, 171–174, 190–191, *53–55, 63–65, 79, 173–174,*
*184–186, 192–193, 202; WB 167–170, 176–177, 187,*
*190, 248, 259; WB 49–50, 94, 142*

Plane shapes, *See* Geometry

Plus, *See* Addition

Position words, **145**, 160–161
above, **151**, 152, 154, 161; *WB 145, 152, 154, 257*
after, **145**, 150, 169; *WB 141, 153, 159*
before, **145**, 160; *WB 141, 153, 159*
behind, **151**, 152, 155, 157; *WB 145, 151, 159, WB 260*
below, **151**, 152, 154, 161; *WB 145, 152, 154*
between, **145**, 146–147, 150, 157, 160;
*WB 141, 144, 148, 151–152, 153, 154, 159, 257*
down, **153**, 155, 161; *WB 146, 153*
far, **153**, 157, 161; *WB 146, 152, 159*
in front of, **151**, 152, 154, 161; *WB 145, 151–152, 159; WB 260*
last, **141**, 143, 146–148, 160; *WB 143–144, 154, 159; WB 260*
left, **146**, 147–150, 156–160; *WB 142–144, 148, 151, 159, 257*
near, **153**, 155, 157, 161; *WB 146, 159*
next to, **146**, 147–148, 150; *WB 143–144, 148, 151,*
*154, 257*
right, **146**, 147–150, 156, 158–160; *WB 142–144, 148, 151,*
*154, 159, 257*
under, **151**, 152–154; *WB 145, 151–152*
up, **153**, 155, 161; *WB 146, 153*

Practice
Guided Practice, *throughout. See for example 7–9,*
*15–17, 20–22, 43–45, 48, 50*
Let's Practice, *throughout. See for example, 12,*
*18–19, 25, 33, 47, 51–52*

Prerequisite skills
Recall Prior Knowledge, 2, 29, 40, 65, 96, 139,
163, 193, 219, 2–3, 28, 53, 54, 81–82, 133–134, 151,
173–174, 205–207, 241, 259
Quick Check, 3, 29, 41, 66, 97, 139, 164, 194, 220, 4–5, 29,
55–56, 83, 135, 152, 174–175, 207–208, 241, 260

Problem solving
Put On Your Thinking Cap!, 26, 37, 61, 90–91,
135, 158–159, 189, 214–215, 247, 23, 49, 76–77,
129, 148, 170, 201, 237, 255, 290–291; *WB 17–18,*
*31–32, 57–58, 127–132, 183–186, 213–216; WB*
*17–18, 39–42, 57–58, 83–86, 105–106, 125–126,*
*149–150, 173–174, 205–206, 239–244*
strategies
act it out, 37, 157–159, 247, 255; *WB 58, 127–129,*
*147–148, 184, 240–241; WB 205–206, 239*
apply data, *WB 126*
raw a diagram, 255; *WB 39*
drawing, interpreting a graph, *WB 40, 42*
guess and check, 37, 61, 90–91, 189, 214–215, 129,
237; *WB 17–18, 31–32, 83, 131–132, 148, 183,*
*185–186, 213–214, 215–216, 242; WB 83–86,*
*105–106, 239, 243*
look for patterns and relationships, 26, 135, 189,
76–77, 201; *WB 18; WB 58, 174*
make a systematic list, 49, 148, 290–291; *WB 57,*
*83–86, 105–106, 125, 241–242*
make suppositions, 237; *WB 127–129*
making 100, *WB 173*
restate the problem another way, *WB 184, 213–214*
simplify the problem, 129, 237
solve part of the problem, *WB 57, 83–84, 131–132*
use a drawing/model/diagram, 61, 157–159, 247;
*WB 239–241; WB 105–106*
work backward, 148; *WB 147*
thinking skills
analyzing parts and whole, 37, 57–58, 61, 90–91,
214–215, 129, 170, 290–291; *WB 31–32, 57,*
*83–84, 184, 213–214, 216; WB 173*
classifying, 26, 127, 49; *WB 17, 127; WB 205–206*
comparing, 26, 189, 247, 23, 49, 76–77, 170, 201,
255, 290–291; *WB 17, 31–32, 131–132, 147,*
*183–184, 185–186, 215, 239–241; WB 39–40,*
*41–42, 105–106, 239, 242–243*
deduction, 37, 61, 157–159, 247, 237; *WB 31–32,*
*57–58, 84, 148, 183–184, 185–186, 239–240,*
*242*
identifying patterns and relationships, 159, 189,
148, 237; *WB 12, 18, 131–132, 215; WB 58, 173*
induction, 247; *WB 84*
interpreting data, *WB 126, 241*
sequencing, 157–159, 23; *WB 147, 241; WB 57, 125*
spatial visualization, *WB 128–129; WB 239*

Pages listed in regular type refer to Student Book A.
Pages listed in blue type refer to Student Book B.
Pages in *italic* type refer to Workbook (WB) A.
Pages listed in *blue italic type* refer to WorkBook (WB) B.
Pages in **boldface** type show where a term is introduced.

Real-world problems, *see Real-world problems*

Put on Your Thinking Cap!, *See* Problem Solving

Pyramid, *See* Geometry

Pages listed in regular type refer to Student Book A.
Pages listed in blue type refer to Student Book B.
Pages in *italic* type refer to Workbook (WB) A.
Pages listed in *blue italic type* refer to WorkBook (WB) B.
Pages in **boldface** type show where a term is introduced.

# Photo Credits

# Acknowledgements

The publisher wishes to thank the following organizations for sponsoring the various objects used in this book:

**Accent Living**
Flower frames p. 4
Plate with fish motifs p. 59
Spoons p. 86

**Growing Fun Pte Ltd**
Math balance pp. 32, 35, 38

**Hasbro Singapore Pte Ltd**
For supplying Play-Doh™
to make the following:
      Clay stars p. 205
      Clay cats pp. 58, 93
      Clay shells p. 210

**Lyves & Company Pte Ltd**
Fish mobile p. 231

**Noble International Pte Ltd**
Unit cubes – appear throughout the book

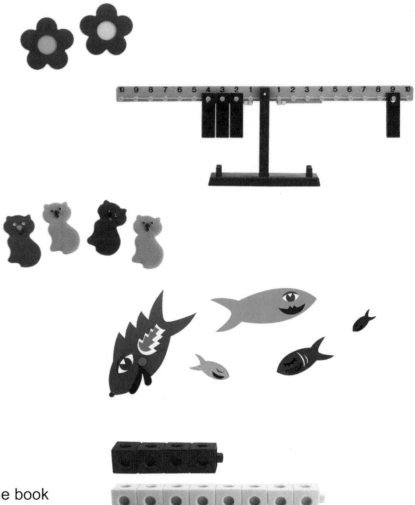

The publisher also wishes to thank the individuals who have contributed in one way or another, namely:
Model Isabella Gilbert
And all those who have kindly loaned the publisher items for the photographs featured.